5 STEPS TO A

500

AP Physics 1 Questions
to Know by Test Day

Second Edition

Anaxos, Inc.

New York Chicago San Francisco Athens London Madrid
Mexico City Milan New Delhi Singapore Sydney Toronto

1 2 3 4 5 6 7 8 9 10   DOC/DOC   1 2 1 0 9 8 7 6 5

ISBN 978-0-07-184910-4
MHID   0-07-184910-6

e-ISBN 978-0-07-184911-1
e-MHID   0-07-184911-4

McGraw-Hill Education, the McGraw-Hill Education logo, 5 Steps to a 5, and related trade dress are trademarks or registered trademarks of McGraw-Hill Education and/or its affiliates in the United States and other countries and may not be used without written permission. All other trademarks are the property of their respective owners. McGraw-Hill Education is not associated with any product or vendor mentioned in this book.

AP, Advanced Placement Program, and College Board are registered trademarks of the College Entrance Examination Board, which was not involved in the production of, and does not endorse, this product.

McGraw-Hill Education products are available at special quantity discounts to use as premiums and sales promotions or for use in corporate training programs. To contact a representative, please visit the Contact Us pages at www.mhprofessional.com.

This book is printed on acid-free paper.

CONTENTS

ABOUT THE AUTHOR

For more than fifteen years, Anaxos, Inc., has been creating educational and reference materials for some of the nation's most respected publishers. Based in Austin, Texas, the company uses writers from across the globe and who offer expertise on an array of subjects just as expansive.

INTRODUCTION

Congratulations! You've taken a big step toward AP success by purchasing *500 AP Questions to Know by Test Day*. We are here to help you take the next step and score high on your AP exam so you can earn college credits and get into the college or university of your choice!

This book gives you 500 AP-style multiple-choice questions that cover all the most essential course material. Each question has a detailed answer explanation. These questions will give you valuable independent practice to supplement your regular textbook and the groundwork you are already doing in your AP classroom. Furthermore, this new edition incorporates both document-based questions and short-response components to help with the updated components of the exam while maintaining the content questions to make this book useful in preparing for other survey course exams.

This and the other books in this series were written by expert AP teachers who know your exam inside out and can identify the crucial exam information as well as questions that are most likely to appear on the exam.

You might be the kind of student who takes several AP courses and needs to study extra questions a few weeks before the exam for a final review. Or you might be the kind of student who puts off preparing until the last weeks before the exam. No matter what your preparation style, you will surely benefit from reviewing these 500 questions, which closely parallel the content, format, and degree of difficulty of the questions on the actual AP exam. These questions and their answer explanations are the ideal last-minute study tool for those final few weeks before the test.

Remember the old saying "Practice makes perfect." If you practice with all the questions and answers in this book, we are certain you will build the skills and confidence needed to do great on the exam. Good luck!

—Editors of McGraw-Hill Education

$\frac{43}{50}$ # Kinematics

1. A 10-g penny is dropped from a building that is 125 m high. The penny is initially at rest. Approximately how long does it take the penny to hit the ground?
   (A) 3.2 s
   (B) 4.5 s
   (C) 10 s
   (D) 15 s
   (E) 20 s

2. A car in a drag race started from rest and accelerated constantly to a velocity of 50 m/s when it reached the end of a 500-m road. What was the car's rate of acceleration?
   (A) -5.0 m/s^2
   (B) -2.5 m/s^2
   (C) 0.5 m/s^2
   (D) 2.5 m/s^2
   (E) 5.0 m/s^2

Questions 3–6 refer to the motion of the car represented in the following graph:

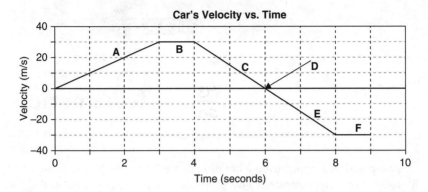

3. Which of the following best describes the motion of the car in regions C, D, and E of the velocity versus time graph?
   (A) It is slowing down until in reverses direction and speeds back up again.
   (B) It moves at a constant velocity in the negative direction.
   (C) It accelerates at a constant, nonzero acceleration except at point C when its acceleration is zero.
   (D) Its position changes at a constant rate.
   (E) It moves at a constant, positive acceleration throughout the trip.

4. What is the magnitude of the acceleration of the car in region A?
   (A) 0 m/s²
   (B) 3 m/s²
   (C) 5 m/s²
   (D) 10 m/s²
   (E) 30 m/s²

5. What is the acceleration rate of the car at the 6-second clock reading?
   (A) 0 m/s²
   (B) −15 m/s²
   (C) −30 m/s²
   (D) +30 m/s²
   (E) −60 m/s²

6. Rank the average velocities of the car in regions A, B, C, and E.
   (A) A > B > C = E
   (B) B = A > C = E
   (C) B > A = C = E
   (D) B > A = C > E
   (E) A > B > C = E

7. An airplane is flying horizontally at a velocity of 50.0 m/s at an altitude of 125 m. It drops a package to observers on the ground below. Approximately how far will the package travel in the horizontal direction from the point that it was dropped?

   (A) 100 m
   (B) 159 m
   (C) 250 m
   (D) 1,020 m
   (E) 1,590 m

8. A placekicker kicks a football at a velocity of 10.0 m/s from a tee on the ground at an angle of 30° from the horizontal. Approximately how long will the ball stay in the air?

   (A) 0.0 s
   (B) 0.6 s
   (C) 0.8 s
   (D) 1.0 s
   (E) 1.8 s

9. This graph depicts the motion of an object. During which time interval is the object at rest?

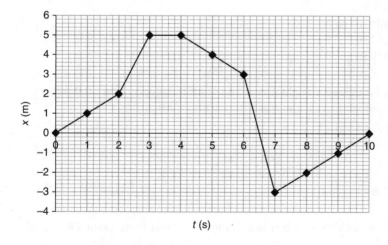

   (A) 0–2 s
   (B) 2–3 s
   (C) 3–4 s
   (D) 4–7 s
   (E) 7–10 s

10. A car is traveling at an unknown velocity. It accelerates constantly over 5.0 seconds at a rate of 3.0 m/s² to reach a velocity of 30 m/s. What was the original velocity of the car?

    (A) 1.0 m/s
    (B) 5.0 m/s
    (C) 10 m/s
    (D) 15 m/s
    (E) 20 m/s

11. A plane takes off from rest and accelerates constantly at a rate of 1.0 m/s² for 5 minutes. How far does the plane travel in this time?

    (A) 15 km
    (B) 30 km
    (C) 45 km
    (D) 90 km
    (E) 150 km

12. A person drops a stone down a well and hears the echo 8.9 s later. If it takes 0.9 s for the echo to travel up the well, approximately how deep is the well?

    (A) 40 m
    (B) 320 m
    (C) 405 m
    (D) 640 m
    (E) 810 m

13. If a ball is thrown straight upward with an initial velocity of 30.0 m/s, how much time does it take to reach its maximum height?

    (A) 1.0 s
    (B) 1.4 s
    (C) 1.5 s
    (D) 3.0 s
    (E) 9.8 s

14. On an airless planet, an astronaut drops a hammer from rest at a height of 15 m. The hammer hits the ground in 1 s. What is the acceleration due to the gravity on this planet?

    (A) 10 m/s²
    (B) 15 m/s²
    (C) 20 m/s²
    (D) 25 m/s²
    (E) 30 m/s²

15. A car uniformly accelerates from rest at 3.0 m/s² down a 150-m track. What is the car's final velocity?
    (A) 30 m/s
    (B) 90 m/s
    (C) 150 m/s
    (D) 450 m/s
    (E) 900 m/s

16. An object's position with time is depicted in the following graph. Based on the graph, at which time points will the object's velocity be closest to zero?

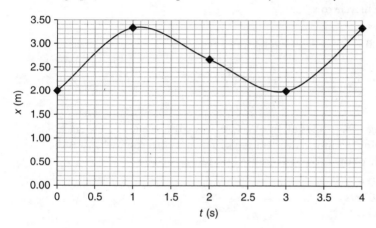

    (A) 0 s and 2 s
    (B) 0 s and 4 s
    (C) 1 s and 2 s
    (D) 1 s and 3 s
    (E) 2 s and 4 s

17. A cannonball is launched at an angle and travels above the flat ground. At what time point does a projectile reach its maximum height?
    (A) One-fifth of the total time in the air
    (B) One-fourth of the total time in the air
    (C) One-half of the total time in the air
    (D) Three-fifths of the total time in the air
    (E) Three-fourths of the total time in the air

18. A boy drops a stone from a cliff and counts the seconds until the stone hits the base. He counts 3 s. About how high is the cliff?
    (A) 3 m
    (B) 10 m
    (C) 15 m
    (D) 45 m
    (E) 90 m

19. A boy is riding a bicycle at a velocity of 5.0 m/s. He applies the brakes and uniformly decelerates to a stop at a rate of 2.5 m/s². How long does it take for the bicycle to stop?
    (A) 0.5 s
    (B) 1.0 s
    (C) 1.5 s
    (D) 2.0 s
    (E) 2.5 s

20. A police officer finds 60 m of skid marks at the scene of a car crash. Assuming a uniform deceleration of 7.5 m/s² to a stop, what was the velocity of the car when it started skidding?
    (A) 20 m/s
    (B) 30 m/s
    (C) 45 m/s
    (D) 60 m/s
    (E) 90 m/s

21. The velocity–time graph of an object's motion is shown in this graph. At 10 s, what is the object's displacement relative to the initial time?

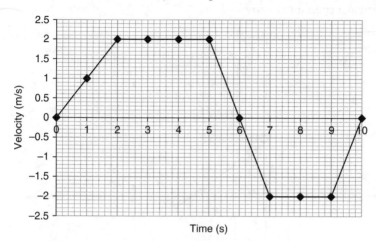

(A) 3 m
(B) 6 m
(C) 9 m
(D) −6 m
(E) −3 m

22. A projectile is launched with an unknown velocity at an angle of 30° from the horizontal of level ground. Which of the following statements is true?

(A) The horizontal component of velocity is less than the vertical component of velocity.
(B) The horizontal component of velocity is greater than the vertical component of velocity.
(C) Both the horizontal and vertical components of velocity are equal.
(D) The horizontal component of velocity is used to calculate the time that the projectile is in the air.
(E) The vertical component of velocity is used to calculate the range of the projectile.

23. From rest, a ball is dropped from the top of a building. It takes 4 s to hit the ground. Approximately how tall is the building?

(A) 40 m
(B) 90 m
(C) 100 m
(D) 160 m
(E) 200 m

24. The position–time graphs of five different objects are shown in these graphs. If the positive direction is forward, then which object is moving backward at a constant velocity?

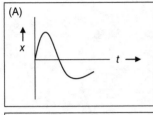

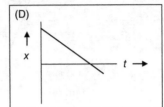

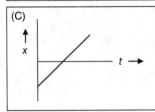

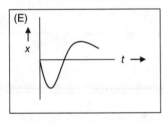

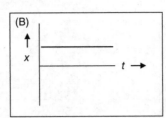

(A) Object A
(B) Object B
(C) Object C
(D) Object D
(E) Object E

25. A student launches projectiles with the same velocity but at different angles (0–90°) relative to the ground. He measures the range of each projectile. Which angle pairs have the same range?
(A) 10° and 20°
(B) 30° and 45°
(C) 30° and 60°
(D) 45° and 60°
(E) 10° and 90°

26. An object free-falls from rest a distance D. How far will the object fall from rest in twice the elapsed time?

(A) D
(B) $\sqrt{2}\,D$
(C) $2\,D$
(D) $3\,D$
(E) $4\,D$

27. A car is traveling at 30 m/s. The driver applies the brakes, and the car uniformly decelerates at 9 m/s². How far does the car travel before coming to a complete stop?

(A) 2 m
(B) 50 m
(C) 100 m
(D) 200 m
(E) 450 m

28. The position–time graph shown here is typical of which type of motion?

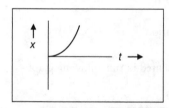

(A) Motion with a constant positive velocity
(B) Motion with zero velocity
(C) Motion with a constant positive acceleration
(D) Motion with zero acceleration
(E) Motion with a constant negative acceleration

29. If you drop a ball from a 100-m-tall building, approximately how far will the ball fall in 2 s?

(A) 10 m
(B) 20 m
(C) 40 m
(D) 50 m
(E) 100 m

30. An ice skater moving at 10 m/s comes to a complete stop in 0.5 s. What is the rate of acceleration?
    (A) 5 m/s^2
    (B) 10 m/s^2
    (C) 20 m/s^2
    (D) −20 m/s^2
    (E) −10 m/s^2

31. The position–time graph shown here is typical of which type of motion?

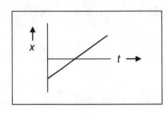

    (A) Motion with a constant negative velocity
    (B) Motion with zero velocity
    (C) Motion with a constant positive acceleration
    (D) Motion with zero acceleration
    (E) Motion with a constant negative acceleration

Questions 32–35 refer to the motion of the car represented in the following graph:

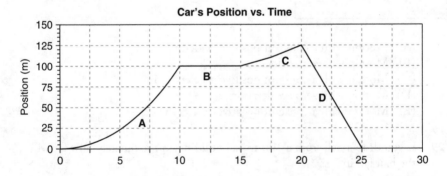

32. Which of the following best describes the motion of the car in region D of the graph?
    (A) The car slows down.
    (B) The car is moving a constant speed in the negative direction.
    (C) The car is moving down an incline.
    (D) The car is speeding up in the negative direction.
    (E) The car moves from a position of 20 to a position of 25.

33. Which of the following best ranks the displacement of the car in each region?
    (A) A > B > C > D
    (B) A > C > B > D
    (C) D > A > C > B
    (D) A > C > D > B
    (E) D > C > B > A

34. Which of the following best ranks the average speed of the car in each region?
    (A) A > B > C > D
    (B) A > C > B > D
    (C) D > A > C > B
    (D) A > C > D > B
    (E) D > C > B > A

35. What is the velocity of the car in regions C and D, respectively?
    (A) +25 m/s, −125 m/s
    (B) 5 m/s, 25 m/s
    (C) 25 m/s, 125 m/s
    (D) 5 s, 5 s
    (E) 5 m/s, −25 m/s

Multi-select: For **questions 36–38**, two of the suggested answers will be correct. Select the two best answers, and record them both on the answer sheet.

36. Which of the following are moving at a constant velocity?
    (A) A tetherball moving in a circle at a constant speed
    (B) A rolling ball constantly accelerating at −0.20 m/s^2
    (C) A jogger continuing to run at a speed of 2 m/s along a straight path
    (D) A truck constantly gaining 2 miles per hour each second
    (E) A box steadily sliding down an incline at a speed of 0.5 m/s

37. Which of the following are moving with a constant, nonzero acceleration?
    (A) A skydiver gaining speed as she falls through the air
    (B) A hammer falling near the surface of the moon
    (C) A box sliding down an incline at a steady speed of 2 m/s.
    (D) A cart moving in a straight line gaining 3 m/s each second
    (E) A truck moving in a circle as it gains 3 m/s each second

38. Which of the following are true about the motion of the carts in the graph below?

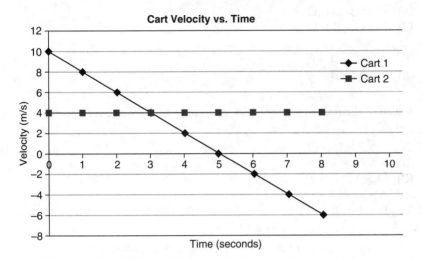

(A) At the 7-second clock reading, Cart 1 was moving with the same speed as Cart 2.
(B) Cart 1 moved at a constant speed in the negative direction.
(C) Cart 1 moved in the negative direction over the entire 8-second trip.
(D) At the 8-second clock reading, Cart 1 was moving faster than Cart 2.
(E) At the 5-second clock reading, Cart 1 was at the origin of the coordinate system.

39. An object is free-falling near the surface of the Earth. At a certain instant in time, it is falling downward at a rate 25 m/s. Two seconds later, what is its acceleration?

(A) 0 m/s^2
(B) 5 m/s^2
(C) 10 m/s^2
(D) 25 m/s^2
(E) 45 m/s^2

40. An object is free-falling near the surface of the Earth. At a certain instant in time, it is falling downward at a rate 25 m/s. Two seconds later, what is its speed?

(A) 0 m/s
(B) 5 m/s
(C) 10 m/s
(D) 25 m/s
(E) 45 m/s

41. A car accelerates at 2 m/s/s. If the car starts with an initial speed of 20 m/s, how much time does it need to accelerate to a speed of 30 m/s?

(A) 2 s
(B) 5 s
(C) 10 s
(D) 20 s
(E) 30 s

42. An object at the 35-m position of a one-dimensional coordinate system is moving in the negative direction at a constant speed of 25 m/s.
Which function below best represents how the car's position (X) on the coordinate system changes with time (t)?

(A) $X = -25t + 35$
(B) $X = -35t + 25$
(C) $X = 10t^2 - 35t + 25$
(D) $X = 10t^2 - 25t + 35$
(E) $X = -10t^2 + 25t - 35$

43. At $t = 0$, an object is at a position of -12 meters of a one-dimensional coordinate system and is moving in the positive direction at 5 m/s.
It constantly gains velocity at a rate of $+2$ m/s each and every second.
Which function below best represents how the car's position (X) on the coordinate system changes with time (t)?

(A) $X = 5t + -12$
(B) $X = 2t^2 + 5t - 12$
(C) $X = t^2 + 5t - 12$
(D) $X = -12t^2 + 5t + 2$
(E) $X = 2t^2 + 2t - 12$

Free Response: An archer stands on a castle wall that is 45 m high. He shoots an arrow with a velocity of 10.0 m/s at an angle of 45° relative to the horizontal.

44. Describe the path of the arrow.

45. Determine the magnitude of the horizontal and vertical components of the arrow's velocity.

46. Determine how much time it takes for the arrow to reach the ground.

47. Determine the maximum range of the arrow.

Free Response: The acceleration versus time of a bicycle rider is shown here:

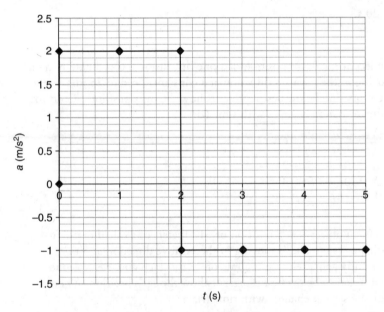

Assuming that the bicycle starts from the origin at an initial velocity of +4 m/s, complete the following questions

48. Sketch a scaled velocity–time graph for the 5-s motion.

49. Describe the motion of the bicyclist in detail during the 5 seconds, commenting on what's happening to the speed and the direction of motion throughout the trip.

50. Determine the total distance traveled during the 5 s of motion.

CHAPTER 2

Dynamics: Newton's Laws

51. Which of Newton's laws describes equilibrium?

(A) The first, which mathematically states that $\Sigma \mathbf{F} = 0$.

(B) The second, which mathematically states that $\Sigma \mathbf{F} = m\mathbf{a}$.

(C) The third, which mathematically states that $\mathbf{F} = -\mathbf{F}$.

(D) The fourth, which mathematically states that $\mathbf{F} = Gm_1m_2/r^2$.

(E) The fifth, which mathematically states that $dx/dt = v$.

52. A student claims that two spheres of different mass dropped from rest above the surface of the Moon will hit the ground at the same time. Which of the following is a correct assessment of this statement?

(A) The more massive sphere will hit the surface first because it's heavier.

(B) Neither sphere will hit the surface because there is no gravity on the Moon and they will both float.

(C) The less massive sphere will hit the surface first because its smaller profile will hit more air, which will slow down its motion.

(D) They will hit the ground at approximately the same time because the net force-to-mass ratio is the same for both.

(E) Physicists have no models to predict which sphere will hit first.

53. A box slides to the right along a horizontal surface. Which is true about the friction force?

(A) It acts perpendicular to the surface.

(B) It is a force in the direction of motion that allows the box to move.

(C) It is a force that is proportional to the normal force that acts in opposition to the direction of motion.

(D) It is a force that is proportional to the normal force and acts in the direction of motion.

(E) It is a force that is proportional to the square of the box's weight and acts in the direction of motion.

54. A rope is strung between two cliffs. A mountain climber weighing 100 kg
is halfway across the rope when the rope forms an angle of 45° with the
horizontal. The tension in the rope is closest to what value? (Assume the
gravitational field strength is 10 N/kg.)

    (A) 1,000 N
    (B) 500 N
    (C) 700 N
    (D) 250 N
    (E) 100 N

55. Object A, when acted upon by a force F, accelerates at a rate of 4.0 m/s/s.
This same force accelerates Object B at a rate of 8.0 m/s/s. Compared to
the mass of Object A, the mass of Object B is:

    (A) Four times as great
    (B) Twice as great
    (C) The same
    (D) One-half as great
    (E) One-fourth as great

56. A 100-kg box is sitting on a 10° incline with a coefficient of friction of 0.5.
At what angle must the incline be raised to start sliding the box?

    (A) 30°
    (B) 33°
    (C) 26°
    (D) 24°
    (E) 15°

57. A six-vertical-strand pulley is used to raise a load weighing 1,000 kg. What
is the tension on the pulley cables?

    (A) 15,000 N
    (B) 1,000 N
    (C) 1,600 N
    (D) 10,000 N
    (E) 170 N

58. An object is supported by a spring attached to the ceiling. What are the forces acting on the object?

    (A) The mass of the object in the downward direction and the supporting force of the spring in the upward direction

    (B) The mass of the object in the downward direction and the supporting force of the spring in the downward direction

    (C) The weight of the object in the upward direction and the supporting force of the spring in the downward direction

    (D) The weight of the object in the downward direction and the supporting force of the spring in the upward direction

    (E) The weight of the object pulling on the Earth and the downward supporting force of the spring

59. A box that is resting on an inclined plane has what forces acting on it?

    (A) The weight of the box, the box's component forces perpendicular to and along the plane, and the friction force along the surface of the plane beneath the box

    (B) The weight of the box, the box's component forces perpendicular to and along the plane, the resultant force of the plane on the box, and the friction force along the surface of the plane beneath the box

    (C) The weight of the box and the friction force along the surface of the plane beneath the box

    (D) The mass of the box and its acceleration along the plane

    (E) The weight of the box, the perpendicular force of the plane on the box, and the friction force along the surface of the plane beneath the box

60. A large 2,000-N cement block is pulled constantly up a frictionless 43° incline using a dual-strand pulley that is attached to the block. One end of the rope is tied to the wall at the top of the plane while a man is pulling the other end of the rope. What is the tension in the pull of the rope if the rope is pulled parallel to the plane?

    (A) 732 N

    (B) 682 N

    (C) 1,463 N

    (D) 1,364 N

    (E) 462 N

61. Two boys push a 5-kg box on a frictionless floor. James pushes the box with a 10-N force to the right. Louis pushes the box with an 8-N force to the left. What is the magnitude and direction of the box's acceleration?

    (A) 0 m/s²; the box does not move
    (B) 0.4 m/s² to the right
    (C) 0.4 m/s² to the left
    (D) 1.6 m/s² to the right
    (E) 1.6 m/s² to the left

62. A box of unknown mass (m) slides down a plane inclined at an angle (θ). The plane has a coefficient of friction (μ). Which of the following expressions would you use to calculate the rate of acceleration (a)?

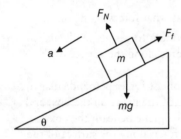

    (A) $a = g(\sin\theta - \mu g \cos\theta)/m$
    (B) $a = g(\cos\theta - \mu g \sin\theta)/m$
    (C) $a = m(\sin\theta - \mu g \cos\theta)/g$
    (D) $a = g(\sin\theta - \mu\cos\theta)$
    (E) $a = g(\cos\theta - \mu\sin\theta)$

63. You pull straight down on one side of a rope stretched across a pulley. Attached to the other side of the rope is a 10-kg box. How much force must you pull down on the rope to get the box to accelerate upward at a rate of 10 m/s²?

    (A) 10 N
    (B) 20 N
    (C) 100 N
    (D) 150 N
    (E) 200 N

64. A jet takes off at an angle of 60° to the horizontal. The jet flies against a wind that exerts a horizontal force of 1,000 N on it. The engines produce 20,000 N of thrust (60° to the horizontal), and the mass of the jet is 90,000 kg. What is the rate of the jet's acceleration in the horizontal direction?

(A) 0.1 m/s²
(B) 0.2 m/s²
(C) 1.0 m/s²
(D) 5.0 m/s²
(E) 10 m/s²

65. Only two forces act on a 0.1-kg object. This graph depicts the magnitudes and directions of those two forces. What is the acceleration of the object at the 2-second clock reading?

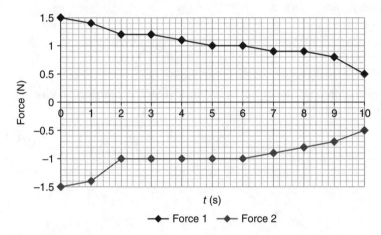

(A) 0 m/s²
(B) 0.2 m/s²
(C) 1 m/s²
(D) 2 m/s²
(E) 4 m/s²

66. A boy pushes a 10-kg crate across the floor with a constant force of 10 N against a force of friction. The box accelerates at a rate of 0.1 m/s². What is the magnitude of the opposing frictional force?

(A) 0 N
(B) 1 N
(C) 5 N
(D) 9 N
(E) 10 N

67. A 10-kg crate is on a plane that is inclined at an angle of 45°. The coefficient of friction is 0.1, and the downward direction is positive. What is the approximate rate of the box's acceleration?

(A) 0 m/s²
(B) 4.2 m/s²
(C) 6.4 m/s²
(D) 8.7 m/s²
(E) 10 m/s²

68. Two masses are hanging vertically by a rope strung through a pulley. The mass on the left of the pulley is 5 kg, while the mass on the right is 10 kg. If the positive direction of the pulley is counterclockwise, what is the magnitude and direction of the acceleration?

(A) 0 m/s²
(B) −3.30 m/s²
(C) −5.0 m/s²
(D) 3.3 m/s²
(E) 5.0 m/s²

69. The acceleration of a 5-kg object over time is shown in this graph. What is the net force at 1 s?

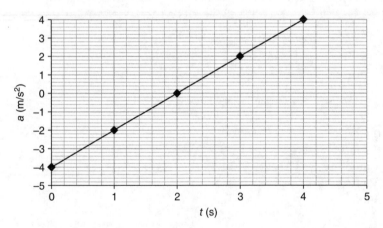

(A) −10 N
(B) −5 N
(C) −2.5 N
(D) 5 N
(E) 10 N

70. A skier weighing 70 kg pushes off from the top of a ski slope with a force of 105 N directed down the slope. The slope is inclined at 30°. Assuming that the slope is frictionless, what is the initial rate of the skier's acceleration during the push-off?

(A) 0.5 m/s²
(B) 1 m/s²
(C) 2 m/s²
(D) 7 m/s²
(E) 11 m/s²

71. A soldier fires a musket with a barrel that is 1 m in length. The gases from the exploding gunpowder exert a constant net force of 50 N on a 0.010-kg bullet as it travels through the musket barrel. What is the bullet's velocity as it leaves the musket barrel?

(A) 10 m/s
(B) 100 m/s
(C) 1,000 m/s
(D) 10,000 m/s
(E) 100,000 m/s

72. An object's position with time is depicted in this graph. At which time range will there be nearly no net force acting on the object?

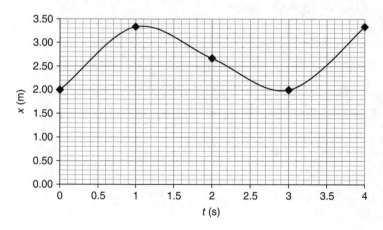

(A) 0.5 to 1.0 s
(B) 1.0 to 1.5 s
(C) 1.8 to 2.2 s
(D) 2.5 to 3.0 s
(E) 1.0 to 1.2 s

73. A block with a mass of 30 kg is located on a horizontal, frictionless tabletop. This block is connected by a rope to another block with a mass of 10 kg. The rope is looped through a pulley on the table's edge so that the less massive block is hanging over the edge. What is the magnitude of the acceleration of the larger block across the table?

    (A) 0.5 m/s²
    (B) 1 m/s²
    (C) 2.5 m/s²
    (D) 3.5 m/s²
    (E) 4.0 m/s²

74. A jet flies at level flight. The engines produce a total of 20,000 N of forward thrust, the jet's mass is 50,000 kg, and it accelerates at 0.3 m/s². What is the magnitude of the air resistance against which the jet flies?

    (A) 1,000 N
    (B) 3,000 N
    (C) 5,000 N
    (D) 10,000 N
    (E) 15,000 N

75. A boy is pushing a 50-kg crate across a frictionless surface. The velocity is changing with time as shown in this graph. What is the magnitude of the force that the boy applies to the crate?

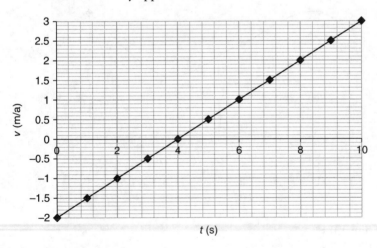

    (A) 5 N
    (B) 10 N
    (C) 15 N
    (D) 20 N
    (E) 25 N

76. A car with a mass of 1,000 kg travels at 30 m/s. The driver applies his brakes for a uniform deceleration and comes to a complete stop in 60 m. Assuming that the forward motion is positive, what is the magnitude and direction of the net force acting on the car?

(A) 7,500 N
(B) 5,000 N
(C) −1,000 N
(D) −5,000 N
(E) −7,500 N

77. A bowler applies a constant net force of 100 N on a 5-kg bowling ball over a time period of 1.5 s before he releases the ball. The ball starts from rest. What is its final velocity?

(A) 5 m/s
(B) 10 m/s
(C) 20 m/s
(D) 30 m/s
(E) 40 m/s

78. A tow truck is pulling a car out of a ditch. Which of the following statements is true about the forces between the truck and the car?

(A) The force of the truck on the car is greater than the force of the car on the truck.
(B) The force of the truck on the car is less than the force of the car on the truck.
(C) The force of the truck on the car is equal in magnitude to the force of the car on the truck.
(D) The force of the truck on the car may be equal to the force of the car on the truck, but only when the system is in a state of constant velocity.
(E) The force of the truck on the car may be greater than the force of the car on the truck, but only when the system is accelerating.

79. This graph depicts the velocity of a skydiver over time during a free fall. Which of the following statements is true?

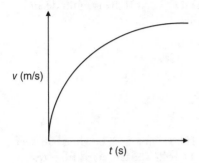

(A) The net forces acting on the skydiver increase until the acceleration reaches its maximum and the velocity becomes constant.

(B) The net forces acting on the skydiver decrease until the acceleration reaches zero and the velocity becomes constant.

(C) There are no net forces acting on the skydiver.

(D) The net forces acting on the skydiver increase until the acceleration reaches zero and the velocity becomes constant.

(E) The net forces acting on the skydiver decrease until the acceleration reaches zero and the velocity becomes zero.

80. A girl pushes a 10-kg box from rest across a horizontal floor with a force of 50 N. The force of friction opposing her is 45 N. If the box uniformly accelerates from rest to a final velocity of 2.0 m/s, how much time did it take to get to that velocity?

(A) 1 s
(B) 2 s
(C) 3 s
(D) 4 s
(E) 5 s

81. A rocket goes from rest to 9.6 km/s in 8 min. The rocket's mass is 8.0×10^6 kg. Assuming a constant acceleration, what is the net force acting on the rocket?

(A) 1.6×10^5 N
(B) 9.6×10^5 N
(C) 9.6×10^6 N
(D) 1.0×10^7 N
(E) 1.6×10^8 N

82. A car travels at a constant velocity of 30 m/s. The mass of the car is 1,000 kg. The forward force of the road on the car is 1,000 N. What is the total amount of backward force on the car from air drag and rolling friction?

    (A) 1,000 N
    (B) 10,000 N
    (C) 9,000 N
    (D) 3,000 N
    (E) 2,000 N

83. A 1,000-kg car is initially traveling at 30 m/s. The driver applies the brakes suddenly, and the friction from the road exerts 9,000 N of force on the car. If the car uniformly decelerates to a complete stop, how far does the car travel during the braking process?

    (A) 2 m
    (B) 50 m
    (C) 100 m
    (D) 200 m
    (E) 450 m

84. This position–time graph is typical of which type of motion?

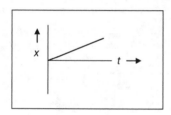

    (A) Motion of an object with an increasing net force acting upon it
    (B) Motion with zero velocity
    (C) Motion with constant positive net force acting upon it
    (D) Motion of an object with no net force acting upon it
    (E) Motion of an object with negative net force acting upon it

85. At the very beginning of a dash, a 70-kg runner accelerates uniformly from rest to 10 m/s in 0.5 s as she moves in the positive direction. What is the net force acting upon the runner?

    (A) −7,000 N
    (B) −1,400 N
    (C) 0 N
    (D) 1,400 N
    (E) 7,000 N

86. Rank the following scenarios from the smallest acceleration to the greatest acceleration:
    I. Net force F applied to a mass M
    II. Net force $2F$ applied to a mass M
    III. Net force F applied to a mass $2M$
    IV. Net force $2F$ applied to a mass $2M$
    (A) II > I = IV > III
    (B) I > II > III > IV
    (C) III > IV = I > II
    (D) IV > II > III > I
    (E) III > I = II > IV

87. The acceleration–time graph of an object's motion is shown in this figure. At what time will the forces acting on it be balanced?

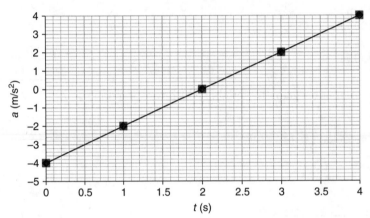

    (A) 0 s
    (B) 1 s
    (C) 2 s
    (D) 3 s
    (E) 4 s

Multi-select: For **questions 88–91**, two of the suggested answers will be correct. Select the two best answers, and record them both on the answer sheet.

88. A book is resting on a table. Which of the following forces act on the book?
    (A) The gravitational force
    (B) The force of the book on the table
    (C) The supporting force of the table on the book
    (D) The net downward force of air on the book
    (E) The force of the table on the floor

89. Consider the forces on a child standing in an elevator. When is the normal force from the elevator equal to the gravitational force?
    (A) When the elevator moves up at a constant speed
    (B) When the elevator accelerates upward
    (C) When the elevator is at rest
    (D) When the elevator accelerates downward at a constant rate
    (E) When the child is jumping up off the floor of the elevator

90. A rope applies 35. N force as shown in the figure. As a result, the box accelerates to the left along the surface. In addition to the gravitational force, which of the following forces act on the box?

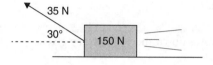

    (A) The downward force of the box on the table
    (B) The frictional force of the surface on the box
    (C) The upward force of the table on the box
    (D) The force of motion to the left on the box
    (E) The tension force of the rope on the box

91. Which of the following are properties of mass?
    (A) Mass is the ratio of weight to volume.
    (B) Masses push on other masses.
    (C) A mass experiences an attractive force with another mass.
    (D) Mass is the amount of space something occupies.
    (E) Mass resists changes in motion.

Free Response: An archer stands on a castle wall that is 45 m high. He shoots an arrow with a velocity of 10.0 m/s at an angle of 45° relative to the horizontal. The arrow is shot into a constant headwind that exerts a force of 0.05 N on the arrow. The arrow has a mass of 0.050 kg.

92. Determine the magnitude of the horizontal and vertical components of the arrow's initial velocity.

93. Determine how much time it takes for the arrow to reach the ground.

94. Determine the maximum range of the arrow into the wind.

95. How much farther would the arrow go if the wind wasn't blowing?

Free Response: A 10-kg box slides down a plane inclined at an angle ($\theta = 30°$). The plane has a coefficient of friction ($\mu = 0.1$). The box starts from rest and slides down the plane for 2.0 s.

96. Draw a free-body diagram of this situation, and label all the forces on the box.

97. Calculate the force of friction on the box.

98. Calculate the acceleration of the box.

99. Calculate the final velocity of the box.

100. Calculate the distance that the box moves down the plane in the given time interval.

CHAPTER 3

Circular Motion and the Universal Law of Gravitation

101. A car moves in a horizontal circle with a radius of 10 m. The tangential velocity of the car is 30 m/s. What is the car's acceleration?

(A) 3 m/s^2 toward the center
(B) 3 m/s^2 away from the center
(C) 90 m/s^2 toward the center
(D) 90 m/s^2 away from the center
(E) 270 m/s^2 toward the center

102. If the car in **the previous question** has a mass of 1,000 kg, then what is the force of friction acting on the car?

(A) 3,000 N toward the center
(B) 3,000 N away from the center
(C) 90,000 N away from the center
(D) 90,000 N toward the center
(E) 90,000 N vertically

103. A satellite orbits the Earth at a distance of 100 km. The mass of the satellite is 100 kg, while the mass of the Earth is approximately 6.0×10^{24} kg. The radius of the Earth is approximately 6.4×10^6 m. What is the approximate force of gravity acting on the satellite?

(A) 4×10^4 N
(B) 6.2×10^6 N
(C) 4×10^8 N
(D) 6.2×10^9 N
(E) 4×10^{14} N

104. Two satellites of equal mass orbit a planet. Satellite B orbits at twice the orbital radius of Satellite A. Which of the following statements is true?
    (A) The gravitational force on Satellite A is four times less than that on Satellite B.
    (B) The gravitational force on Satellite A is two times less than that on Satellite B.
    (C) The gravitational force on the satellites is equal.
    (D) The gravitational force on Satellite A is two times greater than that on Satellite B.
    (E) The gravitational force on Satellite A is four times greater than that on Satellite B.

105. A 70-kg astronaut floats at a distance of 10 m from a 50,000-kg spacecraft. What is the force of attraction between the astronaut and spacecraft?
    (A) 2.4×10^{-6} N
    (B) 2.4×10^{-5} N
    (C) Zero; there is no gravity in space.
    (D) 2.4×10^{5} N
    (E) 2.4×10^{6} N

106. The centripetal acceleration on a 1,000-kg car in a turn is 1×10^{5} m/s². The radius of the turn is 10 m. What is the car's speed?
    (A) 1×10^{1} m/s
    (B) 1×10^{2} m/s
    (C) 1×10^{3} m/s
    (D) 1×10^{4} m/s
    (E) 1×10^{5} m/s

107. An ice skater skates around a circular rink with a diameter of 20 m. If it takes her 62.8 s to go around the rink once, what is the coefficient of friction of the ice?
    (A) 0.01
    (B) 0.10
    (C) 0.20
    (D) 0.30
    (E) 0.50

108. A proposed "space elevator" can lift a 1,000-kg payload to an orbit of 150 km above the Earth's surface. The radius of the Earth is 6.4×10^6 m, and the Earth's mass is 6×10^{24} kg. What is the gravitational potential energy of the payload when it reaches orbit?

(A) 1.0×10^3 J
(B) 2.7×10^6 J
(C) 6.1×10^{10} J
(D) 2.7×10^{12} J
(E) 1.0×10^{15} J

109. A warrior spins a slingshot in a horizontal circle above his head at a constant speed. The sling is 1.5 m long, and the stone has a mass of 50 g. The tension in the string is 3.3 N. When he releases the sling, what will the stone's speed be?

(A) 5 m/s
(B) 10 m/s
(C) 25 m/s
(D) 30 m/s
(E) 50 m/s

Questions 110 and 111 are based on the following graph:

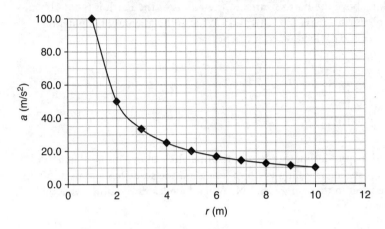

110. Engineers have designed a centrifuge for studying the effects of high gravity environments on plants and animals. This graph shows the results of the relationship between the radius and the centripetal acceleration. If the scientists want to simulate a "3-G environment," then what should the radius of the centrifuge be?

    (A) 1 m
    (B) 2 m
    (C) 3 m
    (D) 5 m
    (E) 10 m

111. If an astronaut with a mass of 70 kg were placed in that centrifuge with a radius of 5 m, what would be the centripetal force acting on him?

    (A) 30 N
    (B) 70 N
    (C) 140 N
    (D) 210 N
    (E) 240 N

112. The Earth is at an average distance of 1 AU from the Sun and has an orbital period of 1 year. Jupiter orbits the Sun at approximately 5 AU. About how long is the orbital period of Jupiter?

    (A) 1 year
    (B) 2 years
    (C) 5 years
    (D) 11 years
    (E) 125 years

113. A satellite orbits the Earth at a distance of 200 km. If the mass of the Earth is 6.0×10^{24} kg and the Earth's radius is 6.4×10^6 m, what is the satellite's speed?

    (A) 1×10^3 m/s
    (B) 3.5×10^3 m/s
    (C) 7.8×10^3 m/s
    (D) 5×10^6 m/s
    (E) 6.1×10^7 m/s

114. A block with a mass of 30 kg is hanging still from a string. If you place another block with a mass of 10 kg at a distance of 2 m away, what is the gravitational attraction between the two blocks?

    (A) 1×10^{-11} N
    (B) 5×10^{-10} N
    (C) 1×10^{-10} N
    (D) 5×10^{-9} N
    (E) 1×10^{-9} N

115. A 1,000-kg car experiences a centripetal force of 1.8×10^5 N while making a turn. The car is moving at a constant speed of 30 m/s. What is the radius of the turn?

    (A) 0.2 m
    (B) 1 m
    (C) 2 m
    (D) 4 m
    (E) 5 m

116. A skater holds out her arms level to the ground as she spins. In one hand she holds a tennis ball. Each of her arms is 1 m long. If the tennis ball travels at 5 m/s, what is its centripetal acceleration?

    (A) 5 m/s^2
    (B) 10 m/s^2
    (C) 15 m/s^2
    (D) 20 m/s^2
    (E) 25 m/s^2

117. Mars orbits the Sun at a distance of 2.3×10^{11} m. The mass of the Sun is 2×10^{30} kg, and the mass of Mars is 6.4×10^{23} kg. Approximately what is the gravitational force that the Sun exerts on Mars?

    (A) 1.6×10^{20} N
    (B) 1.6×10^{21} N
    (C) 3.7×10^{21} N
    (D) 3.7×10^{32} N
    (E) 3.7×10^{42} N

118. A record player has four coins at different distances from the center of rotation. Coin A is 1 cm away, Coin B is 2 cm away, Coin C is 4 cm away, and Coin D is 8 cm away. If the player is spinning 45 rotations/min, what coin has the greatest tangential velocity?

    (A) Coin A
    (B) Coin B
    (C) Coin C
    (D) Coin D
    (E) All the coins have equal tangential velocities.

119. Friction allows a car to make a turn at a speed of 10 miles per hour. By what factor will the friction have to change to allow the driver to make the same turn at twice the speed?

    (A) Four times the friction
    (B) Twice the friction
    (C) The same amount of friction
    (D) One-half the friction
    (E) One-fourth the friction

120. This graph depicts the tangential velocities of several circular space stations with different radii. All the stations are spinning. Which of the following statements is true?

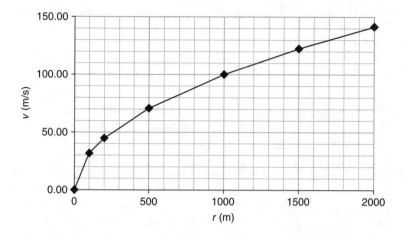

(A) The centripetal accelerations of the three shorter radii space stations are greater than 10 m/s^2; those of the larger ones are less than 10 m/s^2.

(B) The centripetal accelerations of the three shorter radii space stations are greater than 5 m/s^2; those of the larger ones are less than 5 m/s^2.

(C) The centripetal accelerations of all the stations are all nearly 5 m/s^2.

(D) The centripetal accelerations of all the stations are all nearly 10 m/s^2.

(E) The centripetal accelerations of the three shorter radii space stations are less than 10 m/s^2; those of the larger ones are greater than 10 m/s^2.

121. The Moon has a mass of 7.4×10^{22} kg and a radius of 1.7×10^6 m. What is the force of gravity experienced by a 70-kg astronaut standing on the lunar surface?

(A) 10 N
(B) 50 N
(C) 100 N
(D) 120 N
(E) 150 N

122. A bicycle wheel has a radius of 0.5 m. When it spins, it completes one full turn in 1.6 s. A pebble wedged in the tread has a mass of 10 g. What is the centripetal force on the pebble?

(A) 0.01 N
(B) 0.08 N
(C) 0.1 N
(D) 0.8 N
(E) 1 N

123. The Moon has a mass of 7.4×10^{22} kg and a distance from the Earth of 3.8×10^8 m. The Earth's mass is 6×10^{24} kg. What is the magnitude of the gravitational potential energy of the Moon?
    (A) 2.0×10^{20} J
    (B) 7.8×10^{28} J
    (C) 2.0×10^{30} J
    (D) 7.8×10^{30} J
    (E) 2.0×10^{40} J

124. A tetherball swings in a horizontal circle. If the radius of the swing is tripled but the tangential speed remains the same, by what factor does the centripetal force change?
    (A) Nine times greater
    (B) Three times greater
    (C) Remains the same
    (D) One-third as much
    (E) One-ninth as much

125. The coefficient of friction between the rubber tires of a car and dry concrete is $\mu = 0.64$. If a car enters a horizontal turn with a radius of 10.0 m, what is the maximum speed that the car can have and still hold the road?
    (A) 4 m/s
    (B) 8 m/s
    (C) 32 m/s
    (D) 64 m/s
    (E) 144 m/s

126. A spinning top has a radius of 2 cm. If the top takes 0.06 s to complete one rotation, what is the centripetal acceleration at the edge of the top?
    (A) 10 m/s^2
    (B) 22 m/s^2
    (C) 100 m/s^2
    (D) 220 m/s^2
    (E) 1,000 m/s^2

127. You swing a 100-g object attached to a 2-m string in a circle above your head. The speed of the object is 12 m/s. What is the centripetal force on its mass?
    (A) 0.72 N
    (B) 7.2 N
    (C) 72 N
    (D) 720 N
    (E) 7,200 N

128. Four planets, A through D, orbit the same star. The relative masses and distances from the star for each planet are shown in the table. For example, Planet A has twice the mass of Planet B, and Planet D has three times the orbital radius of Planet A. Which planet has the highest gravitational attraction to the star?

Planet	Relative mass	Relative distance
A	$2\,m$	r
B	m	$0.1\,r$
C	$0.5\,m$	$2\,r$
D	$4\,m$	$3\,r$

(A) Planet A
(B) Planet B
(C) Planet C
(D) Planet D
(E) All have the same gravitational attraction to the star.

129. Multi-select: Two of the suggested answers will be correct. Select the two best answers, and record them both on the answer sheet.

The planet Jupiter orbits the Sun at a nearly constant speed. Which of the following statements are true?

(A) There is a force on Jupiter toward the center of the orbit.
(B) There is a force on Jupiter pulling it out from the center of the orbit.
(C) There is a force on Jupiter in the direction of its motion.
(D) Jupiter is accelerating toward the center of the orbit.
(E) There are no forces on Jupiter.

130. A tetherball is whirled in a horizontal circle above your head. If the string breaks, the ball will follow what type of path if it is observed from above?

(A) Straight outward from the center
(B) Straight toward the center
(C) An expanding spiral
(D) A curved path that gradually approaches a straight line
(E) Tangent to the original circular path

131. The driver of a race car takes a turn on a track at a constant speed. What can be said about the acceleration of the driver?
    (A) It is outward from the center of the turn.
    (B) It is in the direction of motion.
    (C) It is toward the center of the turn.
    (D) It is a vector combination of forward and toward the center.
    (E) It has a value of zero.

132. **Multi-select:** Two of the suggested answers will be correct. Select the two best answers, and record them both on the answer sheet.

    What can be said about the Moon as it orbits the Earth at a constant speed?
    (A) The Moon's velocity is constant.
    (B) The Moon experiences acceleration toward the center of the orbit.
    (C) There is an unbalanced force on the Moon.
    (D) The Moon experiences acceleration away from the center of the orbit.
    (E) The Moon experiences a constant acceleration.

133. A pendulum bob is attached to a string that is tied to the ceiling, and the bob is pulled back and released. As the bob moves through the bottom of the swing, how does the magnitude of the tension force from the string compare to the gravitational force on the bob?
    (A) The tension force is less than the gravitational force.
    (B) The tension force is greater than the gravitational force.
    (C) The tension force is equal to the gravitational force.
    (D) The mass of the ball is needed in order to compare these forces.
    (E) The release height of the ball is needed in order to compare these forces.

134. A pendulum bob is attached to a string that is tied to the ceiling, and the bob is pulled back and released from different heights. As the bob moves through the bottom of the swing, how is its centripetal acceleration related to its speed?
    (A) The centripetal acceleration is directly proportional to the speed of the pendulum.
    (B) The centripetal acceleration is inversely proportional to the speed of the pendulum.
    (C) The centripetal acceleration is directly proportional to the square of the speed of the pendulum.
    (D) The centripetal acceleration is inversely proportional to the square of the speed of the pendulum.
    (E) There is no relationship between the centripetal acceleration and the speed.

135. Two satellites orbit the Earth at the same speed in identical orbits. Satellite A is twice the mass of Satellite B. How does the centripetal acceleration of Satellite A compare with that of Satellite B?

(A) Four times as much
(B) Twice as much
(C) The same
(D) One-half as much
(E) One-fourth as much

136. When climbing from sea level to the top of Mount Everest, a hiker changes elevation by 8,848 m. By what percentage will the gravitational field of the Earth change during the climb? (The Earth's mass is 6.0×10^{24} kg, and its radius is 6.4×10^6 m.)

(A) It will increase by approximately 0.3%.
(B) It will decrease by approximately 0.3%.
(C) It will increase by approximately 12%.
(D) It will decrease by approximately 12%.
(E) The gravitational field strength will not change.

Multi-select: For **questions 137–139**, two of the suggested answers will be correct. Select the two best answers, and record them both on the answer sheet.

137. Two masses, M_1 and M_2, are separated a distance d. What changes in the variables will result in NO CHANGE in the gravitational force between the masses?

(A) M_1 is doubled, and d is doubled.
(B) M_2 is tripled, and d is quadrupled.
(C) Both M_1 and M_2 are tripled, and d is tripled.
(D) M_2 is quadrupled, and d is doubled.
(E) M_1 is cut in half, M_2 is cut in half, but d is doubled.

138. A child swings from the end of a rope tied to the branch of a tree. As she swings through the bottom of the arc, which forces act on her?

(A) A downward force of air pressure
(B) A downward centrifugal force
(C) The gravitational force
(D) The forward force of motion
(E) The upward tension from the rope

139. Which of the following affect the strength of the gravitational field on the surface of a planet?

(A) The mass of the object at the surface
(B) The mass of the planet
(C) The radius of the planet
(D) The volume of the object at the surface
(E) The presence of air at the surface of the planet

140. Two identical cars are moving at the same constant speed as they take different exit ramps from the highway. Ramp 1 is a circular arc with a radius of 25 m. Ramp 2 is a circular arc with a radius of 50 m. How does the centripetal force on the car taking Ramp 2 compare with that for the car taking Ramp 1?

(A) Ramp 2 requires four times the centripetal force.
(B) Ramp 2 requires two times the centripetal force.
(C) Ramp 2 requires the same centripetal force.
(D) Ramp 2 requires one-half the centripetal force.
(E) Ramp 2 requires one-fourth the centripetal force.

141. The Moon takes 27.3 days to orbit the Earth at an average radial distance of 385,000 km from the center of the Earth. What is the acceleration of the Moon?

(A) 2.73×10^{-3} m/s^2
(B) 4.96×10^{-3} m/s^2
(C) 9.80×10^{0} m/s^2
(D) 1.94×10^{-3} m/s^2
(E) 6.92×10^{-5} m/s^2

142. In **the previous question,** assign the acceleration of the Moon the symbol a_m and the mass of the Moon M_m. If a satellite with a mass M_s were placed in the same orbit at the same speed, what is the gravitational field strength at the satellite's orbital position?

(A) a_m
(B) $(M_s/M_m)\, a_m$
(C) $(M_m/M_s)\, a_m$
(D) $(M_s + M_m)\, a_m/M_s$
(E) $(M_s + M_m)\, a_m/M_m$

143. The mass, turn radius, and speed of each car in the table below are shown relative to Car A. Which of the following best ranks the centripetal force on the cars?

Car	Mass	Radius	Speed
A	M	R	V
B	$2M$	R	V
C	M	$2R$	V
D	M	$2R$	$2V$

    (A) $D > A = B > C$
    (B) $D > C = B > A$
    (C) $D = A = B > C$
    (D) $D > B > A > C$
    (E) $D = B > A > C$

Free Response: A 1,000-kg satellite orbits the Earth in a circular orbit at an altitude of 1,000 km. The Earth's mass is 6.0×10^{24} kg, and its radius is 6.4×10^6 m.

144. How does the force of gravity on the satellite compare with the centripetal force on the satellite? What is the magnitude of the force of gravity acting on the satellite?

145. What is the magnitude of the satellite's tangential velocity?

146. What is the gravitational potential energy of the satellite?

147. What is the value of the acceleration due to gravity at this altitude?

Free Response: A 1,000-kg car makes a turn on a banked curve. The radius of the turn is 300 m, and the turn is inclined at an angle ($\theta = 30°$). Assume that the turn is frictionless.

148. Draw a free-body diagram of this situation, and label all the forces on the car.

149. Calculate the car's maximum speed.

150. Calculate the centripetal force on the car.

CHAPTER 4

Simple Harmonic Motion

151. A 0.40-kg mass hangs on a spring with a spring constant of 12 N/m. The system oscillates with a constant amplitude of 12 cm. What is the maximum acceleration of the system?

(A) 0.62 m/s^2

(B) 1.4 m/s^2

(C) 1.6 m/s^2

(D) 3.6 m/s^2

(E) 9.8 m/s^2

152. A mass is attached to a spring and allowed to oscillate vertically. Which of the following would NOT change the period of the oscillation?

(A) Double the mass and double the spring constant

(B) Double the amplitude of vibration and double the mass

(C) Double the gravitational field strength and double the mass

(D) Double the gravitational field strength and double the spring constant

(E) Double the gravitational field strength and quadruple the mass

153. The Moon is approximately 384,000 km from the Earth. The Moon revolves around the Earth once every 27.3 days. What is the frequency of the Moon's motion?

(A) 14,100 km each day

(B) 0.0366 revolution each day

(C) 0.036630 revolution each day

(D) 655 hours for each revolution

(E) 27.3 days for each revolution

154. A bell is rung when the dangling clapper within it makes contact with the bell. A poorly designed bell has a clapper that swings with the same period as the bell. How can this design be improved?

(A) Use a clapper with a smaller mass on the end so it is out of period with the bell.

(B) Use a clapper with a bigger mass on the end so it is out of period with the bell.

(C) Force the bell to swing with greater amplitude.

(D) Use a longer clapper so it is out of period with the bell.

(E) Increase the mass of the bell so it makes better contact with the clapper.

155. A meter stick is held at one end by a frictionless pivot and is held horizontally at the other end. Neglecting air resistance, how far will the meter stick swing when released?

(A) It will swing in a circle around the pivot and back to the starting point.

(B) It will swing just short of horizontal on the other side of the pivot.

(C) It will swing just beyond horizontal on the other side of the pivot.

(D) It will swing to horizontal on the other side of the pivot.

(E) It will drop to vertical and stop.

156. A toy nicknamed the "Newton's cradle" consists of five steel balls, each suspended by two strings and each touching the adjacent ball(s). When a ball at the end is raised and then dropped, it hits the adjacent ball and the ball at the other end rises. Why?

(A) The elastic energy of the moving ball is transferred to chemical energy.

(B) The potential energy of the center balls keeps them in place.

(C) The kinetic energy of the moving ball is transferred through the set of balls causing the ball at the end to rise up.

(D) The potential energy of the moving ball is transferred through the set of balls to the only ball that can move, causing it to rise.

(E) The center balls are glued together and do not move.

157. Which choice below best explains why a pendulum does not oscillate in zero gravity?

(A) The pendulum has no mass in zero gravity.

(B) A pendulum requires gravity to create the restoring force.

(C) The pendulum is in orbit and considered weightless.

(D) The pendulum would be too far from the Earth to work properly.

(E) The pendulum must have an oscillating tension in the string to function properly.

158. Some large oil tankers have an antiroll water tank inside the hull that matches the resonant frequency of the ship's hull. When ocean waves hit the ship at the resonant frequency, how does the water tank prevent the ship from capsizing in the waves?

(A) The energy of the waves is used by the water in the tank.
(B) The waves enter the tank and are dampened.
(C) The water tank is 180° out of phase with the ship's hull.
(D) The water tank is 90° out of phase with the ship's hull.
(E) The water in the tank is in phase with the ship's hull.

159. A pendulum has a bob of 28 kg and is 38 cm in diameter. It is hung on a wire that is 67 m long. What are its period and frequency near the surface of the Earth?

(A) 0.061 s and 16 cycles/s
(B) 16 s and 0.061 cycle/s
(C) 0.60869 s and 16.429 cycles/s
(D) 11 s and 0.094 cycle/s
(E) 0.094 s and 11 cycles/s

160. One end of a 50-kg mass is attached to two vertical springs in parallel. Each spring has a spring constant of 20 N/m. When the spring is pulled back and released, what is the system's period?

(A) 14.04962946 s
(B) 7.024814731 s
(C) 14 s
(D) 7.0 s
(E) 0.14 s

161. A mass of 50 kg is held vertically by two springs, one connected to the other in series. Each spring has a spring constant of 20 N/m. When set in motion, what is the system's period?

(A) 0.14 s
(B) 14 s
(C) 7.0 s
(D) 14.04962946 s
(E) 7.024814731 s

162. A mass of 50 kg is held horizontally on a frictionless surface by two springs, one at each end of the mass. Each spring has a spring constant of 20 N/m. When set in motion, what is the system's period?

    (A) 14.04962946 s
    (B) 7.024814731 s
    (C) 14 s
    (D) 7.0 s
    (E) 0.14 s

163. A mass of 50 kg is held horizontally on a frictionless surface by two springs, one connected to the other in series. Each spring has a spring constant of 20 N/m. When set in motion, what is the system's period?

    (A) 0.14 s
    (B) 14 s
    (C) 7.0 s
    (D) 14.04962946 s
    (E) 7.024814731 s

164. A 10-kg mass is placed on a frictionless surface and attached to a spring that is attached to a fixed wall. The spring's constant is 20 N/m. When set in motion, what is the system's period, and what is the period if the system is held vertically?

    (A) 4.4 s and 8.9 s
    (B) 8.885765876 s for both
    (C) 8.885765876 s and 17.77153175 s
    (D) 4.4 s for both
    (E) 13 s for both

165. A 15-kg mass rests on two springs and is held by a spring attached to the ceiling. The spring constant for each of the bottom two springs is 10 N/m, and the spring constant for the upper spring is 25 N/m. When set in motion, what is the system's period?

    (A) 3.6 s
    (B) 7.2 s
    (C) 1.8 s
    (D) 1.2 s
    (E) The mass will not move.

166. A mass of 12 kg is hung onto a spring attached to the ceiling. The spring's constant is 19 N/m. How far will the spring stretch when the weight is hung, and what will be the system's period when activated?

(A) 6.2 cm and 15 s
(B) 6.2 m and 5 min
(C) 62 mm and 15.6 s
(D) 6.2 m and 5.0 s
(E) 6.2 m and 156 s

167. A refrigerator compressor that weighs 8 kg is fixed to three separate springs on the refrigerator frame. Each has a spring constant of 0.01 N/m. What is the natural frequency of the system?

(A) 0.01 cycle/s
(B) 0.03 cycle/s
(C) 0.8 cycle/s
(D) 103 cycles/s
(E) 0.003 cycle/s

168. The pendulum on an old mechanical, weight-driven clock has a period of 3.0 s. What is the length of the clock's pendulum?

(A) 2.2 m
(B) 3.5 m
(C) 22 cm
(D) 35 cm
(E) 3.0 m

169. A blue light wave vibrates at 6.98×10^{14} Hz. What is its period of vibration?

(A) 6.98×10^{14} s
(B) 1.43×10^{-15} s
(C) 2.09×10^{23} m/s
(D) 3.00×10^{8} m/s
(E) 2.09×10^{23} m

170. A steel ball with a mass of 100 g is dropped onto a steel plate. The collision is perfectly elastic. From what height must the ball be dropped for the vibrating system to have a bounce period of 2.0 s?

(A) 100. cm
(B) 20. m
(C) 0.10 m
(D) 9.8 m
(E) 4.9 m

171. A pendulum on the surface of the Moon has a period of 1.0 s. If the length of the pendulum is quadrupled, what is the value of the new period?

    (A) 0.25 s
    (B) 0.50 s
    (C) 1.0 s
    (D) 2.0 s
    (E) 4.0 s

172. A 2.0-m pendulum on a particular planet has a period of 4.6 s. What is the gravitational field strength on that planet?

    (A) 1.6 N/kg
    (B) 3.7 N/kg
    (C) 4.9 N/kg
    (D) 9.8 N/kg
    (E) 25 N/kg

173. A particle oscillates with simple harmonic motion with no damping. Which one of the following statements about the acceleration of the oscillating particle is true?

    (A) It has a value of 9.8 m/s² when the oscillation is vertical.
    (B) It is zero when the speed is the minimum.
    (C) It is proportional to the frequency.
    (D) It is zero throughout the oscillation.
    (E) It is zero when the speed is the maximum.

174. The displacement (in centimeters) of the vibrating cone of a large loudspeaker is represented by the equation $\Delta x = 2.0 \cos(150t)$, where t is the time in seconds. What distance does the tip of the cone move in half a period?

    (A) 0.007 cm
    (B) 1.0 cm
    (C) 2.0 cm
    (D) 4.0 cm
    (E) 150 cm

175. The displacement (in centimeters) of the vibrating cone of a large loudspeaker is represented by the equation $\Delta x = 2.0 \cos(150t)$. What is the frequency of the vibration of the tip of the cone?

    (A) 24 Hz
    (B) 0.042 Hz
    (C) 150 Hz
    (D) 2.0 Hz
    (E) 1.0 Hz

176. The graph shows the displacement versus time for an object. Which equation best describes its displacement in meters?

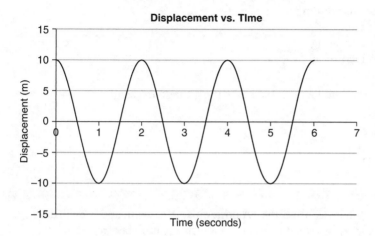

(A) $\Delta x = 20 \cos(0.5t)$
(B) $\Delta x = 10 \cos(2t)$
(C) $\Delta x = 10 \cos(\pi t)$
(D) $\Delta x = 20 \cos(2t)$
(E) $\Delta x = 20 \sin(\pi t)$

Questions 177–180 are based on the figure below of a mass-spring system. Assume the mass is pulled back to position +A and released, and it slides back and forth without friction.

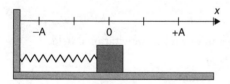

177. When the mass reaches position −A, what can be said about its speed?

(A) It is a minimum.
(B) It is a maximum.
(C) It is zero.
(D) It is decreasing.
(E) It is increasing.

178. When the mass reaches position 0, what can be said about its speed?

(A) It is a minimum.
(B) It is a maximum.
(C) It is zero.
(D) It is decreasing.
(E) It is increasing.

179. At what position does the mass have the greatest acceleration?

(A) −A
(B) −A/2
(C) 0
(D) +A/2
(E) +A

180. The mass is released from the −A position at time $t = 0$, and it oscillates with period T, measured in seconds. Which equation best represents the displacement?

(A) $\Delta x = -A \cos\left(\dfrac{T}{2\pi}t\right)$

(B) $\Delta x = -(A/2) \cos(2\pi T t)$

(C) $\Delta x = -A \cos\left(\dfrac{2\pi}{T}t\right)$

(D) $\Delta x = (A/2) \cos(T t)$

(E) $\Delta x = A \cos\left(\dfrac{2\pi}{T}t\right)$

181. A mass-spring system oscillates up and down in a gravitational field. When is its kinetic energy the greatest?

(A) When it's passing through equilibrium
(B) At the top of its motion
(C) At the bottom its motion
(D) When its gravitational potential energy is the greatest
(E) When its elastic energy is the greatest

182. A mass is suspended from a spring and allowed to oscillate freely. When the amplitude of vibration is doubled, what happens to the frequency of vibration?
    (A) It quadruples.
    (B) It doubles.
    (C) It stays the same.
    (D) It reduces to one-half of what it was.
    (E) It reduces to one-fourth of what it was.

183. Rank the following in regard to the voltage across just one resistor in the circuit. Assume all resistors are identical.
     I. A circuit with a battery of voltage V connected across a resistor
    II. A circuit with a battery of voltage V connected across two resistors in series
   III. A circuit with a battery of voltage V connected across two resistors in parallel
    IV. A circuit with a battery of voltage 2V connected across two resistors in series
    (A) IV > II = III > I
    (B) I = III = IV > II
    (C) I > III > IV = II
    (D) II = III > IV = I
    (E) I = II = III = IV

184. A wave generator in a pool produces one wave every minute. What is the frequency of vibration?
    (A) 60 s
    (B) 1 Hz
    (C) 0.02 Hz
    (D) 60 Hz
    (E) 1 s

185. The Moon has a gravitational field strength that is approximately one-sixth of the field on the Earth. What is the ratio between the period of a pendulum on the Moon and the period of an identical pendulum on the Earth?
    (A) 6
    (B) $\sqrt{6}$
    (C) $\dfrac{1}{6}$
    (D) $\dfrac{1}{\sqrt{6}}$
    (E) 1

186. A mass-spring system oscillates with simple harmonic motion because a compressed or stretched spring has what type of energy?

   (A) Gravitational potential
   (B) Kinetic
   (C) Chemical
   (D) Thermal
   (E) Elastic potential

Multi-select: For **questions 187–191**, two of the suggested answers will be correct. Select the two best answers, and record them both on the answer sheet.

187. Which of the following are NOT examples of simple harmonic motion?

   (A) A tennis ball bouncing on the ground
   (B) A child swinging freely back and forth in a toddler swing
   (C) A plucked guitar string
   (D) A child who continues to jump up and down
   (E) A ball rolling back and forth in a bowl

188. Which of the following best represent periodic motion?

   (A) A skydiver who has reached terminal velocity
   (B) The Moon in orbit about the Earth
   (C) A car driving to each state in the United States
   (D) A cart pushed up a frictionless incline plane
   (E) A pendulum swinging over a 30-min time span.

189. Which of the following significantly affect the period of a simple pendulum?

   (A) The length of the pendulum
   (B) The mass of the pendulum bob
   (C) The amplitude of swing
   (D) The gravitational field strength
   (E) The thickness of the string

190. A mass is suspended from a vertical spring attached to a support. Which of the following significantly affect the frequency of oscillation of this system?

(A) The spring constant
(B) The gravitational field strength
(C) The value of the mass
(D) Friction between the mass and the spring
(E) The surface area of the mass

191. A mass oscillates from the end of a vertical spring. What may be done to increase the frequency of oscillation?

(A) Increase the mass
(B) Decrease the mass
(C) Increase the spring constant
(D) Increase the strength of the gravitational field
(E) Increase the amplitude of vibration

Free Response: A system consists of a 2.0-kg mass hanging from a vertical spring that has a spring constant of 8.0 N/m. The system is displaced 20.0 cm and continues to vibrate with no damping.

192. Determine the amplitude, and calculate the period and frequency of the oscillation.

193. Write an equation for the displacement (in centimeters) of the mass as a function of time.

194. Sketch two oscillations of the displacement versus time graph.

195. Calculate the maximum values of spring force, acceleration, and velocity of the mass.

196. During one full oscillation, explain when the points of maximum acceleration and maximum velocity occur.

Free Response: A student group is conducting a lab to determine the variables that affect the period of a pendulum motion. The group identified three variables to test: the length of the pendulum, the mass of the pendulum bob, and the displacement angle of the swing. Answer the following questions about this experiment.

197. Explain how the period of the pendulum is measured. Identify the instruments that may be used to measure period, and comment on uncertainties in measurement.

198. The group first conducts an experiment to test the effect of the length of the pendulum. Identify the independent variable, the dependent variable, and the controlled variables in this experiment.

199. Sketch the expected shape of the period versus length graph.

200. Next, the group tests the effect of the mass of the bob on the period. Based on your knowledge of the pendulum, make all the necessary calculations and fill in the missing data in this table:

Mass of Bob (g)	Period (s)
10.	
20.	
30.	0.76
40.	
50.	

Angle of swing = 20. °, and the Length of the pendulum = _____ m

201. Because of budgeting issues, the students did not test the effect of the gravitational field on the period of the pendulum. Based on your knowledge of a pendulum, sketch the shape of the graph of period versus the square root of the gravitational field.

CHAPTER 5

Impulse, Linear Momentum, Conservation of Linear Momentum, and Collisions

202. A 70-kg man runs at a constant velocity of 2 m/s. What is the magnitude of his momentum?

(A) 35 kg·m/s
(B) 68 kg·m/s
(C) 70 kg·m/s
(D) 72 kg·m/s
(E) 140 kg·m/s

203. A 10-N force is applied to a hockey puck over a period of 0.1 s. What is the change in momentum of the hockey puck?

(A) 1.0 kg·m/s
(B) 9.9 kg·m/s
(C) 10 kg·m/s
(D) 10.1 kg·m/s
(E) 100 kg·m/s

204. A 1,000-kg car moving at a constant velocity of +11.0 m/s strikes a concrete barrier and comes to a complete stop in 2.0 s. What is the average force acting on the car?

(A) −5,500 N
(B) −180 N
(C) 0.02 N
(D) 180 N
(E) 5,500 N

205. A 1.0-kg ball moving at +10 m/s strikes a wall and bounces back. The collision is perfectly elastic. What is the ball's momentum after the collision? (Assume a frictionless surface.)

    (A) −100 kg·m/s
    (B) −10 kg·m/s
    (C) −1.0 kg·m/s
    (D) 10 kg·m/s
    (E) 100 kg·m/s

206. A 10-kg box is sliding across an ice rink at 10 m/s. A skater exerts a constant force of 10 N against it. How long will it take for the box to come to a complete stop?

    (A) 0.5 s
    (B) 1.0 s
    (C) 10 s
    (D) 50 s
    (E) 100 s

207. Two balls of equal mass collide in a perfectly elastic collision. Ball A moves to the right at 10 m/s. Ball B moves to the left at 5 m/s. After the collision, Ball B moves to the right at 3 m/s. What is the velocity of Ball A after the collision? (Assume a frictionless surface.)

    (A) −10 m/s
    (B) −8.0 m/s
    (C) −5.0 m/s
    (D) 2 m/s
    (E) 3 m/s

208. A 140-kg fullback is running with the football at 10 m/s. A 70-kg defender runs at him in the opposite direction at 5 m/s. The defender wraps his arms around the fullback. What is the velocity of the two players after the collision? (Assume a frictionless surface.)

    (A) −10 m/s
    (B) −5 m/s
    (C) 0 m/s
    (D) 5 m/s
    (E) 10 m/s

209. There are two billiard balls each with a mass of 200 g. A pool player shoots Ball A with a velocity of 1.0 m/s at Ball B, which is at rest. After an elastic collision, Ball A stops and Ball B travels off in a straight line. What is the velocity of Ball B immediately after the collision?

(A) −1.0 m/s
(B) −0.2 m/s
(C) 0 m/s
(D) 0.2 m/s
(E) 1.0 m/s

210. A bullet has a mass of 50 g, and its momentum is 25 kg·m/s. What is the velocity of the bullet?

(A) 2×10^{-3} m/s
(B) 5×10^{-1} m/s
(C) 2.5×10^{1} m/s
(D) 5×10^{1} m/s
(E) 5×10^{2} m/s

211. A firework shell reaches the top of its parabolic trajectory and explodes. What happens to the center of mass of the system of all the shell fragments?

(A) It moves toward the largest fragment.
(B) It moves toward the smallest fragment.
(C) It continues to move in its original parabolic trajectory.
(D) It curves upward before falling back down.
(E) It moves into a larger parabolic trajectory than before.

212. A 150-kg halfback is running down the field carrying the ball at a velocity of 5 m/s. A 50-kg linebacker from the opposing team is running at him in the opposite direction. The linebacker hopes to wrap him in a tackle with a perfectly inelastic collision. Is this possible, and if so, at what velocity must the linebacker run?

(A) Yes, −15 m/s
(B) Yes, −10 m/s
(C) Yes, −5 m/s
(D) Yes, 0 m/s
(E) No, the linebacker cannot stop the fullback.

213. A batter applies a constant force of 10.0 N over a period of 5.00 milliseconds when he strikes a baseball. The mass of the baseball is 145 g. What is the magnitude of the velocity change of the baseball?

(A) 0.100 m/s
(B) 0.345 m/s
(C) 0.500 m/s
(D) 2.00 m/s
(E) 2.90 m/s

214. What is the magnitude of the momentum of an electron moving at 90 percent of the speed of light?

(A) 3.3×10^{-31} kg·m/s
(B) 2.5×10^{-31} kg·m/s
(C) 3.3×10^{-22} kg·m/s
(D) 2.5×10^{-22} kg·m/s
(E) 3.3×10^{-20} kg·m/s

215. A 260-g cue ball moving at 1.0 m/s strikes a 150-g numbered ball at rest. The collision is elastic and the cue ball stops. What is the speed of the numbered ball?

(A) 0.6 m/s
(B) 1.2 m/s
(C) 1.5 m/s
(D) 1.7 m/s
(E) 2.0 m/s

216. A 750-kg aircraft is flying level at 100 m/s. A tailwind blows for 2 min, and the aircraft's speed increases to 120 m/s. What was the average force of the tailwind?

(A) 125 N
(B) 250 N
(C) 2,500 N
(D) 5,000 N
(E) 7,500 N

217. This graph depicts the motion of a box being pushed across the floor. Which of the following statements describes the force upon the box?

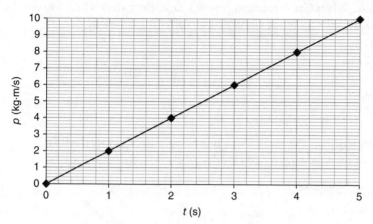

(A) The force on the box is a constant 0.5 N.
(B) The force on the box is a constant 1 N.
(C) The force on the box is a constant 2 N.
(D) The force on the box is 1 N and increasing.
(E) The force on the box is 2 N and increasing.

218. A force of 2.0 N exerted on an object for 100 milliseconds increases the object's velocity by 1.0 m/s. What was the mass of the object?

(A) 0.1 kg
(B) 0.2 kg
(C) 1.0 kg
(D) 20 kg
(E) 200 kg

219. A 70.0-kg stuntman free-falls from a building for 2.5 s and hits an airbag. The airbag exerts a force on him over a time period of 2.0 s, and he comes to a complete stop. What was the approximate magnitude of the average force exerted by the airbag?

(A) 100 N
(B) 280 N
(C) 480 N
(D) 880 N
(E) 1,000 N

220. Two railroad cars (2×10^4 kg each) are traveling in the same direction along a railroad track. Car A is traveling at 14 m/s, and Car B is traveling at 10 m/s. When Car A catches up with Car B, the two cars link together. What is the velocity of the combined cars after the collision?

(A) 10 m/s
(B) 12 m/s
(C) 14 m/s
(D) 20 m/s
(E) 24 m/s

221. This graph depicts the motion of a box being pushed across the floor. Which of the following statements describes the force upon the box?

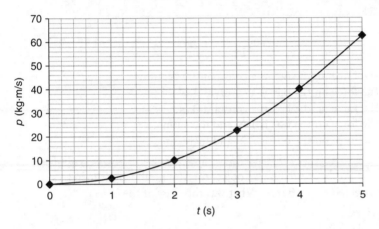

(A) The force on the box is constant.
(B) The force on the box is decreasing.
(C) The force on the box is increasing.
(D) The acceleration of the box is constant.
(E) The force on the box is zero.

222. Two skaters, a 70-kg man and a 50-kg woman, are initially at rest on an ice rink and then "push off" from each other and move in opposite directions. After the push-off, the woman moves with a velocity of +2.5 m/s. What is the velocity of the man?

(A) −2.5 m/s
(B) −1.8 m/s
(C) −1.3 m/s
(D) 0 m/s
(E) 2.5 m/s

223. A 0.5-kg object has a momentum of 10 kg·m/s. What is its speed?

(A) 1.0 m/s

(B) 5.0 m/s

(C) 10 m/s

(D) 20 m/s

(E) 50 m/s

224. A cue ball with a mass of 250 g travels at 1.0 m/s and hits a numbered ball with a mass of 170 g at rest. The numbered ball moves off at an angle of 45°, while the cue ball moves off at an angle of −45°. At what speeds do the balls move?

(A) The cue ball and the numbered ball move at 1.0 m/s.

(B) The cue ball moves at 1.0 m/s, and the numbered ball moves at −1.0 m/s.

(C) The cue ball moves at 0.71 m/s, and the numbered ball moves at 0.71 m/s.

(D) The cue ball moves at 1.04 m/s, and the numbered ball moves at 0.71 m/s.

(E) The cue ball moves at 0.71 m/s, and the numbered ball moves at 1.04 m/s.

225. A 2,000-kg airplane flies at 343 m/s. What is its momentum?

(A) 0.17 kg·m/s

(B) 5.8 kg·m/s

(C) 6,900 kg·m/s

(D) 6.9×10^4 kg·m/s

(E) 6.9×10^5 kg·m/s

226. A marksman fires a 7.5-g bullet from a loosely held 1.2-kg handgun. The bullet travels away at +365 m/s. At what velocity does the handgun recoil?

(A) −2.3 m/s

(B) −1.2 m/s

(C) 0 m/s

(D) +1.2 m/s

(E) +2.3 m/s

227. Two 500-g carts move on a frictionless air track. Cart A is moving at +0.1 m/s when it collides into Cart B at rest. The two carts get stuck together. At what velocity will the combined carts move?

(A) −0.1 m/s
(B) −0.05 m/s
(C) 0 m/s
(D) +0.05 m/s
(E) +0.1 m/s

228. A rifle fires a 4.0-g bullet at a velocity of 950 m/s. If the bullet is in the rifle barrel for only 0.1 s, what average force does the rifle exert on the bullet?

(A) 18 N
(B) 28 N
(C) 38 N
(D) 48 N
(E) 58 N

229. A 1,000-kg cannon fires a 15-kg cannonball. The cannon is mounted on a low-friction carriage that allows it to recoil at −1.5 m/s. What is the speed of the cannonball?

(A) 10 m/s
(B) 50 m/s
(C) 100 m/s
(D) 200 m/s
(E) 500 m/s

230. A 5-kg cart moving with a kinetic energy of 18 joules has an elastic collision with a 10-kg cart at rest. What is the kinetic energy of the system of both carts after the collision?

(A) 9 J
(B) 12 J
(C) 18 J
(D) 27 J
(E) 36 J

231. Which of the following has the greatest magnitude of momentum?

(A) A 500-kg car moving at 40 m/s
(B) A 30,000-kg dump truck at rest
(C) A 1,000-kg SUV moving at 25 m/s
(D) A proton moving at 90 percent of the speed of light
(E) A 90,000,000-kg aircraft carrier moving at 2 cm/s

232. The momentum change of an object exactly equals which of the following?

(A) The force acting on the object

(B) The velocity change of the object

(C) The product of force and the time the force acts

(D) The product of force and the change in velocity

(E) The ratio of net force and mass

233. In a particular crash safety test, engineers study what happens when cars hit solid walls. Which of the following observations best indicates that LESS force is exerted on the car?

(A) The car hits the wall and bounces back.

(B) The car crushes during the collision.

(C) The crash dummy flies through the windshield.

(D) The front seat airbags are deployed.

(E) The wall crumbles upon collision.

234. A 10-kg cart moving to the right at 5 m/s has a head-on collision with a 5-kg cart moving to the left at 7 m/s. If the carts stick together, what is the velocity of the combination?

(A) 1 m/s to the right

(B) 1 m/s to the left

(C) 7 m/s to the right

(D) 9 m/s to the right

(E) 9 m/s to the left

235. A 4-kg cart moving to the right with 18 J of kinetic energy has a head-on collision with a 2-kg cart moving to the left with 1 J of kinetic energy. After the collision, the 4-kg cart continues moving to the right, but its kinetic energy decreases to 2 J. The 2-kg cart is driven to the right, but its kinetic energy increases to 9 J. Which of the following is true about this collision?

(A) This is an inelastic collision that demonstrates momentum conservation.

(B) This is an elastic collision that demonstrates momentum conservation.

(C) This is an inelastic collision where momentum is not conserved.

(D) This is an elastic collision where momentum is not conserved.

(E) This is a perfectly inelastic collision in which energy is conserved.

236. Which of the following results in the cannonball leaving a cannon with the least velocity?

(A) Increase the strength of the gravitational field
(B) Increase the explosive force pushing the cannonball
(C) Decrease the friction in the barrel
(D) Decrease the mass of the ball (keeping its size the same)
(E) Decrease the length of the cannon barrel

237. Measurements and calculations from a slow motion video show a 50.0-g ball hitting the ground at +5.0 m/s and bouncing back up at −4.0 m/s. By how much did the ball's momentum change?

(A) 0.05 kg·m/s
(B) 0.45 kg·m/s
(C) 0.00 kg·m/s
(D) −0.45 kg·m/s
(E) −0.05 kg·m/s

238. The video camera used in the experiment in **the question above** has a frame rate of 30 pictures per second. In the video, the ball makes contact with the floor for three frames. What is the average force that the ball exerts on the floor?

(A) +7.2 N
(B) +4.5 N
(C) −5.0 N
(D) −4.5 N
(E) −7.2 N

Multi-select: For **questions 239–243**, two of the suggested answers will be correct. Select the two best answers, and record them both on the answer sheet.

239. Which of the following may be modeled as an elastic collision?

(A) A ball bounces as high as it's dropped.
(B) Two cars experience a head-on collision.
(C) A piece of soft clay hits a wall and sticks.
(D) A moving cart stops as it hits and pushes a resting cart away at the same speed.
(E) A moving train car links to a resting car, and the combination moves off at a slower speed.

240. Which of the following are FALSE statements for an isolated system of two colliding objects?

(A) The momentum is the same before and after an elastic collision.
(B) The motion center of mass is the same before and after the collision.
(C) The momentum differs before and after an inelastic collision.
(D) The kinetic energy is the same before and after an elastic collision.
(E) The kinetic energy is the same before and after an inelastic collision.

241. When a bat hits a soft tee ball at rest, which of the following will increase the momentum of the tee ball?

(A) The bat contacts the ball for twice the time with half the force.
(B) The bat contacts the ball for the same amount of time but exerts a greater force on the ball.
(C) The bat hits the ball with the same force but contacts it for a greater time.
(D) The bat hits the ball with the same force and contacts it for less time.
(E) The bat hits the ball with less force and contacts it for the same time.

242. Which of the following are NOT necessary to determine the momentum of an object at a particular instant?

(A) Its acceleration
(B) Its speed
(C) Its direction of motion
(D) Its mass
(E) Its gravitational potential energy

243. The momentum of a system is NOT conserved in which of the following scenarios?

(A) An elastic collision within a two-cart system
(B) A net force acting on the system
(C) An inelastic collision within a two-cart system
(D) An explosion within a system
(E) The center of mass of a system accelerating

Free Response: A 2.0-kg box is initially moving at +3.0 m/s and is pushed along a horizontal, frictionless surface with a force that varies with time according to the following graph:

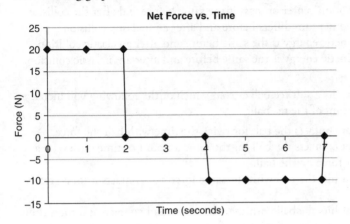

Net Force vs. Time

244. Qualitatively describe what happens to the motion of the box in the following time intervals: 0–2 s, 2–4 s, and 4–7 s.

245. Calculate the momentum change of the box during each second of elapsed time.

246. Plot the velocity versus time graph for this motion.

247. At the 7-second clock reading, the box collides with a wall and bounces backward at 6 m/s. Given that the box is in contact with the wall for 0.20 s, calculate the average force that the wall exerts on the box.

Free Response: An 800.0-kg car is traveling along a wet road at a velocity of 25.5 m/s. A 1,000.0-kg car is traveling along the same road in the same direction at 34.7 m/s. The two cars collide and lock together. Answer the following questions.

248. The two interlocked cars proceed at what velocity after the collision?

249. Compare the kinetic energy of the two-car system immediately before the collision and after the collision.

250. Discuss any transfer of energy that occurs, and explain whether this is an elastic or inelastic collision.

251. If the coefficient of sliding friction between the tires of the cars and the wet pavement is 0.7, calculate the force of friction.

252. How long does it take for the two interlocked cars to come to a complete stop on the wet pavement?

CHAPTER 6

Work, Energy, and Conservation of Energy

253. A 70-kg man runs at a constant velocity of 2 m/s. What is his kinetic energy?
  (A) 35 J
  (B) 70 J
  (C) 105 J
  (D) 140 J
  (E) 210 J

254. A 10-N force is applied horizontally on a box to move it 10 m across a frictionless surface. How much work was done to move the box?
  (A) 0 J
  (B) 10 J
  (C) 50 J
  (D) 100 J
  (E) 1,000 J

255. A constant net force of 500 N moves a 1,000-kg car 100 m. If the car was initially at rest, then what is the car's final velocity?
  (A) 1 m/s
  (B) 5 m/s
  (C) 10 m/s
  (D) 20 m/s
  (E) 100 m/s

256. A mover uses a pulley system to lift a grand piano with a mass of 500 kg from the ground to a height of 10 m. What is the change in the piano's gravitational potential energy?

(A) 5×10^2 J
(B) 5×10^3 J
(C) 5×10^4 J
(D) 5×10^5 J
(E) 5×10^6 J

257. A boy pulls a 10-kg box across an ice rink for a distance of 50 m. He exerts a constant force of 10 N on a rope attached to the box at an angle of 60°. How much work has he done on the box?

(A) 50 J
(B) 100 J
(C) 200 J
(D) 250 J
(E) 500 J

258. A 5-kg box slides down a frictionless incline from a vertical height of 10 m. The box starts from rest. What is the box's velocity at the bottom of the hill?

(A) 5 m/s
(B) 10 m/s
(C) 14 m/s
(D) 24 m/s
(E) 30 m/s

259. An archer pulls a bowstring back a distance of 20 cm with an average force of 75 N. The arrow has a mass of 20.0 g. When he releases the string, what is the velocity of the arrow when it leaves the bow?

(A) 1.2 m/s
(B) 22 m/s
(C) 32 m/s
(D) 39 m/s
(E) 42 m/s

260. A 1,000-kg car traveling at 30 m/s skids 10 m before it stops. What magnitude of force is the frictional force on the car?

(A) 1.5×10^3 N
(B) 3.0×10^3 N
(C) 4.5×10^3 N
(D) 1.5×10^4 N
(E) 4.5×10^4 N

261. A bullet has a mass of 7.5 g. It is fired into a ballistic pendulum. The pendulum's receiving block of wood is 2.5 kg. After the collision, the pendulum swings to a height of 0.1 m. What is the approximate velocity of the bullet?

    (A) 50 m/s
    (B) 100 m/s
    (C) 200 m/s
    (D) 250 m/s
    (E) 500 m/s

262. A 9.0-kg box is attached to a horizontal spring with a spring constant of 2,500 N/m. If the box is pulled 12 cm horizontally from the equilibrium position, what is its maximum kinetic energy?

    (A) 9.0 J
    (B) 18 J
    (C) 25 J
    (D) 50 J
    (E) 60 J

263. A spring with a constant of 300 N/m is stretched by 0.5 m. What is the force on the spring?

    (A) 50 N
    (B) 100 N
    (C) 150 N
    (D) 200 N
    (E) 300 N

264. A spring with a constant of 400 N/m is stretched by 0.5 m. What is the elastic potential energy stored in the spring?

    (A) 50 J
    (B) 100 J
    (C) 150 J
    (D) 200 J
    (E) 300 J

265. A 1-kg block is attached to a spring with a constant of 100 N/m. The spring is displaced 0.2 m from equilibrium. When the block is let go, what is its velocity as it passes the equilibrium point?

    (A) 0.4 m/s
    (B) 1.4 m/s
    (C) 1.6 m/s
    (D) 2.0 m/s
    (E) 4.0 m/s

266. Two cannons fire identical cannonballs with the same amount of powder. The barrel of Cannon 2 is twice as long as the barrel of Cannon 1. How does the velocity of a cannonball fired from Cannon 2 compare with that of the ball fired from Cannon 1?

(A) Four times that of Cannon 1
(B) Twice that of Cannon 1
(C) 1.4 times that of Cannon 1
(D) One-half that of Cannon 1
(E) The same as Cannon 1

267. A 750-kg glider is flying level at 100.0 m/s. A tailwind blows constantly for 1,200 m, and the glider's speed increases to 120.0 m/s. What is the approximate force of the tailwind?

(A) 125 N
(B) 250 N
(C) 1,400 N
(D) 5,000 N
(E) 7,500 N

268. The gravitational potential energy of a box sliding down an incline decreases by 25 J while the kinetic energy increases by 23 J. Which of the following best describes this scenario?

(A) The law of conservation of energy is violated in this situation.
(B) 2 J of energy is transferred to thermal energy.
(C) The momentum of the box system must remain the same.
(D) The total energy of the system must remain at 48 J.
(E) The kinetic energy of the box must be 25 J.

269. An object is initially at rest. A force of 2.0 N exerted on an object for 5.0 m increases the object's velocity by 1.0 m/s. What was the mass of the object?

(A) 0.1 kg
(B) 0.2 kg
(C) 1.0 kg
(D) 20 kg
(E) 200 kg

270. A 70.0-kg stuntman freefalls from a building for 125 m and hits an airbag. The airbag exerts a force on him as he depresses it 5.0 m and comes to a complete stop. What is the average force exerted by the airbag?

(A) 1.0×10^2 N
(B) 2.8×10^2 N
(C) 1.7×10^4 N
(D) 2.8×10^4 N
(E) 1.0×10^4 N

271. A man pushes a 100-kg box with a horizontal force of 100 N across a floor for a distance of 60 m in 2 min. What is his power?

(A) 10 W
(B) 20 W
(C) 30 W
(D) 40 W
(E) 50 W

Questions 272–274 refer to the figure below. For each question, assume that the roller coaster was initially moving to the right as it approaches point A. Also assume air drag and track friction are negligible.

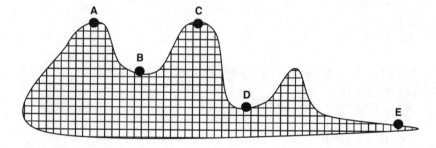

272. The diagram above depicts a frictionless roller-coaster track with various locations labeled A through E. At which locations will a roller-coaster car have the same gravitational potential energy?

(A) A and E
(B) B and C
(C) C and D
(D) B and E
(E) A and C

273. At which location will the roller-coaster car move the fastest?

  (A) A
  (B) B
  (C) C
  (D) D
  (E) E

274. For this diagram, at which point will the total energy be the greatest?

  (A) A
  (B) B
  (C) D
  (D) E
  (E) The total energy is the same at all points.

275. A man pushes a lawn mower with a handle at an angle of 60° to the horizontal. He applies a constant 20-N force along the axis of the handle and moves the lawn mower a horizontal distance of 100 m in 5 min. What is the man's power output?

  (A) 3 W
  (B) 7 W
  (C) 10 W
  (D) 17 W
  (E) 27 W

276. A 2,000.0-kg airplane flies at 343 m/s. What is its kinetic energy?

  (A) 1.18×10^4 J
  (B) 1.18×10^5 J
  (C) 3.43×10^5 J
  (D) 1.18×10^8 J
  (E) 3.43×10^8 J

277. A marksman fires a 7.5-g bullet from a 1.2-kg handgun. The bullet strikes a target and generates 500 J of thermal energy as it stops. If the length of the gun barrel is 125 mm, then how much force did the handgun exert on the bullet?

  (A) 500 N
  (B) 1,000 N
  (C) 2,000 N
  (D) 4,000 N
  (E) 5,000 N

278. Two 500-g air cars are on a frictionless track. Car A is moving at 0.2 m/s when it collides into Car B, which is at rest. Both cars move away at 0.1 m/s. Compared to the total energy of the system before the collision, what percentage of energy is transferred to thermal energy in the collision?

(A) 10 percent
(B) 20 percent
(C) 25 percent
(D) 50 percent
(E) 90 percent

279. A rifle fires a 4.0-g bullet at a velocity of 950 m/s. If the length of the rifle barrel is 1.01 m, then what force does the rifle exert on the bullet?

(A) 180 N
(B) 580 N
(C) 1,800 N
(D) 5,800 N
(E) 18,000 N

280. A 2,700-kg cannon fires an 11-kg cannonball. The length of the cannon's barrel is 2.44 m. If the powder produces 2.25×10^4 N of force, what is the velocity of the cannonball as it leaves the barrel?

(A) 10 m/s
(B) 50 m/s
(C) 100 m/s
(D) 200 m/s
(E) 500 m/s

281. What happens to the kinetic energy of a car if its speed is doubled?

(A) It quadruples.
(B) It doubles.
(C) It stays the same.
(D) It is one-half as much.
(E) It is one-fourth as much.

282. Spring 1 is stretched and stores 2 J of elastic potential energy. An identical spring, Spring 2, is stretched and stores 18 J of elastic potential energy. What is the ratio of the displacement of Spring 2 to the displacement of Spring 1?

(A) 9:1
(B) 3:1
(C) 1:1
(D) 1:3
(E) 1:9

283. A tall sailing ship (m = 1.43×10^4 kg) is initially at rest. A steady wind blows at the 60.0° angle shown in the diagram and moves the ship forward a distance of 850 km. The ship's final speed is 9.0 m/s.

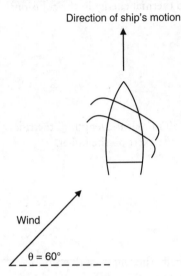

What is the average force of the wind?

(A) 200 N
(B) 390 N
(C) 680 N
(D) 790 N
(E) 1,600 N

284. A car and a pickup truck are moving down the highway. The truck is twice as massive as the car, but it is only moving at half the speed. How does the kinetic energy of the truck compare with that of the car?

(A) Four times as much
(B) Twice as much
(C) The same
(D) One-half as much
(E) One-fourth as much

285. An object has 50 J of gravitational potential energy when it is 10 m off the ground. How much kinetic energy will a twice-as-massive object have if it is held 20 m off the ground?

(A) 50 J
(B) 150 J
(C) 175 J
(D) 200 J
(E) 400 J

286. How much work is done to accelerate a 5.0-kg object from 6.0 m/s to a speed of 12 m/s?

(A) 30 J
(B) 60 J
(C) 135 J
(D) 270 J
(E) 540 J

287. Rank the gravitational potential energy of the object in each of the four scenarios below:

  I. A 2-kg object held at rest 3 m above the ground
  II. A 2-kg object falling down at a rate of 5 m/s at the instant it's 3 m off the ground
  III. A 1-kg object falling down at a rate of 10 m/s at the instant it's 3 m off the ground
  IV. A 3-kg object falling down at rest 2 m above the ground

(A) I = II = IV > III
(B) II > III > I = IV
(C) III > II > I > IV
(D) I = II = III = IV
(E) I = IV > III > II

288. A spring is stretched 5 cm. What happens to its elastic potential energy if it is stretched 20 cm?

(A) It stays the same.
(B) It doubles.
(C) It quadruples.
(D) It increases by a factor of 8.
(E) It increases by a factor of 16.

289. Two cars skid to a stop. How does the skid distance of a 100-kg car moving at 30 miles per hour compare to the skid distance of a 50-kg car moving at 15 miles per hour?

(A) Eight times as much
(B) Four times as much
(C) Twice as much
(D) The same
(E) Half as much

Multi-select: For **questions 290–294**, two of the suggested answers will be correct. Select the two best answers, and record them both on the answer sheet.

290. Which of the following are nonconservative forces?

(A) Spring force
(B) Gravitational forces
(C) The friction force
(D) The force of air drag
(E) The electric force

291. A box is pushed all the way up an incline at a constant speed of 3 m/s. An identical box is pushed all the way up the same incline at a constant speed of 6 m/s. What quantities are the SAME for these two scenarios?

(A) The power required to push the objects
(B) The change in gravitational potential energy
(C) The time it takes to push the box up the incline
(D) The work done on the object by the pushing force
(E) The kinetic energy of the box

292. A stone is propelled vertically off the ground. After it is released, which of the following are true?

(A) Its kinetic energy decreases.
(B) Its total mechanical energy increases.
(C) Its gravitational potential energy increases.
(D) Its total energy is proportional to its distance off the ground.
(E) Its speed decreases linearly with its distance off the ground.

293. Which of the following scenarios result in NO work done on the underlined object?

(A) The gravitational force from the Earth acts on the <u>Moon</u> throughout its circular orbit.

(B) A compressed spring launches a <u>rock</u> into the air.

(C) A child pushes a <u>box</u> across a rough horizontal surface.

(D) A <u>car</u> skids to a stop after panic breaking.

(E) A football player pushes on a stationary <u>wall</u> with all his might.

294. Which of the following statements are true?

(A) The total mechanical energy of an object subject only to conservative forces is constant.

(B) The energy transferred by nonconservative forces is path dependent.

(C) The energy transferred by conservative forces is path dependent

(D) If an object subjected to nonconservative forces follows a closed path, the net amount of work done on the object is zero.

(E) A conservative force is affected by the speed of an object.

Free Response: A 5-kg box slides 10 m diagonally down a frictionless ramp inclined at 45°. At the bottom of the ramp, it slides on a rough horizontal concrete floor with a coefficient of friction of 0.6.

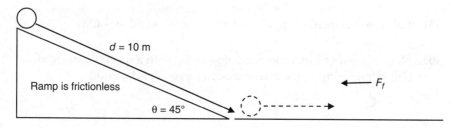

295. Calculate the velocity of the box when it reaches the bottom of the ramp.

296. Calculate the kinetic energy of the box at the bottom of the ramp.

297. How far does the box travel on the concrete before coming to a complete stop?

298. How much time does it take to travel the distance in the **previous question?**

Free Response: The graph below shows the external force applied to a 15-kg object throughout a displacement of 8.0 m.

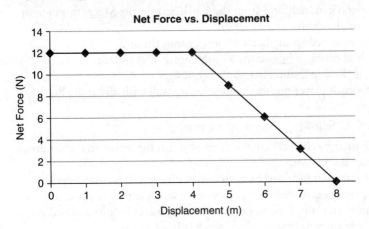

299. How much work was done on the object throughout the 8.0-m displacement?

300. If the object was initially moving at 4.0 m/s (before the force was applied), calculate the object's kinetic energy after the work was done on it.

301. Calculate the speed of the object after the work was done on it.

302. Next, the object hits a compressional spring with a spring constant of 650 N/m. Calculate the maximum compression of the spring.

CHAPTER 7

Rotational Motion

303. A 1-m pry bar is held horizontally and used to open a crate. The tip of the bar, which serves as the fulcrum, is pushed in a distance of 2 cm between the crate lid and the crate. If a 20-N force is applied perpendicularly to the end of the bar, what force is applied on the crate lid?

(A) 1 N
(B) 100 N
(C) 10 N
(D) 1,000 N
(E) 10,000 N

304. A crane is used to pick up a 50.0-m-long steel beam to place in a building. The beam is uniform, but the crane cable is placed 2.0 m off the center of the beam. How much vertical force must be placed on the guide rope to keep the beam level? The beam has a mass of 5.0 kg/m, and the guide rope is placed on the end of the shorter side of the beam.

(A) 210 N
(B) 210 kg
(C) 21 N
(D) 21 kg
(E) 110 N

305. A 2.0-m-long lever is held horizontally with the fulcrum placed at 0.50 m from the left end. How much vertical force must be applied to the right end of the lever to support a 1,000-N rock on the left end?

(A) 67 N
(B) 670 N
(C) 330 N
(D) 1,000 N
(E) 22 N

306. What defines a lever arm?

    (A) The distance parallel to the line of action of the force

    (B) The distance parallel to the line of action of the force from the pivot point

    (C) The length of the lever

    (D) The perpendicular distance from the pivot to the line of action of the force

    (E) $\mathbf{F} = |\mathbf{F}| \cos(\theta)x$

307. A four-wheeled, 5-kg baby carriage carries a 5-kg baby. The front wheels are 60 cm from the back wheels and 90 cm from the carriage handle. Assuming that the center of gravity for the baby and the carriage's center is equidistant between the front and back wheels, what force must the mother apply to tip the carriage back to lift the front wheels?

    (A) 10 kg

    (B) 100 N

    (C) 5 kg

    (D) 50 N

    (E) 1 kg

308. The most general statement of Newton's first law is:

    (A) $\Sigma \mathbf{F} = 0$

    (B) $\Sigma \mathbf{F}_x = 0$, $\Sigma \mathbf{F}_y = 0$, and $\Sigma \mathbf{F}_z = 0$

    (C) All the forces and moments must be zero.

    (D) All the forces added together must be zero.

    (E) $\Sigma \mathbf{F}_x = 0$, $\Sigma \mathbf{F}_y = 0$, $\Sigma \mathbf{F}_z = 0$, $\Sigma \tau_x = 0$, $\Sigma \tau_y = 0$, and $\Sigma \tau_z = 0$

309. When a skater performs a spin on ice with his arms outstretched, what happens when he brings his arms close to his body?

    (A) His angular acceleration decreases because his moment of inertia was decreased.

    (B) His angular acceleration increases because his moment of inertia was decreased.

    (C) His angular velocity decreases because his moment of inertia was decreased.

    (D) His angular velocity increases because his moment of inertia was decreased.

    (E) His angular displacement increases because his moment of inertia was decreased.

310. Why must radians be used in rotational motion problems?

(A) Because radians are the unit of displacement
(B) Because radians are based on the properties of a circle, unlike degrees
(C) Because radians make the numbers come out correctly
(D) Because radians are based on the properties of rotation, unlike degrees
(E) Radians are an alternative to degrees; either can be used.

311. If a ball attached to a string is being twirled in a horizontal circle, what happens to the ball if the string is suddenly cut? (Ignore any effects from the gravitational force.)

(A) The ball spirals away from the center of the circle.
(B) The ball spirals toward the center of the circle.
(C) The ball continues in a circle because of Newton's first law.
(D) The ball flies off tangent to the circle.
(E) The ball falls to the ground.

312. The moment of inertia of a particular thin-walled cylinder around its central axis is given by mR^2. What expression best represents the angular momentum of this cylinder if it spins about the central axis at a rate of 12 revolutions per second?

(A) $(24\ \pi)mR^2$

(B) $(12\ \pi)mR^2$

(C) $12mR^2$

(D) $\left(\dfrac{1}{12}\right)mR^2$

(E) $\left(\dfrac{1}{12\pi}\right)mR^2$

313. The hour hand in a clock makes two revolutions in twenty-four hours while the minute hand makes one revolution each hour. What are the angular velocities (in radians per second) of the hour hand and minute hand, respectively?

(A) 1 and 1/12
(B) 2π and $\pi/6$
(C) $\pi/1{,}800$ and $\pi/30$
(D) $\pi/21{,}600$ and $\pi/1{,}800$
(E) 3,600 and 60

314. A small piece of space junk has a mass of 3 kg and is orbiting the Earth every 90.0 min at an altitude of 300.0 km. The Earth's radius is 6.38×10^6 m. What is the junk's orbital velocity?

(A) 3,710 m/s
(B) 5,160 m/s
(C) 0.001 rad/s
(D) 15,500 m/s
(E) 7,770 m/s

315. What is the translational kinetic energy of the space junk in **Question 314**?

(A) 9.06×10^5 J
(B) 23,200 J
(C) 15,500 J
(D) 9.06×10^7 J
(E) 1.81×10^8 J

316. The Moon orbits the Earth once every 27.3 days with an orbital radius of 385,000 km. What is the orbital speed of the Moon?

(A) 0.163 m/s
(B) 27.3 m/s
(C) 163 m/s
(D) 1,030 m/s
(E) 1.22×10^{12} m/s

317. Newton's first law states that a point particle is in equilibrium if the net forces acting on it are zero. When are torques considered in Newton's first law?

(A) Torques are never included in Newton's first law.
(B) When the forces are unbalanced
(C) When considering objects that have dimensions
(D) Torques are not forces and do not need to be accounted for.
(E) Torques come in pairs and do not need to be accounted for.

318. What happens to the body on which a net torque is acting?

(A) Nothing happens to it.
(B) It causes the body to accelerate linearly.
(C) It causes the body to experience linear and angular acceleration.
(D) It causes the body to experience angular acceleration.
(E) It causes the body to decelerate linearly.

319. A boy and girl are on a rotating merry-go-round. The girl is on the outer edge, while the boy is halfway between the center and the girl. How does the rotational speed of the girl compare to that of the boy?

(A) The girl's rotational speed is four times as much.
(B) The girl's rotational speed is twice as much.
(C) The girl's rotational speed is the same.
(D) The girl's rotational speed is half as much.
(E) The girl's rotational speed is one-fourth as much.

320. A boy and girl are still on a rotating merry-go-round. The girl is on the outer edge, while the boy is halfway between the center and the girl. How does the linear speed of the girl compare to that of the boy?

(A) The girl's linear speed is four times as much.
(B) The girl's linear speed is twice as much.
(C) The girl's linear speed is the same.
(D) The girl's linear speed is half as much.
(E) The girl's linear speed is one-fourth as much.

321. What happens to the magnitude of the angular momentum of an object if its rotational speed is tripled?

(A) The angular momentum is nine times as much.
(B) The angular momentum triples.
(C) The angular momentum stays the same.
(D) The angular momentum is one-third as much.
(E) The angular momentum is one-ninth as much.

322. What happens to the rotational kinetic energy of an object if its rotational speed is tripled?

(A) The rotational kinetic energy is nine times as much.
(B) The rotational kinetic energy triples.
(C) The rotational kinetic energy stays the same.
(D) The rotational kinetic energy is one-third as much.
(E) The rotational kinetic energy is one-ninth as much.

323. As an ice skater is spinning, she extends her arms away from her body. Her angular velocity _____, and her angular momentum _____.

(A) Decreases; increases
(B) Increases; decreases
(C) Decreases; decreases
(D) Remains the same; increases
(E) Decreases; remains the same

324. An object is rotating at a constant angular velocity of 0.50 radians per second. What angle (in degrees) does the object rotate through in 12 s?

(A) 0.10°
(B) 30°
(C) 180°
(D) 340°
(E) 2,160°

325. A propeller, initially at rest, rotates about its midpoint with an angular acceleration of 12 radians/sec². How much time will it take to rotate through a 90.0° angle?

(A) 0.51 s
(B) 0.72 s
(C) 1.2 s
(D) 3.9 s
(E) 4.1 s

326. A spinning sphere has a moment of inertia of 12 kg·m² and has an angular momentum of $18 \frac{kg \cdot m^2}{s}$. What is the angular speed of the sphere?

(A) 0.67 rad/s
(B) 1.5 rad/s
(C) 4 rad/s
(D) 110 rad/s
(E) 220 rad/s

327. A car tire is initially spinning with an angular speed of 150 radians per second. As the brakes are applied, the tire slows down at a rate of 25 rad/s². How much time does it take the car to stop?

(A) 2.0 s
(B) 2.5 s
(C) 3.0 s
(D) 5.0 s
(E) 6.0 s

328. Two children make a seesaw out of a 5.0-m wooden plank. They balance it on a fulcrum located 2.0 m from the left end. The 42.0-kg child sits at the end of the plank on the left side. What distance (measured from the fulcrum) can the 35-kg child sit on the right side of the plank to keep it balanced?

(A) 1.0 m
(B) 1.5 m
(C) 2.0 m
(D) 2.4 m
(E) 3.0 m

329. A cylinder has a moment of inertia, I. How much time does it take a torque, τ, to increase its angular speed from ω_1 to ω_2?

(A) $\dfrac{I\omega_2 - I\omega_1}{\tau}$

(B) $\dfrac{\tau}{I\omega_2 - I\omega_1}$

(C) $(I\omega_2 - I\omega_1)\tau$

(D) $\dfrac{\tau}{\dfrac{1}{2}I\omega_2^2 - \dfrac{1}{2}I\omega_1^2}$

(E) $\left(\dfrac{1}{2}I\omega_2^2 - \dfrac{1}{2}I\omega_1^2\right)\tau$

330. A car wheel has a moment of inertia of 1.5 kg·m². A brake is applied, which decreases its rotational velocity from 25 revolutions per second to zero. How much energy is transferred to thermal energy in the braking process?

(A) 470 J
(B) 940 J
(C) 1,900 J
(D) 19,000 J
(E) 38,000 J

331. A pulley has a radius of 45 cm and a moment of inertia of $0.15 \text{ kg} \cdot \text{m}^2$. A string is wrapped around the pulley, and a 25-g mass is hung from the string on one side of the pulley. Calculate the magnitude of the angular acceleration of the pulley.

(A) 0.075 rad/s^2
(B) 0.15 rad/s^2
(C) 0.74 rad/s^2
(D) 1.6 rad/s^2
(E) 3.3 rad/s^2

332. A barbell consists of a uniform rod with a mass attached to each end. The rod is 2.2 m long and has a moment of inertia about its center of mass of $1.5 \text{ kg} \cdot \text{m}^2$. The center of each 3.0-kg mass is attached to the end of the rod. Calculate the rotational momentum of the barbell when it rotates at 0.50 rad/s about the center of the rod.

(A) $1.1 \dfrac{\text{kg} \cdot \text{m}^2}{\text{s}}$

(B) $2.2 \dfrac{\text{kg} \cdot \text{m}^2}{\text{s}}$

(C) $3.0 \dfrac{\text{kg} \cdot \text{m}^2}{\text{s}}$

(D) $4.4 \dfrac{\text{kg} \cdot \text{m}^2}{\text{s}}$

(E) $6.0 \dfrac{\text{kg} \cdot \text{m}^2}{\text{s}}$

333. Four identical rods shown below experience the forces as shown. Rank the magnitude of the torques about the pivot point on the left end of the rod.

I.

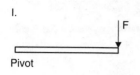

II.

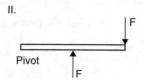

III.

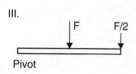

IV.

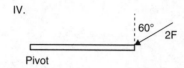

    (A) III > I = IV > II
    (B) II > IV > III > I
    (C) I = III = IV > II
    (D) III > II > I > IV
    (E) II = III > I > IV

334. Starting from rest, a spinning disk accelerates constantly to a final rotational speed, ω, in a period of time, Δt. What expression best represents the revolutions the disk has turned through?

    (A) $\dfrac{\omega \Delta t}{2\pi}$

    (B) $\dfrac{\omega \Delta t}{4\pi}$

    (C) $\dfrac{\omega \Delta t^2}{2}$

    (D) $\dfrac{\omega}{\Delta t}$

    (E) $2\pi \omega \Delta t$

335. A baton of length L rotates with a constant angular velocity, ω, measured in radians per second. What is the period of the baton's rotation?

(A) $\dfrac{2\pi L}{\omega}$

(B) $\dfrac{\omega}{2\pi}$

(C) $\dfrac{1}{\omega}$

(D) $\dfrac{2\pi}{\omega}$

(E) $\dfrac{\omega}{2\pi L}$

336. An object, initially rotating with an angular speed of 15 rad/s, is subjected to a torque of 55 Nm that accelerates it constantly at 5.0 rad/s². What is the moment of inertia of the object?

(A) $3.0 \text{ kg} \cdot \text{m}^2$
(B) $3.5 \text{ kg} \cdot \text{m}^2$
(C) $5.5 \text{ kg} \cdot \text{m}^2$
(D) $11 \text{ kg} \cdot \text{m}^2$
(E) $50 \text{ kg} \cdot \text{m}^2$

337. A sphere (mass = m, radius = R, moment of inertia = $\dfrac{2}{5}mR^2$) is sliding on a frictionless table with linear speed v. An identical sphere is spinning on the same table (not sliding) about its center with an angular velocity, ω. What is the ratio between the kinetic energy of the sliding sphere and the kinetic energy of the rotating sphere?

(A) $\dfrac{5v^2}{2R^2\omega^2}$

(B) $\dfrac{5v^2}{2\omega^2}$

(C) $\dfrac{v^2}{\omega^2}$

(D) 1

(E) $\dfrac{2v^2}{5\omega^2}$

338. A body with a moment of inertia $4 \text{ kg} \cdot \text{m}^2$ accelerates constantly from rest with an angular acceleration of 5 rad/s². How much time does it take to obtain a rotational kinetic energy of 800 J?

(A) 1 s
(B) 2 s
(C) 4 s
(D) 8 s
(E) 10 s

339. A disk, initially rotating at 11 rad/s, slows down at a constant rate of 1.5 rad/s². What is the angular displacement of the disk in 6.0 s of time?

(A) 9.0 rad
(B) 27 rad
(C) 39 rad
(D) 66 rad
(E) 93 rad

340. Object 1 has a moment of inertia of $8 \text{ kg} \cdot \text{m}^2$, and Object 2 has a moment of inertia of $2 \text{ kg} \cdot \text{m}^2$. If Object 1 is rotating with an angular velocity of 1 rad/s, what angular velocity would give Object 2 the same rotational kinetic energy?

(A) 0.25 rad/s
(B) 0.5 rad/s
(C) 1.0 rad/s
(D) 1.5 rad/s
(E) 2 rad/s

Multi-select: For **questions 341–345**, two of the suggested answers will be correct. Select the two best answers, and record them both on the answer sheet.

341. A torque is applied about the axis of rotation in which of the following scenarios?

(A) A force is applied parallel to the lever arm and through the axis of rotation.
(B) A force is applied perpendicular to the lever arm and through the axis of rotation.
(C) A force is applied perpendicular to the lever arm but not through the axis of rotation.
(D) A force is applied at a 45° angle but not through the axis of rotation.
(E) A force is applied at a 45° angle through the axis of rotation.

342. What is moment of inertia?

(A) The resistance something has to rotational motion
(B) The resistance an object has to linear motion
(C) The integral of volume
(D) The rotational equivalent of momentum
(E) The ratio between torque and angular acceleration

343. When an object is moving in circular motion, what accelerations are NOT possible?

(A) Inward radial acceleration
(B) Tangential acceleration
(C) Angular acceleration
(D) Outward radial acceleration
(E) Zero acceleration

344. When a solid object rotates with a constant angular acceleration, which of the following are true?

(A) The net torque on the object is zero.
(B) The net torque on the object is constant and nonzero.
(C) The net torque on the object must increase.
(D) The object's angular velocity changes at a steady rate.
(E) The object's angular velocity is constant.

345. The moment of inertia of a body does NOT depend on which of the following?

(A) The angular acceleration of the body
(B) The distribution of mass in the body
(C) The angular velocity of the body
(D) The axis of rotation of the body
(E) The mass of the body

Free Response: A 3.0-m-long uniform rod with a mass of 12 kg rotates about an axis through its center. There are two applied forces as shown in the diagram below. The moment of inertia for a rod rotating about its center is given by
$I = \dfrac{1}{12} ML^2$.

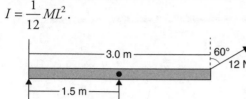

346. Assuming a counterclockwise rotation is positive, calculate the net torque on the rod.

347. Calculate the moment of inertia of the rod.

348. Calculate the angular acceleration of the rod.

349. If the rod accelerates from rest, determine the time it takes the rod to rotate through a 90° angle.

350. How many revolutions does the rod make in 5.0 s?

Free Response: At a carnival, one of the booths has a shooting gallery with spring-loaded guns that fire 12-g suction-cup darts with a muzzle velocity of 2.5 m/s. The 95-g targets are 25 cm tall and hinged at the bottom and may be modeled as a plank pinned at one end ($I = \dfrac{1}{3} ML^2$). In the following questions, assume the dart is moving horizontally when it hits the target 5 cm from the top edge.

351. Calculate the magnitude of the angular momentum of the dart/target system immediately before and immediately after the target is hit. Assume angular momentum is measured relative to the axis of rotation of the target.

352. What is the angular speed of the system immediately after the target is hit?

CHAPTER 8

Electrostatics: Electric Charge and Electric Force

353. An object consists of subatomic particles. It has a net charge of $+8.0 \times 10^{-19}$ C. Which of the following statements best describes this object?

(A) The object has eight more protons than electrons.
(B) The object has eight fewer protons than electrons.
(C) The number of protons and the number of electrons are equal.
(D) The object has five more protons than electrons.
(E) The object has five fewer protons than electrons.

354. Two protons are 1.0 μm apart. What is the electric force between them?

(A) 2.3×10^{-22} N attractive
(B) 2.3×10^{-16} N attractive
(C) 0 N
(D) 2.3×10^{-16} N repulsive
(E) 2.3×10^{-22} N repulsive

355. A negatively charged object is placed near, but not touching, a neutral conductor. As a result, the two objects are attracted to each other. Which of the following is true?

(A) The neutral object gains positive charges to become positively charged.
(B) The neutral object loses negative charges to become positively charged.
(C) The neutral object loses positive charges to become negatively charged.
(D) The neutral object gains negative charges to become negatively charged.
(E) Negative charges of the neutral object move to the side opposite the negatively charged object.

356. A rubber comb is rubbed on hair and then attracts paper bits off the table. Which of the following best compares the forces on the paper bits?

(A) The gravitational force is stronger than the electric force.
(B) The electric force is stronger than the gravitational force.
(C) The strong nuclear force dominates all other forces.
(D) The normal force is stronger than the electric force.
(E) The magnetic force is stronger than the electric force.

357. What is the smallest magnitude of electric charge?

(A) 9.11×10^{-31} C
(B) 8.0×10^{-20} C
(C) 1.6×10^{-19} C
(D) 1 C
(E) 9.0×10^{9} C

358. Two electric objects experience a repulsive force. What happens to that force if the distance between the objects is doubled?

(A) It decreases to one-fourth its value.
(B) It decreases to one-half its value.
(C) It stays the same.
(D) It doubles.
(E) It quadruples.

359. Two electric charges experience an attractive force. What happens to that force if the charge of one of the objects is tripled and the charge of the other object is doubled? (Assume the distance between the objects stays the same.)

(A) The force doubles.
(B) The force triples.
(C) The force is five times greater.
(D) The force is six times greater.
(E) The force is thirty-six times greater.

360. A pith ball is a tiny piece of Styrofoam that is covered with a conductive paint. One pith ball initially has a charge of $+6.4 \times 10^{-8}$ C, and it touches an identical, neutral pith ball. After the pith balls are separated, what is the charge on the pith ball that had the initial charge?

(A) $+6.4 \times 10^{-8}$ C
(B) $+3.2 \times 10^{-8}$ C
(C) 0 C
(D) -3.2×10^{-8} C
(E) -6.4×10^{-8} C

361. Two pith balls each hang from a thread and are suspended from the same hook. If each pith ball is charged -6.4×10^{-8} C and they are separated by a distance of 0.56 cm, what is the force between them?

(A) 1.3×10^{-10} C
(B) 6.6×10^{-3} C
(C) 0.60 N
(D) 1.2 N
(E) 1.8×10^{7} C

362. How many electrons are responsible for a charge of -9.6 C?

(A) 6×10^{19} electrons
(B) 3×10^{19} electrons
(C) 1.1×10^{31} electrons
(D) 3 electrons
(E) Electrons are not responsible for negative charge.

363. A 2-C charge and a -4-C charge attract each other with 100 N of force when placed a certain distance apart. With how much force will a 4-C and a -4-C charge attract each other when placed the same distance apart?

(A) 25 N
(B) 50 N
(C) 100 N
(D) 130 N
(E) 200 N

364. Which of the following may be said about an object that is a good electrical conductor?

(A) The protons are free to move within the object.
(B) The electrons are free to move within the object.
(C) The electrons are bound to their individual atom.
(D) The object cannot maintain its electric charge.
(E) It may be made of materials such as rubber and plastic.

365. Glass becomes positively charged when it is rubbed with silk. Which of the following is the best description of what's happening?

(A) Electrons are rubbed off the glass onto the silk.
(B) Electrons are rubbed off the silk onto the glass.
(C) Protons are rubbed off the glass onto the silk.
(D) Protons are rubbed off the silk onto the glass.
(E) Neutrons in the glass have an affinity for positive charge.

366. Consider an isolated, neutral system consisting of wool fabric and a rubber rod. If the rubber rod is rubbed with wool to become negatively charged, what can be said about the wool fabric?

(A) It becomes equally negatively charged.
(B) It becomes equally positively charged.
(C) It becomes negatively charged but not equally.
(D) It becomes positively charged but not equally.
(E) In a neutral system, neither object can become charged.

367. In an electrostatics experiment, two pieces of transparent tape attract each other. What is the best conclusion one can draw from this observation?

(A) At least one of the pieces of tape is charged.
(B) One of the pieces of tape is neutral.
(C) The two pieces of tape are oppositely charged.
(D) The two pieces of tape have the same charge.
(E) Both pieces of tape are neutral.

368. A helium atom has two protons in its nucleus. If the attractive force between an orbital electron and the nucleus is 4.8×10^{-7} N, what is the atomic radius of a helium atom?

(A) 31 pm
(B) 53 pm
(C) 62 pm
(D) 110 pm
(E) 140 pm

369. Paper is considered an insulator. How does a positively charged piece of tape pick up a neutral paper bit?

(A) The tape makes the protons flow to the opposite end of the paper, causing an attraction between the electrons left behind and the tape.
(B) The tape polarizes the paper atoms, attracting the electrons to the side of the atoms closest to the tape.
(C) The tape forces electrons at the opposite end of the paper to flow through the paper toward the tape.
(D) The tape polarizes the paper atoms, moving the protons within the atoms to the side of the atom farthest from the tape.
(E) It is not possible for a charged object to attract a neutral object.

370. Which of the following statements is NOT correct?

(A) Negatively charged objects have an excess of electrons.

(B) Protons easily move from atom to atom in a solid.

(C) Negatively charged objects typically have the same number of protons as before they were charged.

(D) Positively charged objects have fewer electrons than protons.

(E) The valance electrons in insulators do not move freely from atom to atom.

Questions 371–373 refer to an electroscope. An electroscope is a device used in electrostatics experiments and consists of a metal cap connected by a metal stem to two thin gold leaves that can freely rotate. The following picture shows the parts of an electroscope:

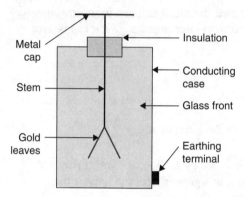

Source: http://www.a-levelphysicstutor.com/field-elect-2.php

371. In the diagram of the electroscope, the gold leaves are standing apart and nothing is interacting with the electroscope. Which of the following best explains this observation?

(A) One leaf is neutral, and the other leaf is negative.

(B) One leaf is neutral, and the other leaf is positive.

(C) The leaves both have opposite charges.

(D) The leaves both have the same charge.

(E) The leaves are both neutral.

372. Why do the two leaves of a neutral electroscope go apart when a positive rod is brought near the cap (but not touching it)?

(A) Protons in the electroscope flow toward the rod, leaving the leaves negative.

(B) Protons in the electroscope flow away from the rod, giving the leaves a positive charge.

(C) Electrons in the electroscope flow away from the rod, giving the leaves a negative charge.

(D) Electrons in the electroscope flow up toward the rod, making the positive leaves repel.

(E) The leaves will actually come together because neutral objects are attracted to charged objects.

373. When a charged rod is brought near the metal ball of a positively charged electroscope, the leaves initially move closer together. What can be said about the charge of the rod?

(A) The rod is positive.

(B) The rod is negative.

(C) The rod is neutral.

(D) The rod is uncharged.

(E) The charge of the rod cannot be determined.

374. An electron and a proton are separated by 1.50×10^{-10} m. If they are released, which one will accelerate at a greater rate, and what is the magnitude of that acceleration?

(A) The electron; 1.12×10^{22} m/s^2

(B) The proton; 1.12×10^{22} m/s^2

(C) The electron; 6.13×10^{18} m/s^2

(D) The proton; 6.13×10^{18} m/s^2

(E) They both accelerate at the same rate; 1.02×10^{-8} m/s^2

375. Three particles are located on a coordinate system. An electron is located at the origin, a proton is located at (0, 1), and an electron is located at (1, 0). What is the direction of the net electrostatic force on the electron located at the origin?

(A) To the right on the coordinate plane

(B) At an angle of 45° (up and to the right on the coordinate plane)

(C) Up on the coordinate plane

(D) At an angle of 135° (up and to the left on the coordinate plane)

(E) To the left on the coordinate plane

376. Calculate the ratio of the electric force to the gravitational force between an electron and a proton.

(A) 4.41×10^{-40}

(B) 1

(C) 9.8

(D) 1.35×10^{20}

(E) 2.27×10^{39}

377. A neutral conductor is touched with a positively charged glass rod. Which of the following best describes what happens?

(A) Electrons flow from the conductor to the glass rod.

(B) Electrons flow from the glass rod to the conductor.

(C) Protons flow from the conductor to the glass rod.

(D) Protons flow from the glass rod to the conductor.

(E) Neutrons flow from the conductor to the glass rod.

378. Two equally charged pith balls are 2.0 cm apart and repel each other with 6.5×10^{-5} N of force. Calculate the charge on each pith ball.

(A) 1.6×10^{-19} C

(B) 1.6×10^{-9} C

(C) 1.6×10^{-7} C

(D) 8.2×10^{-8} C

(E) 8.2×10^{-4} C

379. What can be said about a sphere that has a net charge of $+4.0 \times 10^{-15}$ C?

(A) The sphere has 50,000 more electrons than protons.

(B) The sphere has 50,000 more protons than electrons.

(C) The sphere has 25,000 more electrons than protons.

(D) The sphere has 25,000 more protons than electrons.

(E) This amount of charge is not possible due to the quantization of electric charge.

380. There are four charged objects: A, B, C, and D. Object A is charged positively. Object A is attracted to Object B. Object B is repelled from Object C. Object C is attracted to Object D. What are the charges on Objects B, C, and D?

(A) B is negative, and C and D are positive.
(B) B and C are positive, and D is negative.
(C) B, C , and D are positive.
(D) B, C , and D are negative.
(E) B and C are negative, and D is positive.

381. Conducting Sphere A has a charge of -8 μC, and identical Sphere B has a charge of $+12$ μC. If the spheres are touched and then separated, what is the charge on each sphere?

(A) Sphere A is $+12$ μC, and Sphere B is -8 μC.
(B) Sphere A is -8 μC, and Sphere B is $+12$ μC.
(C) Sphere A is $+10$ μC, and Sphere B is $+10$ μC.
(D) Sphere A is $+2$ μC, and Sphere B is $+2$ μC.
(E) Sphere A is $+4$ μC, and Sphere B is $+4$ μC.

382. Three objects are placed in order from left to right and are not touching: a positive glass rod and two initially neutral, identical conducting spheres. If the spheres are touched and then separated, what can be said about each sphere?

(A) Each sphere is negatively charged.
(B) Each sphere is positively charged.
(C) Each sphere is neutral.
(D) The sphere on the left is positively charged, and the sphere on the right is negatively charged.
(E) The sphere on the left is negatively charged, and the sphere on the right is positively charged.

383. A negatively charged balloon is observed to attract a piece of aluminum foil. What can be concluded about the foil?

(A) The foil must be positively charged.
(B) The foil must be neutral.
(C) The foil must be negatively charged.
(D) The foil is neutral or positively charged.
(E) The foil is neutral or negatively charged.

384. A rubber balloon becomes negatively charged when it is rubbed with a wool cloth. What can be said about the subsequent charge distribution on the balloon?

(A) Excess protons are on the balloon in the location where it was rubbed on the wool.

(B) Excess electrons are on the balloon in the location where it was rubbed on the wool.

(C) Excess protons are spread evenly throughout the balloon.

(D) Excess electrons are spread evenly throughout the balloon.

(E) The balloon is neutral because the wool ground it out.

385. A negative object is brought near the left side of a conducting sphere but does not touch it. Meanwhile, a person briefly touches the right-hand side of the sphere. What happens to the sphere in this process?

(A) The sphere gains electrons from the person.

(B) The sphere gains protons from the person.

(C) The sphere loses electrons to the person.

(D) The sphere loses protons to the person.

(E) The sphere remains neutral.

386. A carbon nucleus has 6 protons. What can be said about the electrostatic force between an orbital electron and the carbon nucleus?

(A) The attractive force of the nucleus on the electron is greater than the force of the electron on the nucleus.

(B) The attractive force of the nucleus on the electron is less than the force of the electron on the nucleus.

(C) The attractive force of the nucleus on the electron is equal to the force of the electron on the nucleus.

(D) The repulsive force of the nucleus on the electron is equal to the force of the electron on the nucleus.

(E) The repulsive force of the nucleus on the electron is greater than the force of the electron on the nucleus.

387. Two identical spheres are initially neutral. Sphere A obtains a charge of -1.28×10^{-13} C by induction and grounding, while Sphere B remains neutral. How does the mass of Sphere A compare with that of Sphere B?

(A) Each sphere has the same mass.

(B) Sphere A has 7.29×10^{-25} kg more mass than Sphere B.

(C) Sphere B has 7.29×10^{-25} kg more mass than Sphere A.

(D) Sphere A has 1.34×10^{-21} kg more mass than Sphere B.

(E) Sphere B has 1.35×10^{-21} kg more mass than Sphere A.

388. A hydrogen nucleus (charge $+e$) and a beryllium nucleus (charge $+4e$) experience a force, F. Which of the following expressions may be used to solve for the distance between the nuclei?

(A) $e\sqrt{\dfrac{5k}{F}}$

(B) $2e\sqrt{\dfrac{k}{F}}$

(C) $\dfrac{4ke^2}{F}$

(D) $6Fe^2$

(E) $3Fe^2$

389. Three identical conducting spheres are on insulated stands and are not touching one another initially. Sphere A has a charge of $+10\ \mu C$, Sphere B has a charge of $-6\ \mu C$, and Sphere C has a charge of $-4\ \mu C$. Sphere A contacts Sphere B, and they are separated. Next, Sphere B contacts Sphere C, and they are separated. What is the final charge on Sphere C?

(A) $-1\ \mu C$
(B) $-2\ \mu C$
(C) $0\ \mu C$
(D) $+2\ \mu C$
(E) $+4\ \mu C$

390. A helium nucleus (charge $+2e$) and a hydrogen nucleus (charge $+e$) are initially separated a certain distance. If the helium nucleus is held in place, describe the motion of the hydrogen nucleus.

(A) It moves away from the helium nucleus with a decreasing acceleration rate.
(B) It moves away from the helium nucleus with an increasing acceleration rate.
(C) It moves away from the helium nucleus with a constant acceleration rate.
(D) It moves toward the helium nucleus with an increasing acceleration rate.
(E) It moves toward the helium nucleus with a constant acceleration rate.

Multi-select: For **questions 391–395**, two of the suggested answers will be correct. Select the two best answers, and record them both on the answer sheet.

391. Which of the following are valid quantities for the net electric charge on an object?

(A) 1.6×10^{-20} C
(B) 3.2×10^{-19} C
(C) 2.4×10^{-19} C
(D) 4.0×10^{-19} C
(E) 2.4×10^{-18} C

392. The magnitude of the electric force between two charges does NOT depend on which of the following?

(A) The charge of the first object
(B) The charge of the second object
(C) The sign of the charges
(D) The distance between the objects
(E) The cross-sectional area of each object

393. Which of the following are the best insulators?

(A) Salt water
(B) Gold
(C) Distilled water
(D) Rubber
(E) Aluminum

394. A balloon is attracted to the wall. Which of the following CANNOT explain this observation?

(A) The wall is positively charged, and the balloon is negatively charged.
(B) The wall is neutral, and the balloon is positive.
(C) The balloon is neutral, and the wall is negative.
(D) The balloon is negative, and the wall is negative.
(E) The balloon is positive, and the wall is positive.

395. Two electrons repel each other. Which of the following changes will keep the force the same?

(A) Each electron is replaced with a proton.
(B) Each electron is replaced with two electrons, and the distance between them is doubled.
(C) One electron is replaced with two electrons, and the distance between them is doubled.
(D) Each electron is replaced with two electrons, and the distance between them is quadrupled.
(E) One electron is replaced with a proton.

Free Response: Three charges are shown in the diagram below:

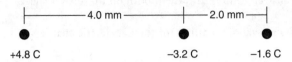

396. Construct a diagram showing arrows that represent the forces on the −3.2 μC charge.

397. Calculate the net force on the −3.2 μC charge.

398. If the −3.2 μC charge has a mass of 75 grams, calculate its initial acceleration.

Free Response: One 24-g conducting pith ball has −6.4 μC of charge and touches an identical pith ball that is initially neutral. The diagram below (not to scale) shows the final configuration of the two pith balls as they hang from threads:

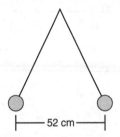

399. Explain the value of the charge on each pith ball after they are separated.

400. Construct a free-body diagram with symbols representing all the forces on the pith ball on the right.

401. Calculate the value of all the forces on the pith ball in your free-body diagram.

402. Determine the angle between the threads in the diagram above.

CHAPTER 9

DC Circuits (Resistors Only)

403. A total charge of 2.4 C passes a point in a circuit in 10.0 milliseconds. What is the magnitude of the electric current?

(A) 0.004 A
(B) 0.04 A
(C) 24 A
(D) 240 A
(E) 2,400 A

404. A 9-V battery drives a circuit containing a 10-Ω resistor. What is the current that flows through this circuit?

(A) 0.9 A
(B) 1.1 A
(C) 9.0 A
(D) 11 A
(E) 90 A

405. A 9.0-V battery drives 3.0 A of electric current through a resistor. What is the power dissipated by the resistor?

(A) 0.30 J
(B) 3.0 J
(C) 6.0 J
(D) 12 J
(E) 27 J

406. Three resistors (20 Ω, 150 Ω, 500 Ω) are linked in series. What is the equivalent resistance?

(A) 0.060 Ω
(B) 17 Ω
(C) 670 Ω
(D) 1.5 kΩ
(E) 1.5 MΩ

Questions 407–410 use the following figure:

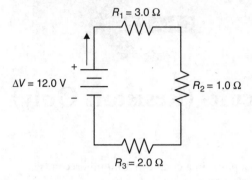

407. What is the current flowing through the circuit shown in the diagram?
    (A) 1 A
    (B) 2 A
    (C) 4 A
    (D) 6 A
    (E) 12 A

408. Which of the following statements is true about the circuit shown in the diagram?
    (A) The voltage drop is greatest across R_1, but R_1 has the least amount of current flowing through it.
    (B) The voltage drop is greatest across R_2, but R_2 has the least amount of current flowing through it.
    (C) The voltage drop is greatest across R_3, but R_3 has the least amount of current flowing through it.
    (D) The voltage drops and current are equal across all resistors.
    (E) The voltage drop is greatest across R_1, but the current is equal at all points in the circuit.

409. In this diagram, what is the power dissipated by all of the resistors in the circuit?
    (A) 2 W
    (B) 6 W
    (C) 12 W
    (D) 24 W
    (E) 48 W

410. In the diagram, what is the voltage drop across the third resistor (R_3)?

(A) 2 V

(B) 3 V

(C) 4 V

(D) 6 V

(E) 12 V

411. Which of the following statements best summarizes a series circuit with three different resistances?

(A) In all parts of the circuit, the resistances are different, the voltage drops are the same, and the current is different.

(B) In all parts of the circuit, the resistances are the same, the voltage drops are the same, and the current is different.

(C) In all parts of the circuit, the resistances are different, the voltage drops are different, and the current is the same.

(D) In all parts of the circuit, the resistances are different, the voltage drops are the same, and the current is the same.

(E) In all parts of the circuit, the resistances are the same, the voltage drops are the same, and the current is the same.

412. When one light in a string of holiday lights goes out, all of the lights go out. Which statement best describes this situation?

(A) The bulb that went out is wired in parallel with the rest of the string.

(B) The light that went out is in series with the rest of the bulbs that are wired in parallel.

(C) The light that went out is in parallel with the rest of the bulbs that are wired in series.

(D) The bulb that went out is wired in series with the rest of the string.

(E) Not enough information is given to make any of the conclusions above.

Questions 413–416 use the following figure:

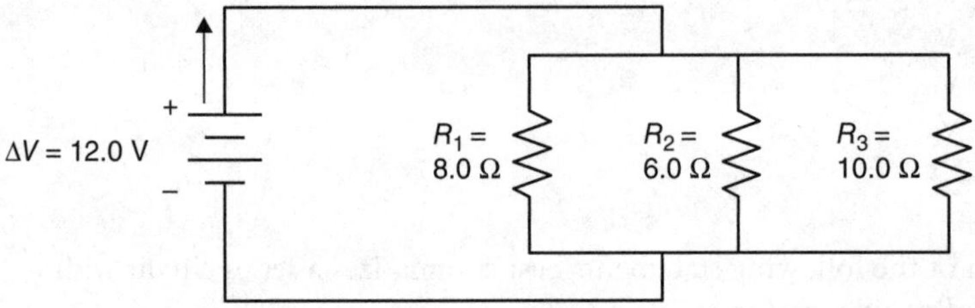

413. For the circuit in the diagram, which of the following expressions will describe the amount of current flowing through the resistors?

(A) $I_1 = I_2 = I_3$
(B) $I_3 > I_2 > I_1$
(C) $I_1 > I_2 < I_3$
(D) $I_2 > I_1 > I_3$
(E) $I_1 < I_2 < I_3$

414. For the circuit in the diagram, what is the equivalent resistance?

(A) 0.040 Ω
(B) 0.40 Ω
(C) 1.0 Ω
(D) 2.6 Ω
(E) 24 Ω

415. For the circuit in the diagram, what is the total current?

(A) 0.5 A
(B) 4.6 A
(C) 12 A
(D) 30 A
(E) 300 A

416. For the circuit in the diagram, the third resistor (R_3) dissipates how much energy each second?

(A) 12 W
(B) 14 W
(C) 46 W
(D) 212 W
(E) 300 W

417. In a circuit, 40 C of charge passes through a 10-Ω resistor in 80 s. What is the voltage that drives the current?

(A) 0.5 V
(B) 1 V
(C) 5 V
(D) 10 V
(E) 20 V

418. A 100-V power supply is wired to a resistor. The current flowing through the circuit is 2.0 A. What is the resistance of the circuit?

(A) 0.05 Ω
(B) 0.5 Ω
(C) 2.0 Ω
(D) 5.0 Ω
(E) 50 Ω

419. A resistor dissipates 100 kW of power when a 5-A current passes through it. What is the value of its resistance?

(A) 1 kΩ
(B) 2 kΩ
(C) 4 kΩ
(D) 5 kΩ
(E) 200 kΩ

420. A 9.0-V battery is wired in series with three resistors (20 Ω, 30 Ω, 15 Ω). What is the sum of the voltages around the entire circuit?

(A) 0 V
(B) 2.1 V
(C) 2.7 V
(D) 4.2 V
(E) 9.0 V

Questions 421–423 use the following figure:

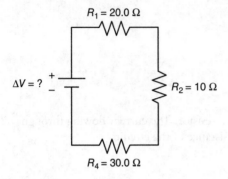

421. For the circuit shown in the figure, what is the voltage of the battery if the current is 2.0 A?

(A) 20 V
(B) 40 V
(C) 50 V
(D) 60 V
(E) 120 V

422. For the circuit shown in the figure, what is the voltage drop across the 30-Ω resistor if the current is 5.0 A?

(A) 0 V
(B) 50 V
(C) 100 V
(D) 150 V
(E) 300 V

423. For the circuit shown in the figure, what must be the sum of the voltages around the complete circuit if the current is 10 A?

(A) 0 V
(B) 200 V
(C) 100 V
(D) 300 V
(E) 600 V

Questions 424 and 425 use the following figure:

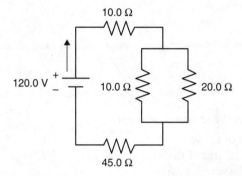

424. For the circuit shown in the diagram, what is the equivalent resistance of the circuit?

  (A) 6.7 Ω
  (B) 61.7 Ω
  (C) 65.0 Ω
  (D) 70.0 Ω
  (E) 85.0 Ω

425. For the circuit shown in the figure, what is the value of the current leaving the parallel branch of the circuit?

  (A) 1.0 A
  (B) 1.9 A
  (C) 5 A
  (D) 10 A
  (E) 12 A

426. In a basic circuit consisting of a battery and a thermal resistor, what happens when the voltage is doubled?

  (A) The current doubles.
  (B) The resistance doubles.
  (C) The power doubles.
  (D) The current is one-half its previous value.
  (E) The current is one-fourth its previous value.

427. What happens to the resistance of a wire when its cross-sectional area is doubled?

(A) Quadruples
(B) Doubles
(C) Stays the same
(D) Reduced to one-half
(E) Reduced to one-fourth

428. Which of the following increases the resistance of a wire?

(A) Increasing the temperature of the wire
(B) Increasing the cross-sectional area of the wire
(C) Decreasing the length of the wire
(D) Decreasing the current in the wire
(E) Decreasing the resistivity of the wire

429. Under certain conditions, the resistivity of copper is 1.7×10^{-8} Ωm. What is the resistance of a 1.5-m-long copper wire with a cross-sectional area of 4.0 mm^2?

(A) 1.6×10^{-3} Ω
(B) 6.4×10^{-3} Ω
(C) 6.4×10^{-6} Ω
(D) 3.2×10^{-6} Ω
(E) 3.2×10^{-9} Ω

430. A space heater with a resistance of 12 Ω is connected to a 120-V power supply. How much energy is transferred to thermal energy as this device operates for 2 hours?

(A) 1.2×10^3 J
(B) 2.4×10^3 J
(C) 8.6×10^6 J
(D) 2.4×10^6 J
(E) 1.2×10^6 J

431. A 3-Ω headlight in a car is attached to the 12-V battery. How much energy transfers from the battery for every coulomb of electric charge that flows through this simple circuit?

(A) 3 J
(B) 4 J
(C) 12 J
(D) 24 J
(E) 36 J

432. Two 40-Ω resistors wired in parallel are connected in series with a 20-Ω resistor and a power supply. The current in each of the parallel resistors is 1.5 A. What is the current flowing through the 20-Ω resistor and the power supply, respectively?

(A) 1.5 A, 1.5 A
(B) 3.0 A, 1.5 A
(C) 1.5 A, 3.0 A
(D) 3.0 A, 3.0 A
(E) 60.0 A, 60.0 A

433. Two identical resistors with resistance R are connected in series with a power supply with a potential difference of ΔV. Which expression represents the power output of the entire circuit?

(A) $\dfrac{\Delta V^2}{4R}$

(B) $\dfrac{\Delta V^2}{2R}$

(C) $\dfrac{\Delta V^2}{R}$

(D) $\dfrac{2(\Delta V)^2}{R}$

(E) $2R(\Delta V)^2$

434. Two identical resistors with resistance R are connected in series with a power supply with a potential difference of ΔV. Which expression represents the rate that the circuit transfers energy to a single resistor?

(A) $\dfrac{\Delta V^2}{4R}$

(B) $\dfrac{\Delta V^2}{2R}$

(C) $\dfrac{\Delta V^2}{R}$

(D) $\dfrac{2(\Delta V)^2}{R}$

(E) $2R(\Delta V)^2$

435. Two identical resistors with resistance R are connected in parallel with a power supply with a potential difference of ΔV. Which expression represents the rate that the circuit transfers energy to a single resistor?

(A) $\dfrac{\Delta V^2}{4R}$

(B) $\dfrac{\Delta V^2}{2R}$

(C) $\dfrac{\Delta V^2}{R}$

(D) $\dfrac{2(\Delta V)^2}{R}$

(E) $2R(\Delta V)^2$

436. What happens to the resistance of a wire if its length is doubled and its cross-sectional area is doubled?

(A) It quadruples.
(B) It doubles.
(C) It stays the same.
(D) It is reduced to one-half.
(E) It is reduced to one-fourth.

437. Kirchhoff's junction rule is based on which of the following?

(A) Coulomb's law
(B) Newton's law
(C) Conservation of energy
(D) Conservation of charge
(E) Conservation of momentum

438. Kirchhoff's loop rule is based on which of the following?

(A) Coulomb's law
(B) Newton's law
(C) Conservation of energy
(D) Conservation of charge
(E) Conservation of momentum

439. As the temperature increases, what happens to the current-carrying ability of a wire?

(A) The current increases.
(B) The current decreases.
(C) The current stays the same.
(D) The current increases and then decreases.
(E) The current decreases and then increases.

Multi-select: For **questions 440–444**, two of the suggested answers will be correct. Select the two best answers, and record them both on the answer sheet.

440. Which of the following can be said about a series circuit of two or more resistors with a power supply?

(A) The current is the same through all the elements.

(B) The current through each element adds up to the current through the power supply.

(C) The voltage is the same across each element.

(D) The resistance increases as devices are added.

(E) The power demand is greater than a parallel circuit with the same elements.

441. The resistance of a wire does NOT depend on which of the following?

(A) Current

(B) Cross-sectional area

(C) The wire material

(D) The length of the wire

(E) Voltage

442. What is true about a basic circuit consisting of a battery and a resistor?

(A) The electrons flow out from the positive terminal of the battery.

(B) The battery provides all the charge for the circuit.

(C) The circuit's electrons stay in the circuit throughout its operation.

(D) More electrons flow into the resistor than out of it.

(E) The electrons flow at the same rate in and out of the battery.

443. Which of the following are true about the power output of a circuit?

(A) Power decreases as devices are added in a parallel circuit.

(B) Power is the product of current and voltage.

(C) Power is the rate at which energy is transferred to or from a device.

(D) Power is inversely proportional to the square of current.

(E) Power is directly proportional to resistance.

444. What is true about the energy in a basic circuit consisting of a battery and a resistor?

(A) The chemical energy in the battery transfers to thermal energy in the resistor.

(B) The battery creates the energy, and the resistors destroy it.

(C) The electrons are turned into energy as the resistor consumes them.

(D) The energy moves from the battery to the resistor and back to the battery.

(E) The circuit does not create or destroy energy.

Free Response: For the circuit depicted in this figure, answer the questions that follow.

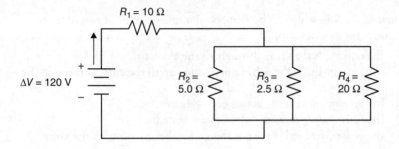

445. What is the equivalent resistance of the circuit?

446. What is the current flowing through the circuit?

447. What is the voltage drop across each resistor?

448. How much current flows through each resistor?

Free Response: An experiment is conducted with a 12-V battery and four 1-Ω resistors.

Experiment 1:
1. Wire the battery to a resistor, calculate the equivalent resistance, measure the total current, and calculate the power dissipated by the resistor in the circuit.
2. Add the second resistor in series, and repeat the measurements and calculations.
3. Add the third resistor in series, and repeat the measurements and calculations.
4. Add the fourth resistor in series, and repeat the measurements and calculations.
5. Graph the results.

Experiment 2:
Follow the same procedure for **Experiment 1**, but wire the resistors in parallel for this second experiment. The following graphs were obtained from the two experiments:

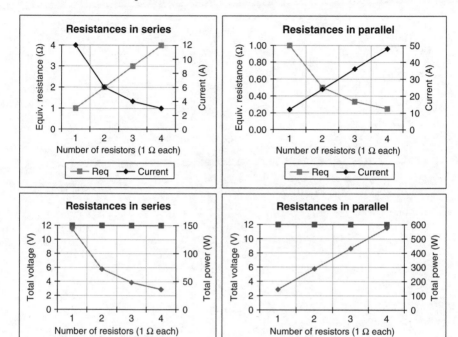

Using the graphs, answer the following questions:

449. (a) Describe the behavior of the equivalent resistance of the circuit as you add resistors in series versus parallel.
  (b) Describe and explain the behavior of the current through the power supply as you add resistors in series versus parallel.

450. (a) Describe and explain the behavior of the power demanded of the power supply as you add resistors in series versus parallel.
  (b) If the resistors were lightbulbs in strings of holiday lights, one wired in series and one in parallel, what can be said about the brightness of an individual bulb as you increase the number of bulbs? Explain your reasoning.

CHAPTER 10

Mechanical Waves and Sound

451. Which of the following is an example of a longitudinal wave?

(A) Water wave
(B) Microwave
(C) Sound wave
(D) Radio wave
(E) X-ray

452. Which of the following distances describes the amplitude of a wave?

(A) Crest to trough
(B) Crest to crest
(C) Trough to trough
(D) Top of crest to bottom of trough
(E) Crest to equilibrium position

453. A wave has a frequency of 100 Hz. What is the period of the wave?

(A) 0.5 s
(B) 0.01 s
(C) 0.1 s
(D) 1 s
(E) 100 s

454. A wave has a frequency of 100 Hz and a wavelength of 1 m. What is the speed of the wave?

(A) 0.01 m/s
(B) 1 m/s
(C) 10 m/s
(D) 100 m/s
(E) 1,000 m/s

455. The highest sound that a human can hear has a wavelength of 17.2 cm. What is the frequency of this wave? (Assume the speed of sound is 343 m/s.)

(A) 20 Hz
(B) 200 Hz
(C) 2,000 Hz
(D) 20 kHz
(E) 20 MHz

456. A jackhammer operator wears a set of protective headphones. Through the headphones, a sound wave is broadcast that is 180° out of phase with the jackhammer sound wave. The result is that he does not hear the sound of the jackhammer. These two sound waves are an example of which of the following?

(A) Standing wave
(B) Transverse wave
(C) Destructive interference
(D) Constructive interference
(E) Doppler effect

457. Half of a sound wave forms in a 0.500-m open tube when the fundamental frequency is played. What is this fundamental frequency when the speed of sound is 343 m/s?

(A) 34 Hz
(B) 86 Hz
(C) 172 Hz
(D) 343 Hz
(E) 686 Hz

Questions 458–460 use the following figure:

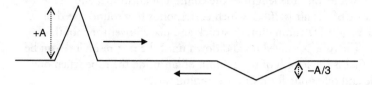

458. Two waves are traveling on a string. The directions and amplitude of each wave are shown in the figure. When the two waves meet, what will be the amplitude of the resulting wave?

   (A) −4A/3
   (B) −2A/3
   (C) 0
   (D) 2A/3
   (E) 4A/3

459. The figure depicts which of the following phenomena?

   (A) Standing wave
   (B) Transverse wave
   (C) Destructive interference
   (D) Constructive interference
   (E) Doppler effect

460. After the waves interact, what will happen?

   (A) One wave (2A/3) will travel to the right.
   (B) One wave (−2A/3) will travel to the left.
   (C) There will be no more waves.
   (D) One wave (+A) will travel to the right, while one wave (−A/3) will travel to the left.
   (E) One wave (−A) will travel to the right, while one wave (+A/3) will travel to the left.

461. A 0.50-m tube is placed in a bucket of water. The tube can be moved up and down to vary the length of the column of air inside, and the temperature of the air is 20°C, which corresponds to a sound speed of 343 m/s. A 440-Hz tuning fork is struck and placed over the mouth of the tube. The tube is moved up and down until the first resonance can be heard. What is the length of the column of air inside the tube when one antinode and one node form in the standing wave?

   (A) 0.09 m
   (B) 0.19 m
   (C) 0.27 m
   (D) 0.38 m
   (E) 0.5 m

462. A tsunami wave travels at 720 km/h and has a period of 10 min. What is the wavelength of the wave?

   (A) 2.0 km
   (B) 7.5 km
   (C) 120 km
   (D) 720 km
   (E) 750 km

463. A favorite radio station is located on the dial at 100 MHz. What is the wavelength of the radio waves emitted from the radio station if the speed of these waves is 3.00×10^8 m/s?

   (A) 3 m
   (B) 30 m
   (C) 300 m
   (D) 3 km
   (E) 300 km

464. What phenomenon describes how sound changes frequency as it passes a receiver?

   (A) Young's modulus
   (B) Maxwell effect
   (C) Michelson shift
   (D) Doppler effect
   (E) Einstein bridge

465. A 440-Hz and a 444-Hz tuning fork are struck simultaneously. What is the beat frequency that you hear?

(A) 1 Hz
(B) 2 Hz
(C) 4 Hz
(D) 221 Hz
(E) 442 Hz

466. Two waves are traveling on a string. The directions and amplitude of each wave are shown in the figure. When the two waves meet, what will be the amplitude of the resulting wave?

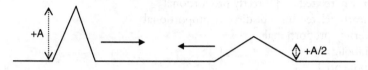

(A) A/2
(B) A
(C) 3A/2
(D) 2A
(E) 4A

467. Which of the following measurements is used to find the wavelength?

(A) Crest to zero displacement
(B) Crest to trough
(C) Trough to zero displacement
(D) Trough to crest
(E) Crest to crest

468. What is true about a loud sound with a low pitch?

(A) It travels faster than a soft sound.
(B) It travels slower than a high-pitch sound.
(C) It has large amplitude and low frequency.
(D) It has small amplitude and high frequency.
(E) It has small amplitude and low frequency.

469. A girl sitting on a beach counts six waves passing a buoy in 3.0 s. She measured the distance between the waves to be 1.5 m. What is the speed of the waves the girl observed?

(A) 3.0 m/s
(B) 9.0 m/s
(C) 0.75 m/s
(D) 1.3 m/s
(E) 0.30 m/s

470. As a wave is formed, what is the relationship between the wavelength and frequency?

(A) Linearly related and directly proportional
(B) Linearly related but not directly proportional
(C) Inversely proportional
(D) Parabolic
(E) Exponential

471. The sound from a loudspeaker vibrating at 256 Hz interferes with a trumpet vibrating at 252 Hz. What sound results?

(A) A 254-Hz pitch with a 4-Hz beat frequency
(B) A 4-Hz pitch with a 254-Hz beat frequency
(C) A melodic chord
(D) Two distinct pitches
(E) A resonance with a frequency of 308 Hz

472. A girl sitting on a beach counts six waves passing a buoy in 3 s. What is the period of the buoy's vibration?

(A) 0.5 s
(B) 0.5 Hz
(C) 2 s
(D) 2 Hz
(E) 6 Hz

473. If a wave disturbance travels 16 m each second and the distance between each crest is 4 m, determine the frequency of the disturbance.

(A) 0.25 Hz
(B) 2 Hz
(C) 4 Hz
(D) 32 Hz
(E) 64 Hz

474. What are the approximate amplitude and wavelength, respectively, of the wave shown in the diagram?

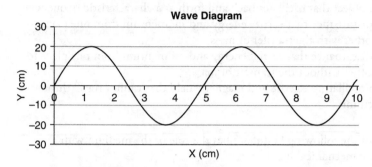

(A) 40 cm; 10 cm
(B) 20 cm; 5 cm
(C) 40 cm; 5 cm
(D) 20 cm; 10 cm
(E) 10 cm; 20 cm

475. Which of the following is observed as a constantly moving source of sound passes a receiver that is at rest?

(A) The frequency and the speed increase.
(B) The frequency decreases, and the speed increases.
(C) The frequency decreases, and the speed stays the same.
(D) The frequency and the speed stay the same.
(E) The frequency increases, and the speed decreases.

476. Which of the following will cause the phenomenon of sound beats to occur?

(A) Two slightly different frequencies sounding together
(B) When the frequency of one object matches the natural frequency of another
(C) A sound wave reflecting off a boundary back onto itself
(D) A source approaching the receiver at a speed faster than its sound wave
(E) When a source varies its amplitude at regular intervals

477. What is observed when sound beats occur?

(A) A rhythmic change in the pitch of the sound
(B) A regular increase and decrease in the speed of the sound
(C) An increase in frequency of the sound
(D) A dramatic growth in amplitude of the sound
(E) A sound that gets louder and softer at regular intervals

478. Which of the following best describes a wave?

(A) A pattern resembling a sine wave

(B) An object that oscillates back and forth at a characteristic frequency

(C) A disturbance that carries energy and momentum from one place to another with the transfer of mass

(D) A disturbance that carries energy and momentum from one place to another without the transfer of mass

(E) An oscillating electric and magnetic field that cannot travel through a vacuum

479. Which of the following best describes the role of the medium with a transverse mechanical wave?

(A) The medium vibrates back and forth parallel to the motion of the wave.

(B) The medium vibrates back and forth perpendicular to the motion of the wave.

(C) The medium oscillates between parallel and perpendicular vibrations.

(D) There is a snakelike slither through the medium.

(E) Oscillating compressions and rarefactions move through the medium.

480. Which of the following quantities is defined as the amount of vibrations a medium experiences in a given amount of time?

(A) Speed

(B) Period

(C) Wavelength

(D) Velocity

(E) Frequency

481. A child dips her finger repeatedly into the water to make waves. If she dips her finger more frequently, the wavelength _____ and the speed _____.

(A) Increases; decreases

(B) Decreases; increases

(C) Increases; stays the same

(D) Decreases; stays the same

(E) Stays the same; increases

482. An observer notices a 2.00-s delay between seeing fireworks and hearing them. How far away are the fireworks if the speed of sound is 344 m/s?

(A) 86 m
(B) 172 m
(C) 344 m
(D) 688 m
(E) 1,376 m

483. A tuning fork vibrates 256 times each second. What is the distance between compressions if the speed of the sound waves is 345 m/s?

(A) 0.70 m
(B) 0.740 m
(C) 1.40 m
(D) 89.0 m
(E) 601 m

484. Two waves have the same frequency. What other characteristic must be the same for these waves?

(A) Speed
(B) Period
(C) Amplitude
(D) Intensity
(E) Wavelength

485. Which of the following best describes the air particles as sound travels through air?

(A) The air particles vibrate along lines perpendicular to the motion of the wave.
(B) The air particles vibrate along lines parallel to the motion of the wave.
(C) The air particles don't move unless the transverse wave has a direct collision with them.
(D) The air particles remain stationary as the wave travels through them.
(E) The air particles move from the source of the wave to the receiver.

486. Which of the following quantities remains constant as a mechanical wave travels from one type of spring into another?

(A) Frequency
(B) Wavelength
(C) Speed
(D) Amplitude
(E) Spring constant

487. A dolphin swimming at the surface of the sea emits an ultrasonic sound wave toward the ocean floor. It takes 0.15 s for the sound to go from the dolphin to the floor of the ocean and back. Determine the depth of the ocean if the speed of sound in the water is 1,400 m/s.

(A) 93 m
(B) 105 m
(C) 186 m
(D) 210 m
(E) 420 m

Multi-select: For **questions 488–492**, two of the suggested answers will be correct. Select the two best answers, and record them both on the answer sheet.

488. Which of the following are true about sound waves?

(A) Their speed increases slightly with temperature.
(B) They travel faster than light waves.
(C) Their speed gets greater as the pitch of the sound increases.
(D) They travel faster in steel than air.
(E) They can travel in the vacuum of space.

489. Which of the following are necessary for a standing wave to form?

(A) A vibration at a natural frequency
(B) Reflection off a boundary
(C) At least two different vibration frequencies
(D) The source must move faster than the speed of the wave.
(E) The wave must be transverse.

490. The speed of a sound wave depends on which of the following?

(A) The loudness and pitch of the sound
(B) The intensity of the vibration
(C) The frequency of the source of vibration
(D) The characteristics of the medium
(E) The type of medium

491. Which of the following may NOT occur when a single wave hits a boundary between one medium and another?

(A) It reflects back into the original medium.
(B) Its frequency changes.
(C) It transmits into the new medium.
(D) It gains energy.
(E) Some of its energy is absorbed as thermal energy.

492. Which of the following are examples of resonance?

(A) A low frequency beat is detected when two tuning forks are played together.

(B) A high frequency is detected when a moving object approaches an observer.

(C) A tuning fork starts vibrating when an identical tuning fork vibrates next to it.

(D) A wineglass vibrates dramatically and shatters when a certain pitch is played on a nearby speaker.

(E) Two waves combine to form a wave with a larger amplitude.

Free Response: The end of a spring is attached to a wall. A student vibrates the end of a spring with 5.0 vibrations each second. The following standing wave forms:

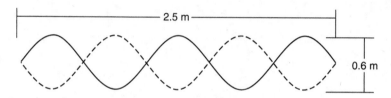

493. Determine the wavelength and amplitude of the wave.

$\lambda = 1\,m$ $A = 0.3\,m$

494. Calculate the period of the wave.

$T = 0.2\,s$

495. Calculate the speed of the wave.

$v = 5\,\frac{m}{s}$

496. How much time does it take a disturbance to travel to the wall and back again?

1 second

497. Explain what happens to the speed and wavelength of the wave if the frequency is doubled.

Since velocity of a wave only depends on the medium which it passes through, the velocity remains at 5 $\frac{m}{s}$, but the wavelength becomes half of what it was. Since $\lambda = \frac{v}{f}$ and f doubles, wavelength changes from $\lambda = 1\,m$ to $\lambda = 0.5\,m$.

Free Response: A particular bat emits a 25,000-Hz ultrasonic sound to navigate in a cave in which the speed of sound is 343 m/s.

498. Determine the distance between compressions of the sound signal.

499. As the bat hovers 3.5 m from the wall of the cave, calculate the amount of time it takes the sound to travel to the wall and back again.

500. As the bat flies toward another bat, explain the frequency that the second bat detects.

Chapter 1: Kinematics

1. (B) The height is (125 m) and the initial velocity (0 m/s). The acceleration due to gravity (9.8 m/s^2) is implied. Solve this equation for t:

$$\Delta x = v_0 t + \frac{1}{2} a t^2$$

$$(125 \text{ m}) = (0 \text{ m/s}) + \frac{1}{2}(9.8 \text{ m/s}^2) t^2$$

$$t = 5.0 \text{ s}$$

2. (D) The distance the car traveled is 500 m, the initial velocity is 0 m/s, and the final velocity is 50 m/s. Solve this equation for a:

$$v_f^2 = v_0^2 + 2a\Delta x$$

$$(50 \text{ m/s})^2 = (0 \text{ m/s})^2 + 2a(500 \text{ m})$$

$$a = 2.5 \text{ m/s}^2$$

3. (A) At the beginning of region C, the velocity gradually decreases to zero, indicating its speed is decreasing. At point D, the velocity has reached zero (resting instantaneously). At the beginning of region E, the negative velocity indicates that the direction is now negative, and the increasing magnitude of the velocity indicates it is speeding up.

4. (D) Acceleration is the slope of the velocity versus clock reading graph. The velocity increases at a rate of 10 m/s each and every second in region A.

5. (B) Acceleration is the slope of the velocity versus clock reading graph (it is not the value of velocity at the 5-second clock reading!). To find the slope at the 6-second clock reading, one must examine the entire (constant) slope from $t = 4$ s to $t = 8$ s:

$$a = \frac{\Delta v}{\Delta t} = \frac{(-30 - 30)\text{m/s}}{(8 - 4)\text{s}} = -15\frac{\text{m}}{\text{s}^2}$$

6. (D) The average velocity of region A is (0 + 30 m/s)/2 = +15 m/s.
Region B is (30 m/s + 30 m/s)/2 = +30 m/s.
Region C is (30 m/s + 0 m/s)/2 = +15 m/s.
Region E is (0 m/s + −30 m/s)/2 = −15 m/s.

7. (C) The horizontal velocity of the package is the same as that of the plane (50.0 m/s). The height of the plane is 125.0 m. First, find the time it takes for the package to reach the ground, and use that time to calculate the horizontal distance that the package travels.

1. Solve for time:

$$\Delta y = y_0 t - \frac{1}{2} g t^2$$

$$(-125 \text{ m}) = (0 \text{ m/s}) - \frac{1}{2}(9.8 \text{ m/s}^2)t^2$$

$$t = 5 \text{ s}$$

2. Solve for horizontal distance:

$$\Delta x = v_x t$$
$$\Delta x = (50.0 \text{ m/s})(5 \text{ s})$$
$$\Delta x = 250 \text{ m}$$

8. (D) Information provided is the angle of the kick (30°) and the initial velocity (10.0 m/s). Find the vertical component of the velocity, and solve for t when the ball hits the ground ($y = 0$).

1. Solve for the vertical component of velocity:

$$v_y = v \sin \theta$$
$$v_y = (10.0 \text{ m/s})(\sin 30°)$$
$$v_y = 5.0 \text{ m/s}$$

2. Solve for time:

$$\Delta y = v_y t + \frac{1}{2} g t^2$$

$$0 = v_y t + \frac{1}{2} g t^2$$

$$0 = t\left(v_y + \frac{1}{2} g t \right) \quad : \quad t = 0 \text{ is not a relevant solution}$$

$$v_y + \frac{1}{2} g t = 0$$

$$t = \frac{-2v_y}{g}$$

$$t = \frac{-2(5.0 \text{ m/s})}{(-9.8 \text{ m/s}^2)}$$

$$t = 1.0 \text{ s}$$

9. (C) The object is at rest during the time interval of 3–4 s when the object's position does not change.

10. (D) Knowing the car's final velocity (30 m/s), the rate of acceleration (3.0 m/s²), and the time interval over which it accelerated (5.0 s), calculate the initial velocity as follows:

$$v_t = v_0 + at$$

$$v_0 = v_f - at$$

$$v_0 = (30 \text{ m/s}) - (3.0 \text{ m/s}^2)(5 \text{ s})$$

$$v_0 = 15 \text{ m/s}$$

11. (C) The airplane's initial velocity was 0 m/s, and it accelerated at 1.0 m/s² for 5 min (300 s). Calculate the distance as follows:

$$\Delta x = v_0 t + \frac{1}{2} at^2$$

$$\Delta x = 0 + \frac{1}{2}(1.0 \text{ m/s}^2)(300 \text{ s})^2$$

$$\Delta x = 45,000 \text{ m, or 45 km}$$

12. (B) By subtracting the echo time, calculate that the stone takes 8 s to reach the bottom of the well. Now, calculate the vertical distance of the well:

$$\Delta x = v_0 t + \frac{1}{2} at^2$$

$$\Delta x = 0 + \frac{1}{2}(9.8 \text{ m/s}^2)(8 \text{ s})^2$$

$$\Delta x = 320 \text{ m}$$

13. (D) The ball is in a free fall, which means it slows down at a constant acceleration rate of about 10 m/s/s, or it loses 10 m/s of speed each and every second. At the maximum height, its final velocity is zero. To determine the time, divide the initial velocity of 30 m/s by the acceleration rate of 10 m/s/s, which gives 3.0 s.

14. (E) The initial velocity is 0 m/s, the height is 15 m, and the time is 1 s. Calculate the acceleration due to gravity:

$$\Delta x = v_0 t + \frac{1}{2} at^2$$

$$15 \text{ m} = 0 + \frac{1}{2}(a)(1 \text{ s})^2$$

$$a = 30 \text{ m/s}^2$$

15. (A) Knowing the car's initial velocity (0 m/s), the rate of acceleration (3.0 m/s²), and the distance of the track (150 m), calculate the final velocity as follows:

$$v_f^2 = v_0^2 + 2a\Delta x$$
$$v_f^2 = (0 \text{ m/s})^2 + 2(3.0 \text{ m/s}^2)(150 \text{ m})$$
$$v_f = 30 \text{ m/s}$$

16. (D) When a position–time graph is horizontal, the velocity of the object is zero. The velocity at any instant in time is the slope of the line tangent to any point on the position–time graph. For this graph, that occurs at 1 s and 3 s.

17. (C) A projectile launched at an angle from the ground follows a parabolic path. The parabola is symmetrical, so the maximum height occurs at one-half of the total time in the air.

18. (D) It takes approximately 3 s for the stone to drop, and the stone started from rest. So, we can calculate the approximate height of the cliff:

$$\Delta x = v_0 t + \frac{1}{2}at^2$$
$$\Delta x = 0 + \frac{1}{2}(9.8 \text{ m/s}^2)(3 \text{ s})^2$$
$$\Delta x = 45 \text{ m}$$

19. (D) The bicycle's initial velocity was 5.0 m/s, and it slowed at an acceleration of −2.5 m/s² to a stop ($v_f = 0$). The time can be determined from this equation:

$$v_f = v_0 + at$$
$$(0 \text{ m/s}) = (5.0 \text{ m/s}) + (-2.5 \text{ m/s}^2)t$$
$$t = 2.0 \text{ s}$$

20. (B) The final velocity of the car was zero, and the rate of deceleration was −7.5 m/s² across a distance of 60 m. Calculate the initial velocity of the car when it started skidding:

$$v_f^2 = v_0^2 + 2a\Delta x$$
$$(0 \text{ m/s})^2 = v_0^2 + 2(-7.5 \text{ m/s}^2)(60 \text{ m})$$
$$v_0 = 30 \text{ m/s}$$

21. (A) To find the displacement, integrate the area under the curve to the t axis. This simply involves adding the areas of two trapezoids, one in the 0–6 s time interval and the other in the 6–10 s time interval.

$$\Delta x = A_{0-6\,s} + A_{6-10\,s}$$

$$\Delta x = \left[\frac{1}{2}(b_1 + b_2)(h) \right] + \left[\frac{1}{2}(b_1 + b_2)(h) \right]$$

$$\Delta x = \left[\frac{1}{2}(3\ s + 6\ s)(2\ m/s) \right] + \left[\frac{1}{2}(2\ s + 4\ s)(-2\ m/s) \right]$$

$$\Delta x = [9\ m] + [-6\ m]$$

$$\Delta x = 3\ m$$

22. (B) The horizontal component of velocity is calculated by $v_x = v \cos \theta$, while the vertical component is calculated by $v_x = v \sin \theta$. For angles less than $45°$, the cosine is larger than the sine. So, the horizontal component of velocity is larger than the vertical component.

23. (B) The dropped ball's initial velocity was zero, and it took 4 s to hit the ground. The height of the building can be calculated:

$$\Delta x = v_0 t + \frac{1}{2} a t^2$$

$$\Delta x = 0 + \frac{1}{2}(9.8\ m/s^2)(4\ s)^2$$

$$\Delta x = 90\ m$$

24. (D) If the positive direction is forward, then an object that is moving backward at a constant velocity would have a position–time graph that is linear with a negative slope.

25. (C) For projectiles launched at the same velocity but at different angles (between $0°$ and $90°$), those with complementary angles will have the same range.

26. (E) When the initial velocity is zero, the following equation is obtained:

$$.x = x_0 + v_{x0} t + \frac{1}{2} a_x t^2 = \frac{1}{2} a_x t^2$$

$$.\Delta x = v_{x0} t + \frac{1}{2} a_x t^2 = \frac{1}{2} a_x t^2$$

$$.\Delta x = \frac{1}{2} a_x t^2$$

So if the elapsed time is doubled (and the acceleration stays the same), the displacement quadruples.

27. (B) The initial velocity of the car is 30 m/s, the final velocity is 0 m/s, and the acceleration is -9 m/s². The distance the car traveled can be calculated:

$$v_f^2 = v_0^2 + 2a\Delta x$$
$$(0 \text{ m/s})^2 = (30 \text{ m/s})^2 + 2(-9 \text{ m/s}^2)\Delta x$$
$$\Delta x = 50 \text{ m}$$

28. (C) The position in the graph is increasing nonlinearly in the positive direction. It is consistent with motion with a constant positive acceleration.

29. (B) The initial velocity of the ball is 0 m/s, and the time is 2 s. The distance it travels can be calculated:

$$\Delta x = v_0 t + \frac{1}{2}at^2$$
$$\Delta x = 0 + \frac{1}{2}(9.8 \text{ m/s}^2)(2 \text{ s})^2$$
$$\Delta x = 20 \text{ m}$$

30. (D) The ice skater has an initial velocity of 10 m/s and a final velocity of 0 m/s. The time interval is 0.5 s. Calculate the rate of acceleration:

$$v_f = v_0 + at$$
$$(0 \text{ m/s}) = (10 \text{ m/s}) + a(0.5 \text{ s})$$
$$a = -20 \text{ m/s}^2$$

31. (D) The position in the graph is increasing linearly in the positive direction. This is consistent with motion with a constant positive velocity and, hence, zero acceleration.

32. (B) The slope of the position–time graph is the velocity of the car. The negative constant slope indicates a constant speed in the negative direction.

33. (B) The displacement is the final position minus the starting position.
The displacement for part A is 125 m − 0 m = +125 m.
The displacement for part B is 100 m − 100 m = 0 m.
The displacement for part C is 125 m − 100 m = +25 m.
The displacement for part D is 0 m − 125 m = −125 m.

34. (C) The average speed is the distance traveled divided by the time for each section.
The average velocity for part A is (125 m)/10 s = 12.5 m/s.
The average velocity for part B is (0 m)/5 s = 0 m/s.
The average velocity for part C is (25 m)/5 s = 5 m/s.
The average velocity for part D is (125 m)/5 s = 25 m/s.

35. **(D)** The velocity is the slope of the position–time graph, which includes direction. The slope of section C is $(+25 \text{ m})/(5 \text{ s}) = +5$ m/s. The slope of section D is $(-125 \text{ m})/(5 \text{ s}) = -25$ m/s.

36. **(C, E)** Velocity is a vector quantity, so constant velocity is achieved when an object moves at a constant speed in a straight line.

37. **(B, D)** Acceleration $\left(\dfrac{\Delta \vec{v}}{\Delta t}\right)$ is a vector quantity, so the direction of the acceleration must remain constant as well as the rate of change of speed. The skydiver's acceleration decreases as she approaches terminal velocity (when $a = 0$), so this choice must be eliminated. The direction of the acceleration of the truck driver is changing throughout the circle (especially with the required centripetal acceleration), so this choice must be eliminated. The box has zero acceleration, which eliminates it from consideration. The hammer is free-falling near the surface of the moon (no atmosphere and a steady gravitational field), which is a constant acceleration model, and the cart is clearly gaining speed at a steady rate while keeping direction constant.

38. **(A, D)** Option A is correct because speed is the absolute value of velocity, and both carts were moving at 4 m/s. Option D is correct because, at the 8-second clock reading, Cart 1 was moving at 6 m/s and Cart 2 was moving at 4 m/s. Option C is tempting but incorrect because it had positive velocity for the first half of the trip, indicating that it was moving in the positive direction. Option E is incorrect because the fact that it has a velocity of 0 m/s does not mean it is at the origin.

39. **(C)** The free-fall acceleration near the surface of the Earth is a constant rate of nearly 10 m/s^2.

40. **(E)** The free-fall acceleration near the surface of the Earth is a constant rate of nearly 10 m/s^2, which means a falling object constantly gains 10 m/s each and every second. Therefore, for 2 seconds, 25 m/s + 10 m/s + 10 m/s = 45 m/s.

41. **(B)** At a constant acceleration rate of 2 m/s each and every second, the car would speed up from 20 m/s to 22 m/s the first second, 22 to 24 the second, 24 to 26 the third, 26 to 28 the fourth, and 28 to 30 the fifth. Thus, it will take 5 seconds.

42. **(A)** At a constant speed, position should change linearly with time, so only options A and B should be considered. At $t = 0$, option A's position is 25 m. Each second after that, its position changes by −25 m each second.

43. **(C)** The initial position is $x_0 = -12$ m. The initial velocity is $v_{x0} = +5$ m/s. The acceleration rate is $a_x = 2$ m/s^2.

$$x = x_0 + v_{x0}t + \frac{1}{2}a_x t^2 = -12 + 5t + 1t^2$$

This is a projectile motion problem where $v = 10.0$ m/s, $\Delta y = -45$ m, and $\theta = 45°$.

44. The arrow follows a parabolic path. It first moves upward and away from the wall. It peaks and then moves downward and away from the wall until it hits the ground.

45. The horizontal component of velocity is vx = v cos q = (10.0 m/s) cos 45° = 7.1 m/s. The vertical component of velocity is vy = v sin q = (10.0 m/s) sin 45° = 7.1 m/s. Because the cosine and sine of 45° are equal, the horizontal and vertical components are equal.

46. The time it takes for the arrow to reach the ground can be calculated as follows:

$$\Delta y = v_y t + \frac{1}{2} g t^2$$

$$-45 \text{ m} = (7.1 \text{ m/s})t + \frac{1}{2}(-9.8 \text{ m/s}^2)t^2$$

When you solve the quadratic equation by the quadratic formula, you get:

$$t = 3.84 \text{ s}$$

47. The range of the arrow can be calculated as follows:

$$\Delta x = v_x t$$
$$\Delta x = (7.1 \text{ m/s})(3.84 \text{ s})$$
$$\Delta x = 27.3 \text{ m}$$

48. Starting with the velocity of +4 m/s, the given graph shows a constant acceleration of 2 m/s each second for the first two seconds; then for the last three seconds the acceleration is −1 m/s each second, as shown in the graph below:

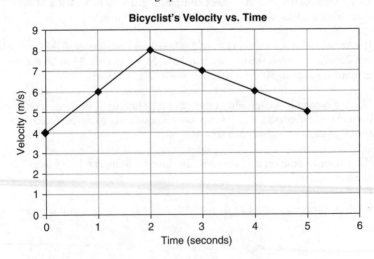

49. The bicyclist starts with a speed of 4 m/s and is moving in the positive direction. She gains 2 m/s each second for two seconds, and for the next three seconds begins to slow down at a rate of 1 m/s each second. Even for the second half of the trip, as she slows down, her velocities are still positive, indicating that she is still moving in the positive direction.

50. During the first half of the trip, her distance traveled was:

$$x - x_0 = v_{x0}t + \frac{1}{2}a_x t^2 = 4(2) + 0.5(2)(2^2) = 12 \text{ m}$$

At the beginning of the second part of the trip, the velocity was +8 m/s, and the distance is calculated as:

$$x - x_0 = v_{x0}t + \frac{1}{2}a_x t^2 = 8(3) + 0.5(-1)(3^2) = 24 - 4.5 = 19.5 \text{ m}$$

The total distance is 12 m + 19.5 m = 31.5 m, or approximately 32 m.

An alternate method of calculating distance is to determine the magnitude of the area bounded by the velocity–time graph above.

Chapter 2: Dynamics: Newton's Laws

51. (A) The first, which mathematically states that $\Sigma\ \mathbf{F} = 0$, shows that the net force is zero, and thus there is no acceleration. Equilibrium describes that state of motion when something is not accelerating.

52. (D) There is a gravitational field on the surface of the Moon that is about one-sixth the strength of the Earth's field, so they will both accelerate. According to Newton's second law, acceleration is the net force-to-mass ratio. The more massive sphere has a greater gravitational force but in ratio to the greater mass yields the same free-fall acceleration as the less massive sphere.

53. (C) Sliding friction acts in opposition to the direction of motion, and its magnitude is directly proportional to the normal force.

54. (E) According to Newton's third law, the forces are equal and opposite between two interacting systems, regardless of motion, mass, or any other variables.

55. (D) According to Newton's second law $\left(\vec{a} = \dfrac{\vec{F}_{net}}{m} \right)$, acceleration is inversely proportional to mass. In order to double the acceleration, the mass must be half as much (for the same net force).

56. (C) 26° is found from the arctan $(0.5) = 26°$.

57. (C) 1,600 N. A six-strand pulley has six supporting cables. Thus, the tension in the cable, which is continuous through the pulleys, is the 9,800-N total load divided by 6.

58. (D) The weight of the object in the downward direction is balanced by the supporting force of the spring in the upward direction in order to maintain equilibrium.

59. (E) The weight of the box, the perpendicular force of the plane on the box (the "normal force"), and the friction force along the surface of the plane beneath the box are the only forces acting on the box. The others mentioned are components, or they are misleading.

60. (B) 682 N. The component of weight acting down the incline is $2,000 \text{ N} * \sin(43) = 1,364 \text{ N}$. To keep the box moving at a constant velocity, the pulley ropes must balance this component of weight. The two ropes of the pulley share this load, giving $1,364 \text{ N}/2 = 682 \text{ N}$.

61. (B) A 10.0-N force pushes the box to the right, while an 8.0-N force pushes it to the left. The mass of the box is 5 kg. Solve this equation for a:

$$F_{net} = ma$$
$$(10.0 \text{ N} - 8.0 \text{ N}) = (5 \text{ kg})a$$
$$a = 0.4 \text{ m/s}^2 \text{ to the right}$$

62. (D) Remember that the force of gravity (mg) must be resolved into x and y components, and that the force of friction (F_f) is related to the normal force (F_N) by $F_f = \mu F_N$. The box does not move above or into the plane, so the forces in the y direction must be balanced. Apply Newton's second law to both the x and y directions to come up with an expression for acceleration:

$$F_{nety} = 0$$
$$F_N = mg \cos \theta = 0$$
$$F_N = mg \cos \theta$$
$$F_{netx} = ma$$
$$mg \sin \theta - F_f = ma$$
$$mg \sin \theta - \mu F_N = ma$$
$$mg \sin \theta - \mu(mg \cos \theta) = ma$$
$$g \sin \theta - \mu(g \cos \theta) = a$$
$$a = g(\sin \theta - \mu \cos \theta)$$

63. (E) The force that you exert on the rope is equal to the rope's tension (T). The acceleration due to gravity is approximately 10 m/s^2. The acceleration of the box is given at 10 m/s^2 upward. Use Newton's second law to calculate the downward force that applies to the rope:

$$F_{net} = ma$$
$$T - mg = ma$$
$$T = ma + mg$$
$$T = m(a + g)$$
$$T = (10 \text{ kg})(10 \text{ m/s}^2 + 10 \text{ m/s}^2)$$
$$T = 200 \text{ N}$$

64. (A) Resolve the jet's thrust into horizontal and vertical components. Then enter the horizontal component of thrust, force of the wind, and the jet's mass into Newton's second law to find the acceleration:

$$F_x = F \cos\theta$$
$$F_x = (20,000 \text{ N})(\cos 60°)$$
$$F_x = 10,000 \text{ N}$$
$$F_{netx} = ma$$
$$a = \frac{F_{netx}}{m}$$
$$a = \frac{(F_x - F_{wind})}{m}$$
$$a = \frac{(10,000 \text{ N} - 1,000 \text{ N})}{(90,000 \text{ kg})}$$
$$a = 0.1 \text{ m/s}^2$$

65. (D) The object accelerates only when the forces acting upon it are unbalanced. The net force on the object at $t = 2$ s is 1.2 N – 1.0 N = 0.2 N. The acceleration is the net force divided by the mass, or (0.2 N/0.1 kg) = 2 m/s^2.

66. (D) The crate's mass is 10 kg, one force is 10 N, and the rate of acceleration is 0.1 m/s^2. Solve for the second force by using Newton's second law:

$$a = \frac{F_{net}}{m}$$
$$a = \frac{(F_1 - F_2)}{m}$$
$$F_1 - F_2 = ma$$
$$F_2 = F_1 - ma$$
$$F_2 = (10 \text{ N}) - (10 \text{ kg})(0.1 \text{ m/s}^2)$$
$$F_2 = 9 \text{ N}$$

67. (C) By applying Newton's second law to the inclined situation, derive an equation in which the crate's acceleration depends only upon the coefficient of friction ($\mu = 0.1$), acceleration due to gravity ($g \approx 10$ m/s^2), and the angle of incline ($\theta = 45°$).

$$F_{nety} = 0$$
$$F_N - mg\cos\theta = 0$$
$$F_N = mg\cos\theta$$
$$F_{netx} = ma$$
$$mg\sin\theta - F_f = ma$$
$$mg\sin\theta - \mu F_N = ma$$
$$mg\sin\theta - \mu(mg\cos\theta) = ma$$
$$g\sin\theta - \mu(g\cos\theta) = a$$
$$a = g(\sin\theta - \mu\cos\theta)$$
$$a = (10 \text{ m/s}^2)[\sin 45° - (0.1)\cos 45°]$$
$$a = (10 \text{ m/s}^2)[0.707) - (0.1)(0.707)]$$
$$a = 6.4 \text{ m/s}^2$$

68. (B) The two masses are designated $m = 5$ kg and $M = 10$ kg. By applying Newton's second law to the pulley system and using the direction of positive as counterclockwise, derive an equation for acceleration and solve the problem:

$$mg - T = ma$$
$$T - Mg = Ma$$
$$T = Ma + Mg$$
$$mg - (Ma + Mg) = ma$$
$$mg - Ma - Mg = ma$$
$$mg - Mg = ma + Ma$$
$$g(m - M) = a(m + M)$$
$$a = g\frac{(m - M)}{(m + M)}$$
$$a = (10 \text{ m/s}^2)\frac{(5 \text{ kg} - 10 \text{ kg})}{(5 \text{ kg} + 10 \text{ kg})}$$
$$a = -3.3 \text{ m/s}^2$$

69. (A) From the graph, the acceleration at $t = 1$ s is -2 m/s^2. The object's mass is 5 kg. So, the net force can be calculated from Newton's second law:

$$F_{net} = ma$$
$$F_{net} = (5 \text{ kg})(-2 \text{ m/s}^2)$$
$$F_{net} = -10 \text{ N}$$

70. (D) Find the x component of the skier's weight. The skier has a mass of 70 kg, the angle of the incline is 30°, and the skier pushes off with an applied force ($F_A = 105$ N). Use Newton's second law to find the rate of acceleration:

$$F_{netx} = ma$$

$$mg \sin\theta + F_A = ma$$

$$a = \frac{mg \sin\theta + F_A}{m}$$

$$a = \frac{(70 \text{ kg})(10 \text{ m/s}^2)\sin 30° + (105 \text{ N})}{(70 \text{ kg})}$$

$$a = \frac{(70 \text{ kg})(10 \text{ m/s}^2)(0.5) + (105 \text{ N})}{(70 \text{ kg})}$$

$$a = 6.5 \text{ m/s}^2$$

$$a \approx 7 \text{ m/s}^2$$

71. (B) Knowing the bullet's initial velocity (0 m/s) and mass (0.010 kg), use Newton's second law to calculate the rate of the bullet's acceleration. The bullet uniformly accelerates over the distance of the musket barrel (1 m) to its final velocity:

$$a = \frac{F_{net}}{m}$$

$$a = \frac{(50 \text{ N})}{(0.010 \text{ kg})}$$

$$a = 5,000 \text{ m/s}^2$$

$$v_f^2 = v_0^2 + 2a\Delta x$$

$$v_f^2 = (0 \text{ m/s}^2) + 2(5,000 \text{ m/s}^2)(1 \text{ m})$$

$$v_f = 100 \text{ m/s}$$

72. (C) A curve on the position versus clock reading graph indicates a changing slope, which is a changing velocity. The straight section between 1.8 and 2.2 s indicates a constant velocity, which is zero acceleration.

73. (C) The two masses are designated $m = 10$ kg and $M = 30$ kg. By applying Newton's second law to the pulley system and using the direction of positive as counterclockwise, derive an equation for acceleration and solve the problem:

$$F_{netx} = 0 - T = Ma : \text{Block } M$$
$$F_{net} = T - mg = ma : \text{Block } m$$
$$(-Ma) - mg = ma$$
$$ma = -Ma - mg$$
$$ma + Ma = -mg$$
$$a(m + M) = -mg$$
$$a = \frac{-mg}{(m + M)}$$
$$a = \frac{-(10 \text{ kg})(10 \text{ m/s}^2)}{(10 \text{ kg} + 30 \text{ kg})}$$
$$a = -2.5 \text{ m/s}^2$$

The magnitude of the acceleration is 2.5 m/s^2

74. (C) The jet has a mass of 50,000 kg, the engines produce 20,000 N of thrust, and the acceleration is 0.3 m/s^2. From Newton's second law, calculate the force of the air resistance:

$$F_{net} = ma$$
$$F_{thrust} - F_{air\ resistance} = ma$$
$$-F_{air\ resistance} = ma - F_{thrust}$$
$$F_{air\ resistance} = F_{thrust} - ma$$
$$F_{air\ resistance} = (20,000 \text{ N}) - (50,000 \text{ kg})(0.3 \text{ m/s}^2)$$
$$F_{air\ resistance} = 5,000 \text{ N}$$

75. (E) The acceleration is the slope of a velocity–time graph. In this case, the slope of the graph yields an acceleration of 0.5 m/s^2. The mass of the crate is 50 kg. From Newton's second law, calculate the force applied:

$$F_{net} = ma$$
$$F_{net} = (50 \text{ kg})(0.5 \text{ m/s}^2)$$
$$F_{net} = 25 \text{ N}$$

76. (E) Knowing the initial velocity of the car (30 m/s), the final velocity of the car (0 m/s), and the distance over which the car uniformly decelerates ($\Delta x = 60$ m), calculate the car's acceleration. Knowing the acceleration and the car's mass (1,000 kg), use Newton's second law to calculate the net force on the car:

$$v_f^2 = v_0^2 + 2a\Delta x$$
$$0 = v_0^2 + 2a\Delta x$$
$$-2a\Delta x = v_0^2$$
$$a = -\frac{v_0^2}{2\Delta x}$$
$$a = -\frac{(30 \text{ m/s})^2}{2(60 \text{ m})}$$
$$a = -7.5 \text{ m/s}^2$$
$$F_{net} = ma$$
$$F_{net} = (1,000 \text{ kg})(-7.5 \text{ m/s}^2)$$
$$F_{net} = -7,500 \text{ N}$$

77. (D) First calculate the acceleration using Newton's second law. The net force is 100 N, and the mass of the ball is 5 kg. Next, calculate the final velocity when the ball starts from rest ($v_0 = 0$ m/s) and the time interval is 1.5 s:

$$a = \frac{F_{net}}{m}$$
$$a = \frac{(100 \text{ N})}{(5 \text{ kg})}$$
$$a = 20 \text{ m/s}^2$$
$$v_f = v_0 + at$$
$$v_f = (0 \text{ m/s}) + (20 \text{ m/s}^2)(1.5 \text{ s})$$
$$v_f = 30 \text{ m/s}$$

78. (C) Newton's third law states that an interaction force between two systems is equal and opposite. During acceleration, each individual system will have unbalanced forces, but the tension interaction between the two systems is always equal and opposite.

79. (B) The forces acting upon the skydiver are the downward gravitational force and upward air resistance force (drag). Initially, the net force is high (gravity > air resistance), the skydiver accelerates, and the velocity increases rapidly. Over time, the air resistance increases with speed and the net force decreases, so the acceleration decreases. At some point in time, there is no net force (gravity = air resistance), acceleration drops to zero, and the skydiver's velocity is constant (e.g., terminal velocity).

80. (D) You know the box's initial velocity (0 m/s) and mass (10 kg), as well as the girl's applied force (50 N) and the force of friction opposing her (45 N). Use Newton's second law to calculate the rate of the box's acceleration. The box uniformly accelerates to its final velocity of 2 m/s. Calculate the time:

$$a = \frac{F_{net}}{m}$$

$$a = \frac{F_A - F_f}{m}$$

$$a = \frac{(50 \text{ N} - 45 \text{ N})}{(10 \text{ kg})}$$

$$a = 0.5 \text{ m/s}^2$$

$$v_f = v_0 + at$$

$$2.0 \text{ m/s} = 0 \text{ m/s} + (0.5 \text{ m/s}^2)t$$

$$t = 4 \text{ s}$$

81. (E) The rocket goes from rest ($v_0 = 0$ m/s) to 9.6 km/s ($v_f = 9,600$ m/s) in 8 min ($t = 480$ s). The rocket's mass is 8.0×10^6 kg. First, determine the rate of acceleration, and then use Newton's second law to determine the net force:

$$v_f = v_0 + at$$

$$9,600 \text{ m/s} = 0 \text{ m/s} + a(480 \text{ s}^2)t$$

$$a = 20 \text{ m/s}^2$$

$$F_{net} = ma$$

$$F_{net} = (8.0 \times 10^6 \text{ kg})(20 \text{ m/s}^2)$$

$$F_{net} = 1.6 \times 10^8 \text{ N}$$

82. (A) The car travels at constant velocity (its value is irrelevant). So, the net force acting on the car is zero according to Newton's first law. Therefore, the resistive forces balance to the forward force on the car (1,000 N).

83. (B) The initial velocity of the car is 30 m/s, the final velocity is 0 m/s, and the net force acting on the car is 9,000 N. The car's mass is 1,000 kg. Use Newton's second law to calculate the rate of acceleration (negative as implied by deceleration). The distance the car traveled can be calculated:

$$a = \frac{F_{net}}{m}$$

$$a = \frac{(-9,000 \text{ N})}{(1,000 \text{ kg})}$$

$$a = -9 \text{ m/s}^2$$

$$v_f^2 = v_0^2 + 2a\Delta x$$

$$(0 \text{ m/s})^2 = (30 \text{ m/s})^2 + 2(-9 \text{ m/s}^2)\Delta x$$

$$\Delta x = 50 \text{ m}$$

84. (D) The position in the graph is increasing linearly in the positive direction. It is consistent with motion with a constant positive velocity. The constant velocity means that acceleration is zero. According to Newton's second law, when acceleration is zero, there is no net force acting upon it.

85. (D) The initial velocity of the runner is 0 m/s, the final velocity is 10 m/s, and the time is 0.5 s. The runner's mass is 70 kg. First, calculate the acceleration, and then use Newton's second law to find the net force:

$$v_f = v_0 + at$$
$$(10 \text{ m/s}) = (0 \text{ m/s}) + a(0.5 \text{ s})$$
$$a = 20 \text{ m/s}^2$$
$$F_{net} = ma$$
$$F_{net} = (70 \text{ kg})(20 \text{ m/s}^2)$$
$$F_{net} = 1,400 \text{ N}$$

86. (A) Acceleration is the ratio between net force and mass:
    I. Net force F applied to a mass M: $a = (F/M)$
    II. Net force $2F$ applied to a mass M: $a = 2F/M = 2(F/M)$
    III. Net force F applied to a mass $2M$: $a = F/(2M) = (F/M)/2$
    IV. Net force $2F$ applied to a mass $2M$: $a = (2F)/(2M) = (F/M)$

87. (C) According to Newton's second law, the forces acting upon an object are balanced when the acceleration is zero. As shown in the graph, this occurs at 2 s.

88. (A, C) The only object touching the book is the table, and it provides the upward support force (normal force) to balance the downward force of gravity from the interaction of the Earth with the book.

89. (A, C) The upward normal force and the downward gravitational force are the only forces acting on the child. These will be balanced ONLY when the elevator is in a state of constant velocity, meaning it moves at a constant speed in a straight line or if it is at a constant zero velocity (i.e., at rest).

90. (B, C) A free-body diagram would show an upward normal force, a downward gravitational force, a tension force up and to the left at a 30° angle, a frictional force to the right parallel to the surface, and possibly an air drag force to the right that is probably negligible. "Motion" is not a force, and the force of the block on the table is a valid force but does not act on the system of interest (which is the box).

91. (C, E) Mass has an inertial property and a gravitational property. Its inertial property is embedded in Newton's second law in the fact that mass is inversely proportional to acceleration. This means that the more massive something is, the more it resists changes in motion. Its gravitational property describes how the gravitational force attracts two masses (like an apple and the Earth).

This is a projectile motion problem where $v = 10.0$ m/s, $\Delta y = -45$ m, and $\theta = 45°$. The arrow ($m = 0.05$ kg) travels against a wind in the x direction with a force of -0.05 N.

92. The horizontal component of velocity is $v_x = v \cos \theta = (10.0$ m/s$) \cos 45° = 7.1$ m/s. The vertical component of velocity is $v_y = v \sin \theta = (10.0$ m/s$) \sin 45° = 7.1$ m/s. Because the cosine and sine of $45°$ are equal, the horizontal and vertical components are equal.

93. Since the wind only acts horizontally, the vertical motion may be modeled as pure free fall. The time it takes for the arrow to reach the ground can be calculated as follows:

$$\Delta y = v_y t + \frac{1}{2} g t^2$$

$$-45 \text{ m} = (7.1 \text{ m/s})t + \frac{1}{2}(-9.8 \text{ m/s}^2)t^2$$

When you solve the quadratic equation by the quadratic formula, you get:

$$t = 3.84 \text{ s}$$

94. While in flight, the wind exerts a constant net force of -0.05 N against the arrow. This will cause the arrow to slow down in the horizontal direction. Calculate the arrow's horizontal acceleration using Newton's second law:

$$a = \frac{F_{\text{net}}}{m}$$

$$a = \frac{-0.05 \text{ N}}{-0.05 \text{ kg}}$$

$$a = -1.0 \text{ m/s}^2$$

The range of the arrow can be calculated as follows:

$$\Delta x = v_{x0} t + \frac{1}{2} a_x t^2$$

$$\Delta x = (7.1 \text{ m/s})(3.84 \text{ s}) + \frac{1}{2}(-1.0 \text{ m/s}^2)(3.84)^2$$

$$\Delta x = 19.7 \text{ m}$$

95. Without the wind, the arrow would travel in the x direction with a constant velocity of 7.1 m/s. So, the range can be calculated as follows:

$$\Delta x = v_x t$$

$$\Delta x = (7.1 \text{ m/s})(3.84 \text{ s})$$

$$\Delta x = 27.3 \text{ m}$$

Therefore, in the absence of a headwind, the arrow would travel 7.6 m farther.

96. The free-body diagram of this situation looks like this:

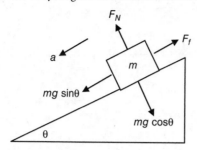

97. We can calculate the force of friction by applying Newton's second law:

$$F_{\text{nety}} = 0$$
$$F_N - mg\cos\theta = 0$$
$$F_N = mg\cos\theta$$
$$F_f = \mu F_N$$
$$F_f = \mu mg\cos\theta$$
$$F_f = (0.1)(10 \text{ kg})(9.8 \text{ m/s}^2)\cos 30°$$
$$F_f = (0.1)(10 \text{ kg})(9.8 \text{ m/s}^2)(0.87)$$
$$F_f = 8.49 \text{ N}$$

98. The box's acceleration can be calculated by applying Newton's second law:

$$F_{\text{nety}} = 0$$
$$F_N - mg\cos\theta = 0$$
$$F_N = mg\cos\theta$$
$$F_{\text{netx}} = ma$$
$$mg\sin\theta - F_f = ma$$
$$mg\sin\theta - \mu F_N = ma$$
$$mg\sin\theta - \mu(mg\cos\theta) = ma$$
$$g\sin\theta - \mu(g\cos\theta) = a$$
$$a = g(\sin\theta - \mu\cos\theta)$$
$$a = (9.8 \text{ m/s}^2)[\sin 30° - (0.1)\cos 30°]$$
$$a = (9.8 \text{ m/s}^2)[(0.5) - (0.1)(0.87)]$$
$$a = 4.05 \text{ m/s}^2$$

99. The box started from rest and accelerated down the plane for 2 s. Calculate the final velocity:

$$v_f = v_0 + at$$
$$v_f = (0) + (4.05 \text{ m/s}^2)(2 \text{ s})$$
$$v_f = 8.1 \text{ m/s}$$

100. Calculate the distance that the box moved:

$$v_f^2 = v_0^2 + 2a\Delta x$$
$$(8.1 \text{ m/s})^2 = (0 \text{ m/s})^2 + 2(4.05 \text{ m/s}^2)\Delta x$$
$$\Delta x = 8.1 \text{ m}$$

or

$$\Delta x = v_0 t + \frac{1}{2}at^2$$
$$\Delta x = 0 + \frac{1}{2}(4.05 \text{ m/s}^2)(2 \text{ s})^2$$
$$\Delta x = 8.1 \text{ m}$$

Chapter 3: Circular Motion and the Universal Law of Gravitation

101. (C) The tangential velocity is 30 m/s, and the radius of the circle is 10 m. Calculate the centripetal acceleration, which is toward the center, as follows:

$$a_c = \frac{v^2}{r}$$
$$a_c = \frac{(30 \text{ m/s})^2}{(10 \text{ m})}$$
$$a_c = 90 \text{ m/s}^2$$

102. (D) The force of friction is what holds the car in the circular motion and is equal to the centripetal force. You calculated the centripetal acceleration in **the previous question**. By knowing the mass of the car (1,000 kg), calculate the centripetal force, which acts toward the center:

$$F_c = ma_c$$
$$F_c = (1,000 \text{ kg})(90 \text{ m/s}^2)$$
$$F_c = 90,000 \text{ N}$$

103. (D) The known quantities include the masses of the satellite (100 kg) and Earth (6×10^{24} kg) and the radius of the satellite's orbit (100 km + radius of the Earth = 100,000 m $+ 6.4 \times 10^6$ m $= 6.5 \times 10^6$ m). The value of G provided on the constants sheet is 6.7×10^{-11} N·m²/kg². Use Newton's law of gravitation to find the force of gravity:

$$F_g = \frac{Gm_1 m_2}{r^2}$$

$$F_g = \frac{(6.7 \times 10^{-11} \text{ N·m}^2/\text{kg}^2)(100 \text{ kg})(6 \times 10^{24} \text{ kg})}{(6.5 \times 10^6 \text{ m})^2}$$

$$F_g = 6.2 \times 10^9 \text{ N}$$

104. (E) Compare the gravitational force on Satellite A to that on Satellite B using the equations of Newton's law of universal gravitation. Note that the radius of Satellite B is twice that of Satellite A.

$$F_{gA} = \frac{Gm_A m_p}{r_A^2}$$

$$F_{gB} = \frac{Gm_B m_p}{r_B^2}$$

$$r_B = 2r_A \text{ and } m_B = m_A$$

$$F_{gB} = \frac{Gm_A m_p}{(2r_A)^2}$$

$$F_{gB} = \frac{Gm_A m_p}{4r_A^2}$$

$$\frac{F_{gA} = \dfrac{Gm_A m_p}{r_A^2}}{F_{gB} = \dfrac{Gm_A m_p}{4r_A^2}}$$

$$\frac{F_{gA}}{F_{gB}} = 4$$

$$F_{gA} = 4F_{gB}$$

105. (A) The known quantities are the mass of the astronaut (70 kg), the mass of the spacecraft (5×10^4 kg), and the distance between them (10 m). Use Newton's law of gravitation to calculate the force of attraction between them:

$$F_g = \frac{Gm_1 m_2}{r^2}$$

$$F_g = \frac{(6.7 \times 10^{-11} \text{ N·m}^2/\text{kg}^2)(70 \text{ kg})(5 \times 10^4 \text{ kg})}{(10 \text{ m})^2}$$

$$F_g = 2.4 \times 10^{-6} \text{ N}$$

106. (A) The centripetal acceleration on the car is 1×10^5 m/s^2, and the radius of the turn is 10 m. Use the centripetal acceleration equation to find the car's velocity:

$$a_c = \frac{v^2}{r}$$

$$v^2 = a_c r$$

$$v = \sqrt{a_c r}$$

$$v = \sqrt{\frac{(1 \times 10^5 \text{ m/s}^2)}{(1,000 \text{ kg})}}$$

$$v = 1 \times 10^1 \text{ m/s}$$

107. (A) The frictional force provides the centripetal force. You know the diameter of the ice rink (20 m), so calculate its circumference. From the circumference and the time it takes her to go around the rink once (62.8 s), calculate the velocity. Using the velocity, the radius, and acceleration due to gravity, calculate the coefficient of friction of the ice:

$$F_{\text{cent}} = \text{friction} = mv^2/r$$

$$\mu F_n = mv^2/r$$

$$\mu mg = mv^2/r$$

$$v = \frac{2\pi r}{t}$$

$$v = \frac{2(3.14)(10 \text{ m})}{(62.8 \text{ s})}$$

$$v = 1 \text{ m/s}$$

$$\mu = \frac{v^2}{gr}$$

$$\mu = \frac{(1 \text{ m/s})^2}{(10 \text{ m/s}^2)(10 \text{ m})}$$

$$\mu = 0.01$$

108. (C) The known quantities are the mass of the payload (1,000 kg), the mass of the Earth (6×10^{24} kg), the Earth's radius (6.4×10^6 m), and the height of the orbit (150 km). Calculate the gravitational potential energy of the payload when it reaches orbit:

$$PE_g = \frac{Gm_1 m_2}{r}$$

$$PE_g = \frac{(6.7 \times 10^{-11} \text{ N} \cdot \text{m}^2/\text{kg}^2)(1,000 \text{ kg})(6 \times 10^{24} \text{ kg})}{(6.4 \times 10^6 \text{ m} + 1.5 \times 10^5 \text{ m})}$$

$$PE_g = 6.1 \times 10^{10} \text{ J}$$

109. (B) The warrior spins a slingshot in a horizontal circle above his head at a constant velocity. When it is released, the stone will fly off at that velocity. The known quantities are the stone's mass (50 g = 0.05 kg) and the sling's radius (1.5 m). The tension in the string is equal to the centripetal force (3.3 N), so calculate the velocity:

$$F_c = \frac{mv^2}{r}$$

$$v^2 = \frac{F_c r}{m}$$

$$v = \sqrt{\frac{F_c r}{m}}$$

$$v = \sqrt{\frac{(3.3 \text{ N})(1.5 \text{ m})}{(0.05 \text{ kg})}}$$

$$v = 10 \text{ m/s}$$

110. (C) An acceleration of 1 G is approximately 10 m/s². So a "3-G environment" would be approximately 30 m/s². On the graph this corresponds to a radius of approximately 3 m.

111. (C) From the graph, notice that a radius of 5 m results in an acceleration of 20 m/s², or approximately 2 G's. Since the astronaut's mass is 70 kg, calculate the magnitude of the centripetal force:

$$F_c = ma_c$$

$$F_c = (70 \text{ kg})(20 \text{ m/s}^2)$$

$$F_c = 140 \text{ N}$$

112. (D) Kepler's third law states that the square of the period of a planet's orbit (T) is proportional to the distance from the Sun (a) cubed. When the period is expressed in Earth years and the orbital radius in AU, then the law is $T^2 = a^3$. Knowing that Jupiter's orbital distance is 5 AU, use Kepler's third law to calculate its orbital period:

$$T^2 = a^3$$

$$T = \sqrt{a^3}$$

$$T = \sqrt{(5 \text{ AU})^3}$$

$$T = 11 \text{ years}$$

113. (C) Starting off you know the satellite's altitude (200 km), the mass of the Earth (6.0×10^{24} kg), and the Earth's radius (6.4×10^6 m). Convert the satellite's altitude to m and add the Earth's radius to it to get the satellite's orbital radius. Then, calculate the satellite's velocity:

$$v = \sqrt{\frac{GM_E}{r}}$$

$$v = \sqrt{\frac{(6.7 \times 10^{-11}\ \text{N} \cdot \text{m}^2/\text{kg}^2)(6 \times 10^{24}\ \text{kg})}{(6.4 \times 10^6\ \text{m} + 2 \times 10^5\ \text{m})}}$$

$$v = 7.8 \times 10^3\ \text{m/s}$$

114. (D) The two masses are designated $m = 10$ kg and $M = 30$ kg. The distance between them is 2 m. So, use Newton's law of universal gravitation to determine the gravitational force between them:

$$F_g = \frac{GmM}{r^2}$$

$$F_g = \frac{(6.7 \times 10^{-11}\ \text{N} \cdot \text{m}^2/\text{kg}^2)(10\ \text{kg})(30\ \text{kg})}{(2\ \text{m})^2}$$

$$F_g = 5 \times 10^{-9}\ \text{N}$$

115. (E) The car's mass is 1,000 kg, the centripetal force is 1.8×10^5 N, and the speed is 30 m/s. Calculate the radius from the equation for centripetal force:

$$F_c = \frac{mv^2}{r}$$

$$r = \frac{mv^2}{F_c}$$

$$r = \frac{(1{,}000\ \text{kg})(30\ \text{m/s})^2}{(1.8 \times 10^5\ \text{N})}$$

$$r = 5\ \text{m}$$

116. (E) The skater's arm length (1 m) is the radius. She spins with a tangential velocity of 5 m/s. Calculate the centripetal acceleration:

$$a_c = \frac{v^2}{r}$$

$$a_c = \frac{(5\ \text{m/s})^2}{(1\ \text{m})}$$

$$a_c = 25\ \text{m/s}^2$$

117. (B) Mars's orbital distance is 2.3×10^{11} m. The mass of the Sun is 2×10^{30} kg, and the mass of Mars is 6.4×10^{23} kg. Use Newton's law of universal gravitation to calculate the gravitational force that the Sun exerts on Mars:

$$F_g = \frac{Gm_1 m_2}{r^2}$$

$$F_g = \frac{(6.7 \times 10^{-11} \text{ N} \cdot \text{m}^2/\text{kg}^2)(6.4 \times 10^{23} \text{ kg})(2 \times 10^{30} \text{ kg})}{(2.3 \times 10^{11} \text{ m})^2}$$

$$F_g = 1.6 \times 10^{21} \text{ N}$$

118. (D) All the coins complete a circle of rotation in the same time period. Coin D traverses the greatest circumference, so it is traveling with the fastest tangential velocity.

119. (A) Centripetal force is directly proportional to centripetal acceleration. Centripetal acceleration is directly proportional to the square of speed. Thus, twice the speed requires four times the centripetal acceleration and friction force.

120. (D) Pick any two points on the graph and calculate the centripetal acceleration. Square the velocity, and divide it by the radius. You will find that all of them have approximately the same centripetal acceleration, i.e., 10 m/s^2.

121. (D) The Moon's mass is 7.4×10^{22} kg, and its radius is 1.7×10^6 m. The force of gravity experienced by a 70-kg astronaut standing on the lunar surface can be calculated with Newton's law of universal gravitation:

$$F_g = \frac{Gm_1 m_2}{r^2}$$

$$F_g = \frac{(6.7 \times 10^{-11} \text{ N} \cdot \text{m}^2/\text{kg}^2)(7.4 \times 10^{23} \text{ kg})(70 \text{ kg})}{(1.7 \times 10^6 \text{ m})^2}$$

$$F_g = 120 \text{ N}$$

122. (B) The velocity of the wheel is its circumference divided by the period ($T = 1.6$ s). The wheel's radius is 0.5 m. Next, calculate the wheel's centripetal acceleration. Using the acceleration and the pebble's mass (10 g = 0.01 kg), calculate the centripetal force on the pebble:

$$v = \frac{2\pi r}{T}$$

$$v = \frac{2\pi(0.5 \text{ m})}{(1.6 \text{ s})}$$

$$v = 2 \text{ m/s}$$

$$a_c = \frac{v^2}{r}$$

$$a_c = \frac{(2 \text{ m/s})^2}{(0.5 \text{ m})}$$

$$a_c = 8 \text{ m/s}^2$$

$$F_c = ma_c$$

$$F_c = (0.01 \text{ kg})(8 \text{ m/s}^2)$$

$$F_c = 0.08 \text{ N}$$

123. (B) The Moon's mass is 7.4×10^{22} kg, and its distance from the Earth is 3.8×10^8 m. The Earth's mass is 6×10^{24} kg. Calculate the gravitational potential energy of the Moon:

$$PE_g = \frac{Gm_1m_2}{r}$$

$$PE_g = \frac{(6.7 \times 10^{-11} \text{ N} \cdot \text{m}^2/\text{kg}^2)(7.4 \times 10^{22} \text{ kg})(6 \times 10^4 \text{ kg})}{(3.8 \times 10^8 \text{ m})}$$

$$PE_g = 7.8 \times 10^{28} \text{ J}$$

124. (D) Centripetal acceleration and centripetal force are inversely proportional to radius. Thus, tripling the radius (while keeping tangential speed the same) will require one-third the centripetal force.

125. (B) The coefficient of friction between the rubber tires of a car and dry concrete is $\mu = 0.64$. The radius of the turn is 10.0 m. Calculate the maximum velocity of the car as follows:

$$F_{cent} = \text{friction} = mv^2/r$$

$$\mu F_n = mv^2/r$$

$$\mu mg = mv^2/r$$

$$\mu = \frac{v^2}{gr}$$

$$v^2 = \mu gr$$

$$v = \sqrt{\mu g r}$$
$$v = \sqrt{(0.64)(10 \text{ m/s}^2)(10 \text{ m})}$$
$$v = 8 \text{ m/s}$$

126. (D) The radius of the top is 2 cm. The period of the top's spin is 0.06 s. Calculate the velocity first and then the centripetal acceleration:

$$v = \frac{2\pi r}{T}$$
$$v = \frac{2\pi(0.02 \text{ m})}{(0.06 \text{ s})}$$
$$v = 2.1 \text{ m/s}$$
$$a_c = \frac{v^2}{r}$$
$$a_c = \frac{(2.1 \text{ m/s})^2}{(0.02 \text{ m})}$$
$$a_c = 220 \text{ m/s}^2$$

127. (B) The known quantities are the mass (100 g = 0.1 kg), the radius of the circle (2 m), and the speed (12 m/s). Calculate the centripetal force:

$$a_c = \frac{v^2}{r}$$
$$a_c = \frac{(12 \text{ m/s})^2}{(2 \text{ m})}$$
$$a_c = 72 \text{ m/s}^2$$
$$F_c = ma_c$$
$$F_c = (0.1 \text{ kg})(72 \text{ m/s}^2)$$
$$F_c = 7.2 \text{ N}$$

128. (B) Applying Newton's law of universal gravitation to each planet and the equations for each planet using constant terms, G, and the mass of the star (M_s), the following data about relative gravitation are obtained:

Planet	Relative mass	Relative distance	Relative gravitational force ($GM_s m/r^2$)
A	$2\ m$	r	2
B	m	$0.1\ r$	100
C	$0.5\ m$	$2\ r$	1/8
D	$4\ m$	$3\ r$	4/9

The planet with the highest gravitational attraction is Planet B.

129. (A, D) The only force on Jupiter is the gravitational force from the Sun. This force provides the centripetal force that allows it to stay in orbit. This net force results in a centripetal acceleration toward the center of the orbit.

130. (E) According to Newton's first law, objects maintain constant velocity unless acted upon by an unbalanced force. The string provides the centripetal force that originally keeps the ball moving in a circle. When that force vanishes, the object must maintain a constant, straight-line velocity, which is tangent to the original path. (Note that gravity will also pull the ball toward the Earth, but this curve is not viewable from above.)

131. (C) All objects moving in a circle must experience a centripetal acceleration toward the center. Since the speed is constant, there is no tangential component of acceleration.

132. (B, C) All objects moving in a circle must experience a centripetal force and centripetal acceleration (directed toward the center of the orbit). The centripetal force is an unbalanced, or net, force toward the center. Whereas the magnitude of the centripetal acceleration may remain constant, it changes in direction because it is a vector pointed toward the center of the circle. The velocity is not constant because the Moon is constantly changing direction.

133. (B) There must be a force toward the center of the circular arc. At the bottom of the swing, the center of the arc is upward, which means the tension force must be greater than the gravitational force.

134. (C) For a fixed radius, centripetal acceleration is directly proportional to the square of speed according to $a_c = v^2/r$.

135. (C) For a fixed radius and fixed speed, centripetal acceleration is independent of mass according to $a_c = v^2/r$. (However, the centripetal force would be twice as much.)

136. (B) The field will decrease the farther you get away from the center of the Earth, but the decrease is small:

$$\frac{g_{top}}{g_{sea\,level}} = \frac{\left(\dfrac{GM_e}{r_{Earth}^2}\right)}{\left(\dfrac{GM_e}{(r_{Earth}+8,848)^2}\right)} = \frac{(r_{Earth}+8,848)^2}{r_{Earth}^2} = 0.997$$

$$\% = (1-0.9976)*100 = 0.28\%$$

137. (C, D) Using $F_g = \dfrac{GM_1M_2}{r^2}$, examine the effect of changing each variable on the gravitational force. Tripling each mass and tripling the distance will result in no change $\left(\dfrac{3\times3}{3^2}=1\right)$. Quadrupling the second mass and doubling the distance will result in no change $\left(\dfrac{1\times4}{2^2}=1\right)$.

138. **(C, E)** Only the rope and the Earth are interacting with the child. A free-body diagram will show an upward tension force and downward gravitational force. The tension will be larger in order to provide the required centripetal force toward the center of the arc.

139. **(B, C)**

$$g = \left(\frac{GM_{planet}}{r_{planet}^2}\right) \text{ where G is the universal gravitational constant.}$$

140. **(D)** Centripetal force is calculated by $\frac{mv^2}{r}$, showing that the centripetal force is inversely proportional to the radius. If the mass and speed remain the same, the doubling of the radius will result in one-half the centripetal force.

141. **(A)** Since the Moon is moving in a circle, it experiences a centripetal acceleration that can be calculated from v^2/r:

$$v = \frac{2\pi r}{T} = \frac{2\pi(385,000,000)\text{m}}{(27.3*24*60*60)\text{s}} = 1,026 \text{ m/s}$$

$$a_c = \frac{v^2}{r} = \frac{\left(\frac{1,026 \text{ m}}{\text{s}}\right)^2}{(385,000,000 \text{ m})} = 2.73 \times 10^{-3} \text{ m/s}^2 \text{(toward the Earth)}$$

142. **(A)** The satellite and the Moon are both moving in circles and experiencing the same centripetal acceleration as **in the previous question** (same speed and same radius of orbit). Since the gravitational force from the Earth is the only force acting on them, the centripetal acceleration is the gravitational acceleration.

143. **(E)** Centripetal force is the net force on the car toward the center of the circle and is calculated as follows:

$$F_{cent} = \frac{mv^2}{r}$$

$$F_A = \frac{MV^2}{R}$$

$$F_B = \frac{(2M)V^2}{R} = 2\left(\frac{MV^2}{R}\right)$$

$$F_C = \frac{MV^2}{2R} = \frac{1}{2}\left(\frac{MV^2}{R}\right)$$

$$F_D = \frac{M(2V)^2}{R} = 4\left(\frac{MV^2}{R}\right)$$

Thus, D = B > A > C.

The known quantities are the mass of the satellite (1,000 kg), the altitude of the orbit (1,000 km), the Earth's mass (6.0×10^{24} kg), and the Earth's radius (6.4×10^6 m). Use this information in Newton's law of universal gravitation.

144. The force of gravity on the satellite is the centripetal force on the satellite. The two are equal. The magnitude of the force of gravity is calculated as follows:

$$F_g = \frac{Gm_1m_2}{(R_E + r)^2}$$

$$F_g = \frac{(6.7 \times 10^{-11}\,\text{N} \cdot \text{m}^2/\text{kg}^2)(1{,}000\,\text{kg})(6 \times 10^{24}\,\text{kg})}{(6.4 \times 10^6\,\text{m} + 1.0 \times 10^6\,\text{m})^2}$$

$$F_g = 7{,}300\,\text{N}$$

145. Here is the magnitude of the satellite's tangential velocity:

$$v = \sqrt{\frac{GM_E}{r}}$$

$$v = \sqrt{\frac{(6.7 \times 10^{-11}\,\text{N} \cdot \text{m}^2/\text{kg}^2)(6 \times 10^{24}\,\text{kg})}{(6.4 \times 10^6\,\text{m} + 1 \times 10^6\,\text{m})}}$$

$$v = 7.4 \times 10^3\,\text{m/s}$$

146. Calculate the gravitational potential energy of the satellite:

$$PE_g = \frac{Gm_1m_2}{(R_E + r)}$$

$$PE_g = \frac{(6.7 \times 10^{-11}\,\text{N} \cdot \text{m}^2/\text{kg}^2)(1{,}000\,\text{kg})(6 \times 10^{24}\,\text{kg})}{(6.4 \times 10^6\,\text{m} + 1 \times 10^6\,\text{m})}$$

$$PE_g = 5.4 \times 10^{10}\,\text{J}$$

147. Here is the value of the acceleration due to gravity (g') at this altitude:

$$g' = \frac{GM_E}{(R_E + r)^2}$$

$$g' = \frac{(6.7 \times 10^{-11}\,\text{N} \cdot \text{m}^2/\text{kg}^2)(6 \times 10^{24}\,\text{kg})}{(6.4 \times 10^6\,\text{m} + 1 \times 10^6\,\text{m})^2}$$

$$g' = 7.3\,\text{m/s}^2$$

148. The free-body diagram of this situation looks like the following figure:

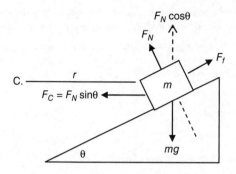

149. Calculate the car's maximum velocity by applying Newton's second law to the situation. The car's centripetal force is provided by the horizontal component of normal force ($F_c = F_N \sin \theta = mv^2/r$), which is provided by the road surface. The car does not move on or off the surface of the road, so the vertical component of the normal force must balance the weight of the car ($mg = F_N \cos \theta$). By dividing these two equations, we get an equation that we can solve for velocity:

$$F_c = F_N \sin \theta = \frac{mv^2}{r}$$

$$mg = F_N \cos \theta$$

$$\frac{F_N \sin \theta = \dfrac{mv^2}{r}}{F_N \cos \theta = mg}$$

$$\tan \theta = \frac{v^2}{rg}$$

$$v^2 = rg \tan \theta$$

$$v = \sqrt{rg \tan \theta}$$

$$v = \sqrt{(300 \text{ m})(10 \text{ m/s}^2) \tan 30°}$$

$$v = 41 \text{ m/s}$$

150. Calculate the centripetal force on the car:

$$F_c = \frac{mv^2}{r}$$

$$F_c = \frac{(1{,}000 \text{ kg})(41 \text{ m/s}^2)}{(300 \text{ m})}$$

$$F_c = 5{,}600 \text{ N}$$

Chapter 4: Simple Harmonic Motion

151. (D) The maximum force and acceleration occur when the spring is displaced the greatest distance from equilibrium, i.e., when the displacement equals the amplitude. The values are calculated as follows:

$$F_{max} = k\Delta x_{max} = \left(12\frac{N}{m}\right)(0.12 \text{ m}) = 1.44 \text{ N}$$

$$a_{max} = \frac{\vec{F}_{net}}{m} = \frac{1.44 \text{ N}}{0.40 \text{ kg}} = 3.6\frac{m}{s^2}$$

152. (A) The period of a spring-mass system is given by:

$$T_s = 2\pi\sqrt{\frac{m}{k}}$$

If you double the mass and double the spring constant, there will be no change in the period of oscillation. The gravitational field strength does not affect the period of vibration.

153. (B) The period of rotation is 27.3 days. Since the frequency is the inverse of the period, the period is F = 1 ÷ 27.3, or 0.0366 revolution/day (3 significant figures).

154. (D) The clapper may be modeled as a simple pendulum, and the period of a pendulum depends on its length. So, by making the clapper longer, its period would be longer and out of phase with the bell. Therefore, the bell will ring with a longer clapper. Mass and amplitude of swing have no significant effect on the period of a pendulum.

155. (D) Without friction, it will swing until its potential energy is equal to the original potential energy, i.e., the horizontal, or 180°.

156. (C) The initial gravitational potential energy in the raised ball first transforms to kinetic energy just before it hits the first ball at the bottom of the swing. This kinetic energy is transferred through the balls to the only ball that can move. Thus, it moves with kinetic energy that transforms back to gravitational potential energy as it swings back to the top.

157. (B) Because the pendulum's mass moves in response to gravity, the restoring force depends on the gravitational force.

158. (C) The water tank is 180° out of phase with the ship's hull, so the rolling of the ship is canceled by the rolling of the water in the tank.

159. (B) Using the formula for the period of a pendulum, $T = 2\pi\sqrt{L \div g}$, the period is 16 s and the frequency is the inverse of the period, or 0.061 cycle/s.

160. (D) The answer is found by using the formula for the period of a mass-spring system, $T = 2\pi \times \sqrt{M \div K}$, and by using the formula for two springs in parallel, $k_{eg} = k_1 + k_2$.

161. (B) The answer is found by using the formula for the period of a mass-spring system, $= 2\pi \times \sqrt{M \div K}$, and by using the formula for two springs in series, $1/k_{eg} = 1/k_1 + 1/k_2$.

162. (D) The answer is found by using the formula for the period of a mass-spring system, $= 2\pi \times \sqrt{M \div K}$, and by using the formula for two springs in parallel, $k_{eg} = k_1 + k_2$. This is because two springs on either side of the mass behave as if they were in parallel (not series).

163. (B) The answer is found by using the formula for the period of a mass-spring system, $= 2\pi \times \sqrt{M \div K}$, and by using the formula for two springs in series, $1/k_{eg} = 1/k_1 + 1/k_2$.

164. (D) 4.4 s for both cases. The answer is found by using the formula for the period of a mass-spring system, $= 2\pi \times \sqrt{M \div K}$, and knowing that both cases are frictionless.

165. (A) Determine the answer by using the formula for the period of a mass-spring system, $= 2\pi \times \sqrt{M \div K}$. You also know that the three springs are parallel, so $k_{eq} = k_1 + k_2 + k_3$.

166. (D) The spring constant determines the stretch of the spring, $= M \times g/k$, and the period of a mass-spring system, $T = 2\pi \times \sqrt{M \div K}$.

167. (A) The springs are supporting the compressor in parallel, so $k_{eq} = k_1 + k_2 + k_3 = 0.3$ N/m. Therefore, the period of a mass-spring system is $T = 2\pi \times \sqrt{M \div K} = 103$ s. The period is the inverse of frequency and equals 0.01 cycle per second (one significant figure).

168. (A) Using the formula for the period of a pendulum, $T = 2\pi\sqrt{L \div g}$, solve for L as follows:

$$L = \frac{T^2}{4\pi^2}(g) = \frac{3.0^2}{4\pi^2}(9.8) = 2.2$$

169. (B) The frequency of vibration is given, and the period is the inverse of frequency:

$$T = \frac{1}{f} = \frac{1}{6.98 \times 10^{14} \text{ cycles/s}} = 1.43 \times 10^{-15} \text{ s/cycle}$$

170. (E) From the falling-body equations, $-x_0 = v_0 \times t + 0.5 \times a \times t^2$, where x_0 is zero, v_0 is zero, a is the acceleration of gravity, and t is one-half of the period of the periodic motion. Because the collision of the ball with the plate is elastic, the full energy of the dropped ball is returned to the ball. So, inserting $t = 1$ into the falling-body equation and solving for x, you get $x = 4.9$ m.

171. (D) The period of a simple pendulum is directly proportional to the square root of the length. If the length is quadrupled, then the period will increase as the square root of 4, or twice as much.

172. (B) The pendulum period equation must be solved for g, the gravitational field strength:

$$T = 2\pi\sqrt{\frac{L}{g}}$$

$$T^2 = 4\pi^2\frac{L}{g}$$

$$g = (4\pi^2)\frac{L}{T^2} = (4\pi^2)\frac{2.0\text{ m}}{(4.6\text{ s})^2} = 3.7\frac{\text{m}}{\text{s}^2} = 3.7\text{ N/kg}$$

173. (E) The maximum speed during an oscillation occurs when the mass moves through equilibrium. At equilibrium, the forces are balanced and the acceleration is instantaneously zero.

174. (D) A simple equation for oscillation is $\Delta x = A\cos(2\pi f\ t)$, where A is the amplitude and f is the frequency of vibration. The amplitude of vibration is 2.0 cm, which means the cone vibrates forward 2.0 cm from equilibrium and back 2.0 cm from equilibrium. This is half a cycle, and the distance traveled is 4.0 cm.

175. (A) A simple equation for oscillation is $\Delta x = A\cos(2\pi f\ t)$, where A is the amplitude and f is the frequency of vibration. Setting $2\pi f = 150$ and solving for f gives 24 Hz.

176. (C) The general equation for this oscillation is $\Delta x = A\cos(2\pi f\ t)$, where A is the amplitude and f is the frequency of vibration. According to the graph, a complete cycle occurs every 2 seconds, which is a frequency of 0.5 cycle per second. The graph also shows an amplitude of vibration of 10 m. This gives the following equation: $\Delta x = 10\cos(\pi t)$.

177. (C) The speed is zero at the position $-A$ because it has to stop as it changes direction.

178. (B) As the mass passes through equilibrium, it has accelerated to its maximum speed.

179. (A) At position $-A$ the compression of the spring is the greatest, giving the largest magnitude of force. This force is to the right (the positive direction) and yields the largest positive net force. Thus, acceleration, the ratio of net force to mass, is a maximum at this position.

180. (C) At $t = 0$, the equation $\Delta x = -A\cos\left(\frac{2\pi}{T}t\right)$ yields $\Delta x = -A$, which is the initial displacement. One cycle later, when $t = T$, it also yields $\Delta x = -A$. At a quarter of the way into the cycle, when $t = T/4$, it is at a position of zero, which is consistent with the oscillation.

181. (A) The kinetic energy is the greatest when the speed is the greatest, which is when the mass passes through equilibrium.

182. (C) The period and frequency of the vibration are independent of amplitude.

183. (B) Voltage across the resistors is as follows:

I. The same potential difference, V, will be measured for the battery and the resistor.

II. According to Kirchhoff's loop rule (conservation of energy), the voltages must add up to the voltage provided by the battery, so each resistor will measure the voltage V/2.

III. Voltage is constant in parallel, so each resistor will get the full voltage of the battery, V.

IV. According to Kirchhoff's loop rule (conservation of energy), the voltages must add up to the voltage provided by the battery, so since the battery has a voltage 2V, each resistor will measure the voltage V.

184. (C) Frequency is the inverse of period, $f = 1/T = 1/60 = 0.02$ Hz.

185. (B) $\dfrac{T_m}{T_e} = \dfrac{2\pi\sqrt{\dfrac{l}{g_m}}}{2\pi\sqrt{\dfrac{l}{g_e}}} = \sqrt{\dfrac{g_e}{g_m}} = \sqrt{\dfrac{g_e}{\dfrac{g_e}{6}}} = \sqrt{6}$

186. (E) Mass-spring systems involve transfer of energy between elastic potential and kinetic. The energy in compressed or stretched springs is classified as elastic potential energy.

187. (A, D) In order to achieve simple harmonic motion, there must be a restoring force that maintains an oscillation about an equilibrium state. Gravity provides the restoring force for the swinging child and the ball in the bowl. The elastic force in the string provides the restoring force for it to continue to vibrate. The bouncing ball and the jumping child rely on gravity and the force from the ground, but these are not considered restoring forces, and the motion is not oscillating about equilibrium.

188. (B, E) Periodic motion repeats itself at regular time intervals. The moon's orbit has a consistent time period, and the pendulum also has a consistent time period as it swings.

189. (A, D) The most significant variables in the list are the length and the gravitational field strength $\left(T_p = 2\pi\sqrt{\dfrac{\ell}{g}}\right)$. Mass has absolutely no effect, and amplitude and string characteristics may have only a negligible effect.

190. (A, C) The value of the mass and the spring constant are the variables that have a significant effect on the period of a spring-mass system $\left(T_s = 2\pi\sqrt{\dfrac{m}{k}}\right)$.

191. (B, C) The oscillation frequency of a string mass is the inverse of frequency as follows:
$f_s = \dfrac{1}{T_s} = \dfrac{1}{2\pi\sqrt{\dfrac{m}{k}}} = \dfrac{1}{2\pi}\sqrt{\dfrac{k}{m}}$. Therefore, decreased mass increases the frequency, and increased spring constant (k) also increases the frequency.

192. The amplitude of vibration remains at 20.0 cm. The period and frequency are calculated as follows:

$$T_s = 2\pi\sqrt{\dfrac{m}{k}} = 2\pi\sqrt{\dfrac{2\text{ kg}}{\left(8\dfrac{N}{m}\right)}} = \pi = 3.1 \text{ s}$$

$$f_s = \dfrac{1}{T_s} = \dfrac{1}{\pi} = 0.32 \text{ Hz}$$

193. The standard equation for displacement is $\Delta x = A \cos(2\pi f\ t)$. Plugging in amplitude and frequency yields displacement in $\Delta x = 20 \cos(2\ t)$ cm.

194. Graphing the equation from part (b) yields the following graph:

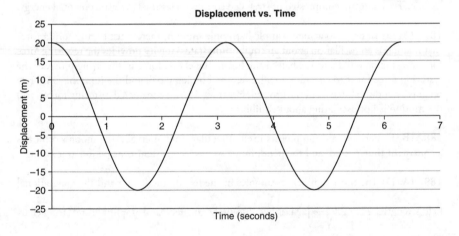

195. $F_{max} = k\Delta x_{max} = \left(8\dfrac{N}{m}\right)(0.20 \text{ m}) = 1.6 \text{ N}$

$$a_{max} = \dfrac{\overrightarrow{F}_{net}}{m} = \dfrac{1.6 \text{ N}}{2.0 \text{ kg}} = 0.8 \ \dfrac{m}{s^2}$$

One way to calculate maximum speed is to analyze how much elastic potential energy in the spring transfers to kinetic energy as it passes through equilibrium (the gravitational energy transfer may be ignored in this analysis because a vertical spring oscillation behaves in the same manner as a horizontal oscillation). As it's released, the elastic potential energy is $U_s = \frac{1}{2}kx^2 = \frac{1}{2}\left(8\frac{N}{m}\right)(0.20\ m)^2 = 0.16\ Nm = 0.16\ J.$

When this energy is completely transferred to kinetic energy, the speed is maximized:

$$K = \frac{1}{2}mv^2$$

$$v_{max} = \sqrt{\frac{2K_{max}}{m}} = \sqrt{\frac{2*0.16\ J}{2\ kg}} = 0.40\frac{m}{s}$$

An alternate method is to use the maximum speed relationship for a mass-spring system (not provided in the AP equations sheet):

$$v_{max} = 2\pi Af = 2\pi(0.20\ m)\left(\frac{1}{\pi}Hz\right) = 0.40\frac{m}{s}.$$

196. The maximum speed occurs at the positions where the mass passes through equilibrium ($\Delta x = 0$) because the restoring force had acted for a quarter-period and is switching directions. The maximum magnitude of acceleration occurs at the points when the magnitude spring force (the net force, since gravity is ignored) is maximized, which is at the points of greatest displacement. When the displacement is −20 cm, the spring force is positive, and this represents the point of maximum (positive) acceleration.

197. The period is the time for one full swing of the pendulum, back and forth. It may be measured with a stopwatch, which has an uncertainty close to the human reaction time (approximately +/− 0.2 or +/− 0.3 s). A photogate placed at the bottom of the swing may also be used to give periods with uncertainties of one-thousandth of a second or better.

198. The independent variable is the length of the pendulum, which is purposely changed. The dependent variable is the variable of interest, which is the period of the pendulum. Controlled variables that are held constant include the mass of the bob, the displacement angle of the swing, and the location (gravitational field).

199. The period is directly proportional to the square root of length and has a shape as follows:

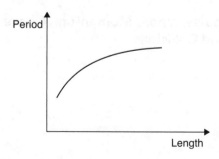

200. The period is independent of mass, so all the periods should be nearly 0.76 s (within the envelope of the measurement uncertainty).

Mass of Bob (g)	Period (s)
10.	0.76
20.	0.76
30.	0.76
40.	0.76
50.	0.76

The length of the pendulum that gives a period of 0.76 may be calculated by solving $T_p = 2\pi\sqrt{\dfrac{\ell}{g}}$ for ℓ:

$$\ell = \frac{g(T_p)^2}{(2\pi)^2} = \frac{\left(9.80\,\dfrac{m}{s^2}\right)(0.76^2\ s^2)}{(2\pi)^2} = 0.14338\ m \approx 14\ cm$$

201. According to the relationship $T_p = 2\pi\sqrt{\dfrac{\ell}{g}}$, the period is inversely proportional to the square root of the gravitational field:

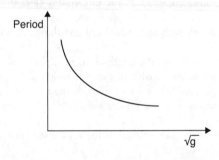

Chapter 5: Impulse, Linear Momentum, Conservation of Linear Momentum, and Collisions

202. **(E)** The mass of the man is 70 kg, and his velocity is 2 m/s. Calculate his momentum as follows:

$$p = mv$$
$$p = (70\ kg)(2\ m/s)$$
$$p = 140\ kg \cdot m/s$$

203. (A) The force (F) applied to the hockey puck is 10 N. The time interval (Δt) is 0.1 s, so the impulse, which is equal to the change in momentum (Δp), can be calculated as follows:

$$\Delta p = F\Delta t$$
$$\Delta p = (10\ \text{N})(0.1\ \text{s})$$
$$\Delta p = 1.0\ \text{kg}\cdot\text{m/s}$$

204. (A) The mass of the car is 1,000 kg. It's moving at a constant velocity ($v = +11.0$ m/s). It comes to a complete stop; therefore, the change in velocity ($\Delta v = 0$ m/s − 11 m/s = −11 m/s) occurs over a time interval ($\Delta t = 2.0$ s). Use the impulse–momentum theorem to calculate the force acting upon the car:

$$\Delta p = F\Delta t$$
$$\Delta p = m\Delta v$$
$$F\Delta t = m\Delta v$$
$$F = \frac{m\Delta v}{\Delta t}$$
$$F = \frac{(1,000\ \text{kg})(-11\ \text{m/s})}{(2.0\ \text{s})}$$
$$F = -5,500\ \text{N}$$

205. (B) The ball has a mass of 1.0 kg. It moves at +10 m/s. When it hits the wall, the collision is perfectly elastic. This means the ball's direction of motion is changed and its velocity is now −10 m/s. Calculate the ball's momentum as follows:

$$p = mv$$
$$p = (1.0\ \text{kg})(-10\ \text{m/s})$$
$$p = -10\ \text{kg}\cdot\text{m/s}$$

206. (C) The mass of the box is 10 kg, and the box's change in velocity is −10 m/s. The force applied to the box is constant at −10 N. Use the impulse–momentum theory to calculate the time it takes the box to stop:

$$\Delta p = F\Delta t$$
$$\Delta p = m\Delta v$$
$$F\Delta t = m\Delta v$$
$$\Delta t = \frac{m\Delta v}{F}$$
$$\Delta t = \frac{(10\ \text{kg})(-10\ \text{m/s})}{(-10\ \text{N})}$$
$$\Delta t = 10\ \text{s}$$

207. **(D)** The balls are of equal mass ($m_A = m_B$). Initially, Ball A moves at a velocity (v_A) of 10 m/s, while Ball B moves at a velocity (v_B) of −5 m/s. After the collision, Ball B moves with a velocity (v'_B) of 3 m/s. Calculate the final velocity of Ball A by conservation of momentum in a perfectly elastic collision:

$$p_A + p_B = p'_A + p'_B$$
$$m_A V_A + m_B v_B = m_A v'_A + m_B v'_B$$
$$m_A = m_B$$
$$v_A + v_B = v'_A + v'_B$$
$$v'_A = v_A + v_B - v'_B$$
$$v'_A = (10 \text{ m/s}) + (-5 \text{ m/s}) - (3 \text{ m/s})$$
$$v'_A = 2 \text{ m/s}$$

208. **(D)** The mass of the fullback (m_A) is 140 kg, while the mass of the defender (m_B) is 70 kg. Initially, A is moving at 10 m/s and B at −5 m/s. They collide inelastically because the defender wraps his arms around the fullback and they travel together. As a consequence, use conservation of momentum for inelastic collisions to find their combined velocity after contact:

$$p_A + p_B = p'_{(A+B)}$$
$$m_A v_A + m_B v_B = (m_A + m_B) v'_{(A+B)}$$
$$v'_{(A+B)} = \frac{m_A v_A + m_B v_B}{(m_A + m_B)}$$
$$v'_{(A+B)} = \frac{(140 \text{ kg})(10 \text{ m/s}) + (70 \text{ kg})(-5 \text{ m/s})}{(140 \text{ kg} + 70 \text{ kg})}$$
$$v'_{(A+B)} = 5 \text{ m/s}$$

209. **(E)** The mass of Ball A equals the mass of Ball B, which is 200 g ($m_A = m_B = 0.2$ kg). Initially, Ball A travels at a velocity (v_A) of 1.0 m/s, while Ball B is at rest ($V_B = 0$ m/s). After the collision, Ball A is at rest ($V'_A = 0$ m/s). The collision is perfectly elastic, so calculate Ball B's velocity after the collision by conservation of momentum:

$$p_A + p_B = p'_A + p'_B$$
$$m_A v_A + m_B v_B = m_A v'_A + m_B v'_B$$
$$m_A = m_B$$
$$v_A + v_B = v'_A + v'_B$$
$$v_B = v'_A = 0$$
$$v_A = v'_B$$

210. **(E)** The bullet's mass was 50 g (0.05 kg). Its momentum was 25 kg·m/s. You can calculate the bullet's velocity as follows:

$$p = mv$$

$$v = \frac{p}{m}$$

$$v = \frac{(25 \text{ kg} \cdot \text{m/s})}{(0.05 \text{ kg})}$$

$$v = 500 \text{ m/s, or } 5 \times 10^2 \text{ m/s}$$

211. **(C)** The explosion of the shell results in forces on all the fragments, but the forces have equal and opposite forces within the system. Thus, there is no net force on the system, and the center of mass will continue on its original parabolic trajectory, although the fragments each have unique trajectories.

212. **(A)** The two masses (m_A, m_B) are 150 kg and 50 kg, respectively. The velocity of the halfback (v_A) is 5 m/s. Calculate the velocity that the linebacker (v_B) must have to stop the two of them after contact ($v'_{A+B} = 0$). Do this by using the conservation of momentum for inelastic collisions:

$$p_A + p_B = p'_{(A+B)}$$

$$m_A v_A + m_B v_B = (m_A + m_B)v'_{(A+B)}$$

$$v'_{(A+B)} = 0$$

$$m_A v_A + m_B v_B = 0$$

$$m_B v_B = -m_A v_A$$

$$v_B = \frac{-m_A v_A}{m_B}$$

$$v_B = \frac{-(150 \text{ kg})(5 \text{ m/s})}{(50 \text{ kg})}$$

$$v_B = -15 \text{ m/s,}$$

Yes, the linebacker can stop the halfback.

213. **(B)** The bat exerts a force of 10.0 N over a time of $\Delta t = 0.005$ s when it strikes a 145-g baseball ($m = 0.145$ kg). Calculate the baseball's change in velocity by the impulse–momentum theorem:

$$\Delta p = F\Delta t$$

$$\Delta p = m\Delta v$$

$$F\Delta t = m\Delta v$$

$$\Delta v = \frac{F\Delta t}{m}$$

$$\Delta v = \frac{(10.0 \text{ N})(0.005 \text{ s})}{(0.145 \text{ kg})}$$

$$\Delta v = 0.345 \text{ m/s}$$

214. (D) The mass of an electron is 9.11×10^{-31} kg. The speed of light is 3.00×10^8 m/s, so 90 percent of the speed of light is 2.70×10^8 m/s. The momentum can be calculated as follows:

$$p = mv$$
$$p = (9.1 \times 10^{-31} \text{ kg})(2.7 \times 10^8 \text{ m/s})$$
$$p = 2.5 \times 10^{-22} \text{ kg} \cdot \text{m/s}$$

215. (D) The mass of the cue ball is 260 g ($m_A = 0.26$ kg), and the mass of the numbered ball is 150 g ($m_B = 0.15$ kg). The initial velocity of the cue ball is 1.0 m/s, and the final velocity is zero. The initial velocity of the numbered ball is zero. The velocity of the numbered ball after the elastic collision can be found by conservation of momentum:

$$p_A + p_B = p'_A + p'_B$$
$$m_A v_A + m_B v_B = m_A v'_A + m_B v'_B$$
$$v_B = v'_A = 0$$
$$m_A v_A = m_B v'_B$$
$$v'_B = \frac{m_A v_A}{m_B}$$
$$v'_B = \frac{(0.26 \text{ kg})(1.0 \text{ m/s})}{(0.15 \text{ kg})}$$
$$v'_B = 1.7 \text{m/s}$$

216. (A) The mass of the aircraft is 750 kg. The plane's velocity increases from 100 m/s to 120 m/s ($\Delta v = 20$ m/s). The wind blows for 2 min ($\Delta t = 120$ s). Find the force by the impulse–momentum theorem:

$$\Delta p = F \Delta t$$
$$\Delta p = m \Delta v$$
$$F \Delta t = m \Delta v$$
$$F = \frac{m \Delta v}{\Delta t}$$
$$F = \frac{(750 \text{ kg})(20 \text{ m/s})}{(120 \text{ s})}$$
$$F = 125 \text{ N}$$

217. (C) The slope of a momentum–time graph is force. Another way of looking at this is with the momentum–impulse theorem: The change in momentum divided by the time interval is the average force exerted on an object:

$$\vec{F} = \frac{\Delta \vec{p}}{\Delta t} = \frac{(10 - 0) \text{ kg} \cdot \text{m/s}}{(5 - 0) \text{s}} = 2 \text{ N}$$

218. (B) The force was 2.0 N and was applied for 100 milliseconds ($\Delta t = 0.1$ s). The object's change in velocity (Δv) was 1.0 m/s. Calculate the mass of the object by the impulse–momentum theorem:

$$\Delta p = F \Delta t$$
$$\Delta p = m \Delta v$$
$$F \Delta t = m \Delta v$$
$$m = \frac{F \Delta t}{\Delta v}$$
$$m = \frac{(2.0 \text{ N})(0.1 \text{ s})}{(1.0 \text{ m/s})}$$
$$m = 0.2 \text{ kg}$$

219. (D) To answer this, find the 70.0-kg stuntman's velocity when he hits the airbag. He has been free-falling from rest for 2.5 s, so his $v \approx (10 \text{ m/s/s}) \ t \approx 25$ m/s. He comes to a complete stop ($|\Delta v| = 25$ m/s) after a time interval of 2 s ($\Delta t = 2$ s). Use the impulse–momentum theorem as follows:

$$\Delta p = F \Delta t$$
$$\Delta p = m \Delta v$$
$$F \Delta t = m \Delta v$$
$$F = \frac{m \Delta v}{\Delta t}$$
$$F = \frac{(70 \text{ kg})(25 \text{ m/s})}{(2 \text{ s})}$$
$$F = 875 \text{ N}$$

220. (B) Two railroad cars ($m_A = m_B = 2 \times 10^4$ kg) are traveling in the same direction along a railroad track. The cars are moving at different velocities ($v_A = 14$ m/s, $v_B = 10$ m/s). The collision is inelastic, and the velocity of the combined cars (v'_{A+B}) can be calculated by conservation of momentum:

$$p_A + p_B = p'_{(A+B)}$$
$$m_A v_A + m_B v_B = (m_A + m_B) v'_{(A+B)}$$
$$v'_{(A+B)} = \frac{m_A v_A + m_B v_B}{(m_A + m_B)}$$
$$v'_{(A+B)} = \frac{(2 \times 10^4 \text{ kg})(14 \text{ m/s}) + (2 \times 10^4 \text{ kg})(10 \text{ m/s})}{(2 \times 10^4 \text{ kg} + 2 \times 10^4 \text{ kg})}$$
$$v'_{(A+B)} = 12 \text{ m/s}$$

221. (C) The slope of a momentum–time graph is force. Another way of looking at this is with the momentum–impulse theorem: The change in momentum divided by the time interval is the average force exerted on an object: $\vec{F} = \dfrac{\Delta \vec{p}}{\Delta t}$. Notice that the momentum is changing more and more rapidly as time elapses (i.e., the slope is greater), which means the force is increasing.

222. (B) The masses of the skaters are 70 kg (m_A) and 50 kg (m_B), respectively. The total momentum before the push-off was 0. The velocity (v_B) of the woman after the push-off is +2.5 m/s. Calculate the man's velocity by the conservation of momentum:

$$p_A + p_B = 0$$
$$m_A v_A + m_B v_B = 0$$
$$m_A v_A = -m_B v_B$$
$$v_A = \frac{-m_B v_B}{m_A}$$
$$v_A = \frac{-(50\ \text{kg})(2.5\ \text{m/s})}{(70\ \text{kg})}$$
$$v_A = -1.8\ \text{m/s}$$

223. (D) The object's momentum is 10 kg·m/s, and its mass is 0.5 kg. Find the object's velocity from the definition of momentum equation:

$$p = mv$$
$$v = \frac{p}{m}$$
$$v = \frac{(10\ \text{kg}\cdot\text{m/s})}{(0.5\ \text{kg})}$$
$$v = 20\ \text{m/s}$$

224. (E) A cue ball ($m_A = 250$ g $= 0.25$ kg) travels at 1.0 m/s ($V_x = 1.0$ m/s, $V_y = 0$ m/s) and hits a numbered ball ($m_B = 170$ g $= 0.17$ kg) at rest ($V_x = V_y = 0$ m/s). The balls move off at angles. The numbered ball moves off at 45°, while the cue ball moves off at −45°. You need to apply the law of conservation of momentum to the x components and the y components of momentum. You will get two equations that solve simultaneously to get each ball's speed:

$$p_{Ax} + p_{Bx} = p'_{Ax} + p'_{Bx}$$
$$m_A v_{Ax} + 0 = m_A v'_{Ax} + m_B v'_{Bx}$$
$$m_A v_{Ax} = m_A v'_A \cos(-45°) + m_B v'_B \cos(45°)$$
$$(0.25\ \text{kg})(1.0\ \text{m/s}) = (0.25\ \text{kg})v'_A (0.707) + (0.17\ \text{kg})v'_B (0.707)$$
$$(0.25\ \text{kg}\cdot\text{m/s}) = (0.177\ \text{kg})v'_A + (0.12\ \text{kg})v'_B$$
$$p_{Ay} + p_{By} = p'_{Ay} + p'_{By}$$
$$0 + 0 = m_A v'_{Ay} + m_B v'_{By}$$

$$0 = m_A v'_A \sin(-45°) + m_B v'_B \sin(45°)$$
$$0 = (0.25 \text{ kg})v'_A(-0.707) + (0.17 \text{ kg})v'_B(0.707)$$
$$0 = (-0.177 \text{ kg})v'_A + (0.12 \text{ kg})v'_B$$

Add the two equations:

$$(0.25 \text{ kg} \cdot \text{m/s}) = (0.177 \text{ kg})v'_A + (0.12 \text{ kg})v'_B$$
$$0 = (-0.177 \text{ kg})v'_A + (0.12 \text{ kg})v'_B$$
$$(0.25 \text{ kg} \cdot \text{m/s}) = (0.24 \text{ kg})v'_B$$
$$v'_B = \frac{(0.25 \text{ kg} \cdot \text{m/s})}{(0.24 \text{ kg})}$$

$v'_B = 1.04$ m/s, Now substitute this value into one of the above equations:

$$0 = (-0.177 \text{ kg})v'_A + (0.12 \text{ kg})(1.04 \text{ m/s})$$
$$(0.177 \text{ kg})v'_A = (0.125 \text{ kg} \cdot \text{m/s})$$
$$v'_A = \frac{(0.125 \text{ kg} \cdot \text{m/s})}{(0.177 \text{ kg})}$$
$$v'_A = 0.71 \text{ m/s}$$

225. (E) The mass of the airplane is 2,000 kg, and the velocity is 343 m/s. Calculate the momentum:

$$p = mv$$
$$p = (2,000 \text{ kg})(343 \text{ m/s})$$
$$p = 6.9 \times 10^5 \text{ kg} \cdot \text{m/s}$$

226. (A) The mass of the handgun (m_A) is 1.2 kg, and the mass of the bullet (m_B) is 7.5 g (0.0075 kg). The bullet travels away at a velocity (v_B) of + 365 m/s. Calculate the recoil velocity of the handgun by conservation of momentum:

$$0 = p_A + p_B$$
$$0 = m_A v_A + m_B v_B$$
$$m_A v_A = -m_B v_B$$
$$v_A = \frac{-m_B v_B}{m_A}$$
$$v_A = \frac{-(0.0075 \text{ kg})(365 \text{ m/s})}{(1.2 \text{ kg})}$$
$$v_A = -2.3 \text{ m/s}$$

227. (D) The two carts have equal masses ($m_A = m_B = 0.5$ kg). Cart A moves at 0.1 m/s, and Cart B is at rest ($v_B = 0$ m/s). The two carts collide and interlock. This is an inelastic collision. Find the velocity of the combined carts (v'_{A+B}) by conservation of momentum:

$$p_A + p_B = p'_{(A+B)}$$
$$m_A v_A + 0 = (m_A + m_B)v'_{(A+B)}$$
$$v'_{(A+B)} = \frac{m_A v_A}{(m_A + m_B)}$$
$$v'_{(A+B)} = \frac{(0.5 \text{ kg})(0.1 \text{ m/s})}{(0.5 \text{ kg} + 0.5 \text{ kg})}$$
$$v'_{(A+B)} = 0.05 \text{ m/s}$$

228. (C) The bullet's mass is 4 g (0.004 kg), and its velocity is 950 m/s. The time interval that the rifle exerts on the bullet is ($\Delta t = 0.1$ s). Find the force from the impulse–momentum theorem:

$$\Delta p = F\Delta t$$
$$\Delta p = m\Delta v$$
$$F\Delta t = m\Delta v$$
$$F = \frac{m\Delta v}{\Delta t}$$
$$F = \frac{(0.004 \text{ kg})(950 \text{ m/s})}{(0.1 \text{ s})}$$
$$F = 38 \text{ N}$$

229. (C) The masses of the cannon ($m_A = 1{,}000$ kg) and cannonball ($m_B = 15$ kg) are known. The recoil velocity of the cannon (v_A) is -1.5 m/s. Calculate the velocity of the cannonball (v_B) by conservation of momentum:

$$0 = p_A + p_B$$
$$0 = m_A v_A + m_B v_B$$
$$m_B v_B = -m_A v_A$$
$$v_B = \frac{-m_A v_A}{m_B}$$
$$v_B = \frac{-(1{,}000 \text{ kg})(-1.5 \text{ m/s})}{(15 \text{ kg})}$$
$$v_B = 100 \text{ m/s}$$

230. (C) In elastic collisions, the total kinetic energy of a system is the same before and after the collision. Thus, the system must have a total of 18 joules of kinetic energy.

231. (E) The momentum magnitude is calculated as follows:
  (A) $p = (500 \text{ kg}) * (40 \text{ m/s}) = 20,000 \text{ kg} \cdot \text{m/s}$
  (B) $p = (30,000 \text{ kg}) * (0 \text{ m/s}) = 0 \text{ kg} \cdot \text{m/s}$
  (C) $p = (1,000 \text{ kg}) * (25 \text{ m/s}) = 25,000 \text{ kg} \cdot \text{m/s}$
  (D) $p = (1.67 \times 10^{-27}) * (0.90 * 3.0 \times 10^8) = 4.5 \times 10^{-19} \text{ kg} \cdot \text{m/s}$
  (E) $p = (90,000,000 \text{ kg}) * (0.02 \text{ m/s}) = 2 \times 10^6 \text{ kg} \cdot \text{m/s}$

  (Note: These values are provided on the AP test.)

232. (C) The impulse theorem states that the momentum change of an object exactly equals the product of the force acting on the object and the time of application of that force.

233. (B) The impulse momentum theorem is solved for force as follows: $\vec{F} = \dfrac{\Delta \vec{p}}{\Delta t}$. To change the car's momentum to zero, the greater the time of the collision, the less the force will be. The process of crushing the car increases the time of impact and decreases the force.

234. (A) Assume that an object moving to the right is going in the positive direction. The 10-kg cart has a momentum of $+50 \text{ kg} \cdot \text{m/s}$, and the 5-kg cart has $-35 \text{ kg} \cdot \text{m/s}$. The system has $+15 \text{ kg} \cdot \text{m/s}$ of momentum before the collision. After the collision, the combined carts (mass = 15 kg) must have the same momentum. Solving for velocity as the ratio of the systems momentum to mass: $\vec{v} = \dfrac{\vec{p}}{m} = \dfrac{+15 \text{ kg} \dfrac{\text{m}}{\text{s}}}{15 \text{ kg}} = +1 \dfrac{\text{m}}{\text{s}}$.

235. (A) It may be assumed that in all collisions there is no net force on the system; therefore *momentum will be conserved*, regardless of whether it's an elastic or inelastic collision. In an elastic collision, the total kinetic energy of the system must remain the same before and after the collision. Before the collision, the system has $18 \text{ J} + 1 \text{ J} = 19 \text{ J}$ of kinetic energy. After the collision, the system has $2 \text{ J} + 9 \text{ J} = 11 \text{ J}$ of kinetic energy. Apparently, 8 J of energy has transferred into other storage modes (e.g., thermal energy), thus classifying this as an *inelastic* collision.

236. (E) According to the impulse–momentum theorem, $\vec{F} \Delta t = \Delta \vec{p}$. In order to change the momentum of the ball the least (i.e., have the smallest exit velocity), a small explosive force would be applied for the least time. *Decreasing the length of the cannon barrel would decrease the time and result in the least velocity.* Decreasing the mass of the cannon ball would actually increase the exit velocity (for the same force and time).

237. (D) $\Delta \vec{p} = \vec{p}_f - \vec{p}_i = 0.050 \text{ kg} \left(-4 \dfrac{\text{m}}{\text{s}} \right) - 0.050 \text{ kg} \left(+5 \dfrac{\text{m}}{\text{s}} \right) = -0.45 \text{ kg} \dfrac{\text{m}}{\text{s}}$

238. (B) With 30 frames per second, a picture is taken each thirtieth of a second. Three frames will be three-thirtieths of a second, or 0.1 second. To find the average force, solve the momentum–impulse theorem for force as follows: $\vec{F} = \dfrac{\Delta \vec{p}}{\Delta t} = \dfrac{-0.45 \text{ kg} \cdot \text{m/s}}{0.1 \text{ s}} = -4.5 \text{ N}$. This is the force of the floor on the ball, which is in the negative direction (up). According to Newton's third law, *the force of the ball on the floor* is equal and opposite, or $+4.5 \text{ N}$ (down!).

239. (A, D) In an elastic collision, the system's kinetic energy is the same before and after the collision. Since $K = \frac{1}{2}mv^2$, the kinetic energy will be the same for the ball before and after the bounce because the speed is the same and the collision is elastic. The moving cart, similarly, transfers all its kinetic energy to the other cart; thus the system of both carts maintains its kinetic energy and is elastic. All the other collisions involve losses in kinetic energy of the system.

240. (C, E) Regardless of the type of collision, momentum is the same before and after the collision, making Option C a FALSE statement. Also, in inelastic collisions, the kinetic energy does not remain the same, making option E the other FALSE statement.

241. (B, C) According to the impulse–momentum theorem, the momentum change of a system equals the product of force and time. An increase in either one (or both) will increase the momentum change of the ball. For the same hit, changing the properties of the ball will have no significant effect.

242. (A, E) Momentum is the product of mass and velocity, and velocity includes both speed and direction. Acceleration and gravitational energy may be related to the current speed, but are NOT particularly helpful for finding the instantaneous momentum, and these negative choices were asked for.

243. (B, E) The momentum of a system is conserved as long as there is no net force on the system, and this applies to both elastic and inelastic collisions. Also, if the center of mass of a system accelerates, then there must be a net force on the system.

244. From 0–2 seconds, the box will gain speed at a constant rate because the constant net force will accelerate the box. From 2–4 seconds, the box will maintain constant velocity because no net force is on the box. From 4–7 seconds, the constant negative net force will slow the box down at a constant rate.

245. Use $\vec{F}\Delta t = \Delta\vec{p}$ as follows (the last column is included to help with part [c]):

Time Interval	$\vec{F}\Delta t$	$\Delta\vec{p}$	$\Delta\vec{v} = \dfrac{\Delta\vec{p}}{m}$
01 second	+20 Ns	+20 kg·m/s	+10 m/s
1–2 seconds	+20 Ns	+20 kg·m/s	+10 m/s
2–3 seconds	0 Ns	0 kg·m/s	0 m/s
3–4 seconds	0 Ns	0 kg·m/s	0 m/s
4–5 seconds	–10 Ns	–10 kg·m/s	–5 m/s
5–6 seconds	–10 Ns	–10 kg·m/s	–5 m/s
6–7 seconds	–10 Ns	–10 kg·m/s	–5 m/s

246. The velocity change in each time interval is calculated in the last column in the table above. Starting with a velocity of +3 m/s, 10 m/s is added each of the first two seconds, no velocity is added for the next two seconds, and 5 m/s of velocity is taken away for each of the last three seconds. This gives a final velocity of +8 m/s.

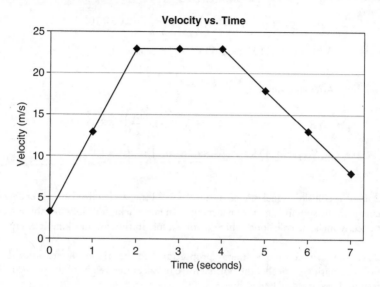

247. The velocity of the box at the 7-second clock reading is +8 m/s as it strikes the wall for 0.20 second and bounces back at a velocity of −6 m/s. The momentum–impulse theorem is solved for average force as follows:

$$\vec{F} = \frac{\Delta \vec{p}}{\Delta t} = \frac{2 \text{ kg}\left(-6\,\frac{\text{m}}{\text{s}}\right) - 2 \text{ kg}\left(+8\,\frac{\text{m}}{\text{s}}\right)}{0.20 \text{ s}} = \frac{-28 \text{ kg}\,\frac{\text{m}}{\text{s}}}{0.2 \text{ s}} = -140 \text{ N}$$

248. Designate Car B as the 800-kg car ($v_B = 25.5$ m/s) and Car A as the 1,000-kg car ($v_A = 34.7$ m/s). The two cars collide in a sticky collision (perfectly inelastic). Find the combined velocity (v'_{A+B}) by the conservation of momentum:

$$p_A + p_B = p'_{(A+B)}$$
$$m_A v_A + m_B v_B = (m_A + m_B)v'_{(A+B)}$$
$$v'_{(A+B)} = \frac{m_A v_A + m_B v_B}{(m_A + m_B)}$$
$$v'_{(A+B)} = \frac{(1,000 \text{ kg})(34.7 \text{ m/s}) + (800 \text{ kg})(25.5 \text{ m/s})}{(1,000 \text{ kg} + 800 \text{ kg})}$$
$$v'_{(A+B)} = 30.6 \text{ m/s}$$

249. Before the collision:

$$K_a = \frac{1}{2}mv^2 = \frac{1}{2}(1{,}000.\ \text{kg})\left(34.7\frac{\text{m}}{\text{s}}\right)^2 = 6.02 \times 10^5\ \text{J}$$

$$K_b = \frac{1}{2}mv^2 = \frac{1}{2}(800.\ \text{kg})\left(25.5\frac{\text{m}}{\text{s}}\right)^2 = 2.60 \times 10^5\ \text{J}$$

$$K_{a+b} = 6.02 \times 10^5\ \text{J} + 2.60 \times 10^5\ \text{J} = 8.62 \times 10^5\ \text{J}$$

After the collision:

$$K_{a+b} = \frac{1}{2}mv^2 = \frac{1}{2}(1{,}800.\ \text{kg})\left(30.6\frac{\text{m}}{\text{s}}\right)^2 = 8.43 \times 10^5\ \text{J}$$

$$\Delta(K_{a+b}) = 8.43 \times 10^5\ \text{J} - 8.62 \times 10^5\ \text{J} = -1.9 \times 10^4\ \text{J}$$

250. The collision is inelastic because 1.9×10^4 J transferred from kinetic energy to internal energy in the system (e.g., thermal energy). In fact, sticky collisions like this are classified as perfectly inelastic collisions, which involve a loss in the system's kinetic energy.

251. The normal force is directly proportional to the friction force. Since the system is not accelerating vertically, the normal force balances the weight of the two-car system. The friction force is calculated as final.

$$F_f = \mu_k F_N$$
$$F_N = (m_A + m_B)g$$
$$F_f = \mu_k(m_A + m_B)g$$
$$F_f = (0.7)(1{,}000\ \text{kg} + 800\ \text{kg})(9.8\ \text{m/s}^2)$$
$$F_f = 1.23 \times 10^4\ \text{N}$$

252. The force of friction is negative because it opposes motion. Calculate the time (Δt) it takes for the interlocked cars to stop ($\Delta v = -30.6$ m/s) by using the impulse–momentum theorem:

$$\Delta p = F\Delta t$$
$$\Delta p = m\Delta v$$
$$F\Delta t = m\Delta v$$
$$F_f\Delta t = (m_A + m_B)\Delta v$$
$$\Delta t = \frac{(m_A + m_B)\Delta v}{F_f}$$
$$\Delta t = \frac{(1{,}000\ \text{kg} + 800\ \text{kg})(-30.6\ \text{m/s})}{(-1.23 \times 10^4\ \text{N})}$$
$$\Delta t = 4.46\ \text{s}$$

Chapter 6: Work, Energy, and Conservation of Energy

253. (D) The mass of the man is 70 kg, and his velocity is 2 m/s. Calculate his kinetic energy as follows:

$$KE = \frac{1}{2}mv^2$$

$$KE = \frac{1}{2}(70 \text{ kg})(2 \text{ m/s})^2$$

$$KE = 140 \text{ J}$$

254. (D) The force (F) applied to the box is 10 N in the direction of motion. The force is applied over a 10-m distance. So the work can be calculated as follows:

$$W = Fd$$

$$W = (10 \text{ N})(10 \text{ m})$$

$$W = 100 \text{ J}$$

255. (C) The mass of the car is 1,000 kg. Its initial velocity is 0 m/s. The net force is 500 N, and it acts constantly over a distance (d) of 100 m. Use the work–energy theorem to calculate the car's final velocity:

$$W = \Delta KE$$

$$Fd = \frac{1}{2}m(v_f)^2 - \frac{1}{2}m(v_i)^2$$

$$v_i = 0$$

$$2Fd = m(v_f)^2$$

$$2Fd = mv_f^2$$

$$v_f^2 = \frac{2Fd}{m}$$

$$v_f = \sqrt{\frac{2Fd}{m}}$$

$$v_f = \sqrt{\frac{2(500 \text{ N})(100 \text{ m})}{(1,000 \text{ kg})}}$$

$$v_f = 10 \text{ m/s}$$

256. (C) The piano has a mass of 500 kg. Its change in height (h) is 10 m. Calculate the piano's change in potential energy (ΔPE) as follows:

$$\Delta PE = mgh$$

$$\Delta PE = (500 \text{ kg})(10 \text{ m/s}^2)(10 \text{ m})$$

$$\Delta PE = 5 \times 10^4 \text{ J}$$

257. (D) The force on the box is 10 N at an angle ($\theta = 60°$) over a distance (d) of 50 m. Only the component of force in the horizontal direction contributes to the work done on the box. Find the x component of force, and use it to calculate the work:

$$W = F_x d$$
$$F_x = F \cos\theta$$
$$W = F \cos\theta d$$
$$W = (10 \text{ N})(\cos 60°)(50 \text{ m})$$
$$W = 250 \text{ J}$$

258. (C) The mass of the box is 5 kg, but this information is irrelevant. The height of the hill (h) is 10 m. The box starts from rest and reaches an unknown final velocity (v_f). The box's change in gravitational potential energy is equal to its change in kinetic energy. Calculate the box's final velocity from conservation of energy:

$$\text{KE}_i + \text{PE}_i = \text{KE}_f + \text{PE}_f$$
$$0 + \text{PE}_i = \text{KE}_f + 0$$
$$\text{KE}_f = \text{PE}_i$$
$$\frac{1}{2}mv_f^2 = mgh$$
$$\frac{1}{2}v_f^2 = gh$$
$$v_f^2 = 2gh$$
$$v_f = \sqrt{2gh}$$
$$v_f = \sqrt{2(10 \text{ m/s}^2)(10 \text{ m})}$$
$$v_f = 14 \text{ m/s}$$

259. (D) The mass of the arrow (m) is 20 g, or 0.02 kg. The archer exerts an average force ($F = 75$ N) to pull the bowstring back ($d = 20$ cm $= 0.20$ m), and so it is assumed that the bow will apply the same force back on the arrow through the same displacement. Calculate the final velocity of the arrow by using the work–energy theorem:

$$W = \Delta \text{KE}$$
$$Fd = \frac{1}{2}m(v_f)^2 - \frac{1}{2}m(v_i)^2$$
$$v_i = 0$$
$$2Fd = m(v_f)^2$$
$$2Fd = mv_f^2$$
$$v_f^2 = \frac{2Fd}{m}$$

$$v_f = \sqrt{\frac{2Fd}{m}}$$

$$v_f = \sqrt{\frac{2(75 \text{ N})(0.20 \text{ m})}{(0.02 \text{ kg})}}$$

$$v_f = 39 \text{ m/s}$$

260. (E) The mass of the car is 1,000 kg. As the car skids to rest, its kinetic energy transfers to thermal energy over a distance (d) of 10 m. Calculate the force by the work–energy theorem:

$$W = \Delta K$$

$$F_{\parallel}d = \frac{1}{2}mv_f^2 - \frac{1}{2}mv_i^2$$

$$F_{\parallel} = \frac{\frac{1}{2}mv_f^2 - \frac{1}{2}mv_i^2}{d}$$

$$F_{\parallel} = \frac{\frac{1}{2}m(v_f^2 - v_i^2)}{d}$$

$$F_{\parallel} = \frac{\frac{1}{2}(1{,}000 \text{ kg})(0^2 - 30^2)}{10}$$

$$F_{\parallel} = -4.5 \times 10^4 \text{ N}$$

$$\left| F_{\parallel} \right| = 4.5 \times 10^4 \text{ N}$$

261. (E) The bullet's mass was 7.5 g (0.0075 kg). The block's mass was 2.50 kg. It swung to a height of 0.1 m. When the bullet strikes the wood, it is an inelastic collision. The kinetic energy of the bullet and the block get converted to potential energy. Calculate the bullet's velocity as follows:

First, calculate the initial velocity of the block and bullet by conservation of energy:

$$KE_i + KE_f = PE_i + PE_f$$

$$KE_i + 0 = 0 + PE_f$$

$$KE_i = PE_f$$

$$\frac{1}{2}(m_A + m_B)v_i^2 = (m_A + m_B)gh$$

$$\frac{1}{2}v_i^2 = gh$$

$$v_i^2 = 2gh$$

$$v_i = \sqrt{2gh}$$

$$v_i = \sqrt{2(10 \text{ m/s}^2)(0.1 \text{ m})}$$

$$v_i = 1.44 \text{ m/s} = v'_{(A+B)}$$

Now, use conservation of momentum for an inelastic collision to calculate the bullet's initial velocity:

$$p_A + p_B = p'_{(A+B)}$$
$$m_A v_A + m_B v_B = (m_A + m_B)v'_{(A+B)}$$
$$v_B = 0$$
$$m_A v_A + 0 = (m_A + m_B)v'_{(A+B)}$$
$$m_A v_A = (m_A + m_B)v'_{(A+B)}$$
$$v_A = \frac{(m_A + m_B)v'_{(A+B)}}{m_A}$$
$$v_A = \frac{(0.0075 \text{ kg} + 2.50 \text{ kg})(1.44 \text{ m/s})}{(0.0075 \text{ kg})}$$
$$v_A = 481 \text{ m/s} ; 500 \text{ m/s}$$

262. **(B)** When released, the elastic potential energy stored in the spring will transfer to kinetic energy in the moving box. Assuming the horizontal surface is frictionless, the maximum kinetic energy will occur when all the elastic potential energy is transferred to the motion of the box:

$$U_s = \frac{1}{2}k \; x^2 = \frac{1}{2}\left(2,500\frac{\text{N}}{\text{m}}\right)(0.12 \text{ m})^2 = 18 \text{ J}$$

263. **(C)** The spring constant (k) is 300 N/m. The spring is stretched (x) by 0.5 m. Calculate the force on the spring by Hooke's law:

$$F = kx$$
$$F = (300 \text{ N/m})(0.5 \text{ m})$$
$$F = 150 \text{ N}$$

264. **(A)** The spring constant (k) is 400 N/m. The spring is stretched (x) by 0.5 m. Calculate the potential energy on the spring:

$$PE = \frac{1}{2}kx^2$$
$$PE = \frac{1}{2}(400 \text{ N/m})(0.5 \text{ m})^2$$
$$PE = 50 \text{ J}$$

265. (D) The spring has a constant of 100 N/m and is displaced ($x = -0.2$ m). The mass of the block is 1 kg. Calculate the block's velocity as it passes equilibrium by conservation of energy:

$$KE_i + PE_i = KE_f + PE_f$$

$$0 + PE_i = KE_f + 0$$

$$KE_f = PE_i$$

$$\frac{1}{2}mv_f^2 = \frac{1}{2}kx^2$$

$$mv_f^2 = kx^2$$

$$v_f^2 = \frac{kx^2}{m}$$

$$v_f = \sqrt{\frac{kx^2}{m}}$$

$$v_f = \sqrt{\frac{(100 \text{ N/m})(-0.2 \text{ m})^2}{(1 \text{ kg})}}$$

$$v_f = 2 \text{ m/s}$$

266. (C) Both cannons fire balls of the same mass (m) and use the same amount of powder to supply identical forces (F). The length of Cannon 2 (d_2) is two times longer than that of Cannon 1 (d_1). Solve this problem by applying the work–energy theorem to both cannons:

$$Fd_1 = \frac{1}{2}mv_1^2$$

$$Fd_2 = \frac{1}{2}mv_2^2$$

$$d_2 = 2d_1$$

$$F(2d_1) = \frac{1}{2}mv_2^2$$

$$Fd_1 = \frac{1}{4}mv_2^2$$

$$\frac{1}{4}mv_2^2 = \frac{1}{2}mv_1^2$$

$$\frac{1}{4}v_2^2 = \frac{1}{2}v_1^2$$

$$v_2^2 = 2v_1^2$$

$$v_2 = \sqrt{2v_1^2}$$

$$v_2 = \sqrt{2}\sqrt{v_1^2}$$

$$v_2 = \sqrt{2}v_1 = 1.4v_1$$

267. (C) The mass of the aircraft is 750 kg. The plane's velocity increases from 100 m/s to 120 m/s. The wind blows for 1,200 m (Δd). The work done by the tailwind on the aircraft equals the increase of kinetic energy of the aircraft, and from this the force may be found:

$$W = \Delta K$$

$$F_{\parallel}d = \frac{1}{2}mv_f^2 - \frac{1}{2}mv_i^2$$

$$F_{\parallel} = \frac{\frac{1}{2}mv_f^2 - \frac{1}{2}mv_i^2}{d}$$

$$F_{\parallel} = \frac{\frac{1}{2}m(v_f^2 - v_i^2)}{d}$$

$$F_{\parallel} = \frac{\frac{1}{2}(750 \text{ kg})(120^2 - 100^2)}{1,200}$$

$$F_{\parallel} = 1,375 \text{ N, or approximately } 1,400 \text{ N.}$$

268. (B) According to the law of conservation of energy, all energy must be accounted for. Since all of the gravitational potential energy did not transfer to kinetic energy, then 25 J − 23 J = 2 J that must be stored as thermal energy due to friction as the box slides down the incline.

269. (D) The force was 2.0 N and was applied for 5.0 m. The object's final velocity was 1.0 m/s. Calculate the mass of the object by the work–energy theorem:

$$W = \Delta K$$

$$Fd = \frac{1}{2}m(v)^2$$

$$2Fd = m(v)^2$$

$$m = \frac{2Fd}{(v)^2}$$

$$m = \frac{2(2.0 \text{ N})(5.0 \text{ m})}{(1.0 \text{ m/s})^2}$$

$$m = 20 \text{ kg}$$

270. (C) According to conservation of energy, the gravitational potential energy of the stuntman gets converted to kinetic energy as he falls. The maximum kinetic energy occurs when he hits the airbag. The airbag must do work to stop the stuntman's kinetic energy. So, solve this by applying conservation of energy and the work–energy theorem to the situation:

$$KE_i + PE_i = KE_f + PE_f$$
$$0 + PE_i = KE_f + 0$$
$$KE_f = PE_i$$
$$\frac{1}{2}mv_f^2 = mgh$$
$$W = \Delta KE$$
$$Fd = \frac{1}{2}mv_f^2$$
$$Fd = mgh$$
$$F = \frac{mgh}{d}$$
$$F = \frac{(70\ kg)(9.8\ m/s^2)(125\ m)}{(5.0\ m)}$$
$$F = 1.7 \times 10^4\ N$$

271. (E) The force exerted by the man is 100 N in the direction of motion. The mass of the box is 100 kg, which is irrelevant to the solution. The distance is 60 m, and the time interval is 2 min ($\Delta t = 120$ s). Calculate the power as follows:

$$P = \frac{W}{t}$$
$$P = \frac{Fd}{t}$$
$$P = \frac{(100\ N)(60\ m)}{(120\ s)}$$
$$P = 50\ W$$

272. (E) Points A and C are at the same height and would have the same gravitational potential energy: $U_g = mg\Delta y$.

273. (E) The car will move the fastest at the point with the most kinetic energy, which is the lowest point, E, where most of the gravitational energy has transferred to the car.

274. (E) The total energy is the sum of the kinetic energy and potential energy. It is the same at all points.

275. (A) The man exerts a component (F_x) of the 20-N force (F) in the horizontal by applying the force at an angle ($\theta = 60°$). The lawn mower moves a horizontal distance (d) of 100 m in a time interval (Δt) of 5 min (300 s). Only the horizontal component of force does work, so resolve the force into components, and use that to calculate the power:

$$P = \frac{W}{\Delta t}$$

$$W = F_x d$$

$$F_x = F \cos\theta$$

$$W = F \cos\theta d$$

$$P = \frac{F \cos\theta d}{\Delta t}$$

$$P = \frac{(20\text{ N})(\cos 60°)(100\text{ m})}{(300\text{ s})}$$

$$P = 3\text{ W}$$

276. (D) The mass of the airplane is 2,000 kg, and the velocity is 343 m/s. Calculate the kinetic energy:

$$KE = \frac{1}{2}mv^2$$

$$KE = \frac{1}{2}(2,000\text{ kg})(343\text{ m/s})^2$$

$$KE = 1.18 \times 10^8\text{ J}$$

277. (D) The handgun does work on the bullet and gives it kinetic energy. All the kinetic energy ($\Delta KE = 500$ J) is lost as heat. The length of the gun barrel is 125 mm ($d = 0.125$ m). Calculate the force that the handgun exerts on the bullet using the work–energy theorem:

$$W = \Delta KE$$

$$Fd = \Delta KE$$

$$F = \frac{\Delta KE}{d}$$

$$F = \frac{(500\text{ J})}{(0.125\text{ m})}$$

$$F = 4,000\text{ N}$$

278. (D) The two cars have equal masses ($m_A = m_B = 0.5$ kg). Car A moves at 0.2 m/s, and Car B is at rest ($v_B = 0$ m/s). The two cars collide in an elastic collision. Both cars move away at 0.1 m/s. Calculate the kinetic energies of the cars before and after the collision. Since knowing that energy must be conserved, the difference between the kinetic energies before and after represents energy lost as heat. (No cars have potential energy because they are at the same height on the track.)

$$KE_A + KE_B = KE'_A + KE'_B + \text{Heat}$$
$$KE_A + 0 = KE'_A + KE'_B + \text{Heat}$$
$$KE_A = KE'_A + KE'_B + \text{Heat}$$
$$\text{Heat} = KE_A - KE'_A - KE'_B$$
$$\text{Heat} = \frac{1}{2}m_A v_A^2 - \frac{1}{2}m_A v_A'^2 - \frac{1}{2}m_B v_B'^2$$
$$m_A = m_B$$
$$\text{Heat} = \frac{1}{2}m_A v_A^2 - \frac{1}{2}m_A v_A'^2 - \frac{1}{2}m_A v_B'^2$$
$$\text{Heat} = \frac{1}{2}m_A \left(v_A^2 - v_A'^2 - v_B'^2\right)$$
$$\text{Heat} = \frac{1}{2}(0.5 \text{ kg})[(0.2 \text{ m/s})^2 - (0.1 \text{ m/s})^2 - (0.1 \text{ m/s})^2]$$
$$\text{Heat} = 0.005 \text{ J}$$
$$KE_A = \frac{1}{2}m_A v_A^2 = \frac{1}{2}(0.5 \text{ kg})(0.2 \text{ m/s})^2 = 0.01 \text{ J}$$
$$\frac{\text{Heat}}{KE_A} = \frac{(0.005 \text{ J})}{(0.01 \text{ J})} = 0.5 = 50\%$$

279. (C) The bullet's mass is 4 g (0.004 kg), and its velocity is 950 m/s. The length of the rifle barrel is 1.01 m. Find the force from the work–energy theorem:

$$W = \Delta KE$$
$$Fd = \frac{1}{2}mv^2$$
$$F = \frac{mv^2}{2d}$$
$$F = \frac{(0.004 \text{ kg})(950 \text{ m/s})^2}{2(1.01 \text{ m})}$$
$$F = 1,800 \text{ N}$$

280. (C) The mass of the cannon is irrelevant. The mass of the cannonball is known ($m = 11$ kg). The powder charge exerts a force of 2.25×10^4 N over the length of the cannon's barrel ($d = 2.44$ m). Calculate the velocity of the cannonball (v) by using the work–energy theorem:

$$W = \Delta KE$$

$$Fd = \frac{1}{2}mv^2$$

$$2Fd = mv^2$$

$$v^2 = \frac{2Fd}{m}$$

$$v = \sqrt{\frac{2Fd}{m}}$$

$$v = \sqrt{\frac{2(2.25\times10^4 \text{ N})(2.44 \text{ m})}{(11 \text{ kg})}}$$

$$v = 100 \text{ m/s}$$

281. (A) Kinetic energy is directly proportional to the square of the speed. Thus, when the speed doubles, the kinetic energy quadruples.

282. (B) The ratio is found as follows:

$$\frac{U_{s2}}{U_{s1}} = \frac{18 \text{ J}}{2 \text{ J}} = 9$$

$$\frac{U_{s2}}{U_{s1}} = \frac{\frac{1}{2}kx_2^2}{\frac{1}{2}kx_1^2} = \frac{x_2^2}{x_1^2} = \left(\frac{x_2}{x_1}\right)^2 = 9$$

$$\left(\frac{x_2}{x_1}\right) = \sqrt{9} = 3$$

283. (D) The work done by the wind equals the change in kinetic energy of the boat:

$$W = \Delta K$$

$$F_\| d = \frac{1}{2} m v_f^2 - \frac{1}{2} m v_i^2$$

$$F_\| = \frac{\frac{1}{2} m v_f^2 - \frac{1}{2} m v_i^2}{d}$$

$$F_\| = \frac{\frac{1}{2} m (v_f^2 - v_i^2)}{d}$$

$$F_\| = \frac{\frac{1}{2} (14,300 \text{ kg}) \left(9^2 \dfrac{m^2}{s^2} \right)}{850 \text{ m}}$$

$$F_\| = 680 \text{ N}$$

The total force of the wind, F, is found as follows:

$$\sin(60) = \frac{F_\|}{F}$$

$$F = \frac{F_\|}{\sin(60)} = \frac{680 \text{ N}}{\sin(60)} = 790 \text{ N}$$

284. (D) Kinetic energy is directly proportional to mass and directly proportional to the square of speed:

$$\frac{K_{truck}}{K_{car}} = \frac{\frac{1}{2}(2M)\left(\dfrac{v}{2}\right)^2}{\frac{1}{2}(M)(v)^2} = 2\left(\frac{1}{4}\right) = \frac{1}{2}$$

285. (D) The gravitational potential energy is $\Delta U_g = mg\Delta y$. If mass is doubled and the vertical height is also doubled, the kinetic energy must quadruple: $4 \times 50 \text{ J} = 200 \text{ J}$.

286. (D) Work transfers energy from one storage mode to another storage mode. Thus, work is done to increase the kinetic energy of the object. According to the work–energy theorem, the amount of work is the difference between its final kinetic energy and its initial kinetic energy:

$$W = K_f - K_i$$

$$W = \frac{1}{2} m v_f^2 - \frac{1}{2} m v_i^2$$

$$W = \frac{1}{2}(5.0 \text{ kg})(12^2 - 6^2)\frac{m^2}{s^2}$$

$$W = 270 \text{ J}$$

287. (A) The gravitational potential energy is calculated using $\Delta U_g = mg\Delta y$.

I. A 2-kg object held at rest 3 m above the ground: $\Delta U_g = (2 \text{ kg})\left(10\dfrac{\text{N}}{\text{kg}}\right)(3 \text{ m}) = 60 \text{ J}$

II. A 2-kg object falling down at a rate of 5 m/s at the instant it's 3 m off the ground:

$$\Delta U_g = mg\Delta y = (2 \text{ kg})\left(10\dfrac{\text{N}}{\text{kg}}\right)(3 \text{ m}) = 60 \text{ J}$$

III. A 1-kg object falling down at a rate of 10 m/s at the instant it's 3 m off the ground:

$$\Delta U_g = mg\Delta y = (1 \text{ kg})\left(10\dfrac{\text{N}}{\text{kg}}\right)(3 \text{ m}) = 30 \text{ J}$$

IV. A 3-kg object falling down at rest 2 m above the ground:

$$\Delta U_g = mg\Delta y = (3 \text{ kg})\left(10\dfrac{\text{N}}{\text{kg}}\right)(2 \text{ m}) = 60 \text{ J}$$

Therefore, I = II = IV > III

288. (E) The elastic potential energy of a spring is given by $U_s = \dfrac{1}{2}kx^2$, so the energy is directly proportional to the square of the stretch distance. Thus, if you quadruple stretch from 5 cm to 20 cm, you'll increase the energy storage by 4^2, or 16 times the original amount.

289. (B) The friction force provides the net force stop for each car. The work–energy theorem is used as follows:

$$Fd = \Delta K$$

$$(F_{\text{friction}})d = \frac{1}{2}mv_f^2 - \frac{1}{2}mv_i^2$$

$$(-\mu F_N)d = -\frac{1}{2}mv_i^2$$

$$(\mu \cancel{mg})d = \frac{1}{2}\cancel{m}v_i^2$$

$$\mu g d = \frac{1}{2}v_i^2$$

$$d = \left\{\frac{1}{2\mu g}\right\}v_i^2$$

Since skid distance (d) is directly proportional to the square of the initial speed (and independent of mass), the car going at twice the speed will have four times the skid distance.

290. (C, D) When nonconservative forces act on an object, the work done (energy transferred) depends on the path taken from the initial to the final state. *The energy transferred to thermal energy through friction and air drag depends on the length of the path, so these are the nonconservative forces.* The transfer of gravitational potential energy, electric potential energy, and elastic potential energy depends only on the initial and final states and, thus, are not path dependent.

291. (B, D) In both cases, identical objects are pushed the same vertical distance up the incline, so the change in gravitational potential energy ($\Delta U_g = mg\Delta y$) is the same. Work is the product of force and displacement, and displacement is the same as well as the applied force, since the object is not accelerating and the applied force must balance the friction force in order to maintain constant velocity. Since it will take twice the amount of time pushing the box at 3 m/s, the power required is different, and the different speeds have different kinetic energies.

292. (A, C) As the stone rises, its speed decreases, so its *kinetic energy will decrease.* As its height off the ground increases, its gravitational potential energy will increase. Its total mechanical energy ($K + U_g$) stays constant.

293. (A, E) Work is the amount of energy transferred from one storage mode to another storage mode. It occurs when a force is applied through a displacement, but only if a component of the force is parallel with that displacement ($W = F_\parallel\, d = F\, d\, \cos\theta$). In circular motion, the force is toward the center and is always perpendicular to the displacement along the circular path; thus the gravitational force on the Moon does no work. The football player pushing on the wall does no work because there is no displacement. The other three options all involve a force applied in the direction of a displacement, resulting in work done on the object.

294. (A, B) When only conservative forces act on an object, the work done (energy transferred) is independent of the path taken from the initial to the final state, and the sum of the potential and kinetic energies (the mechanical energy) will remain constant, so option A is true. Option B is true for nonconservative forces because the energy transferred depends on the path taken. Options C and D contradict the statements above. Option E is incorrect because conservative forces are a function of position, not speed.

295. Find the height of the ramp, and use conservation of energy to find the velocity of the box:

$$KE_i + PE_i = KE_f + PE_f$$
$$0 + PE_i = KE_f + 0$$
$$KE_f = PE_i$$
$$\frac{1}{2}mv_f^2 = mgh$$

$$\sin \theta = \frac{h}{d}$$

$$h = d \sin \theta$$

$$\frac{1}{2} v_f^2 = gd \sin \theta$$

$$v_f^2 = 2gd \sin \theta$$

$$v_f = \sqrt{2gd \sin \theta}$$

$$v_f = \sqrt{2(10 \text{ m/s}^2)(10 \text{ m})(\sin 45°)}$$

$$v_f = 12 \text{ m/s}$$

296. Using the velocity, calculate the box's kinetic energy:

$$KE = \frac{1}{2} mv^2$$

$$KE = \frac{1}{2}(5 \text{ kg})(12 \text{ m/s})^2$$

$$KE = 360 \text{ J}$$

297. The force of friction works on the box to bring it to a stop. First calculate the force of friction, and then use the work–energy theorem to find the distance the box travels:

$$W = F_f d$$

$$\Delta K = \frac{1}{2} m(v_f)^2 - \frac{1}{2} m(v_i)^2 = -\frac{1}{2} m(v_i)^2$$

$$W = \Delta K$$

$$F_f d = -\frac{1}{2} m(v)^2$$

$$F_f = \mu F_N$$

$$F_N = mg$$

$$F_f = -\mu mg$$

$$2 \mu mgd = m(v_i)^2$$

$$2 \mu gd = (v_i)^2$$

$$d = \frac{(v_i)^2}{2 \mu g}$$

$$d = \frac{(12 \text{ m/s})^2}{2(0.6)(10 \text{ m/s}^2)}$$

$$d = 12 \text{ m}$$

298. Knowing the change in velocity of the box and the force of friction, calculate the time it takes to stop by the impulse–momentum theorem:

$$\Delta p = F \Delta t$$

$$\Delta p = m \Delta v$$

$$F \Delta t = m \Delta v$$

$$F_f \Delta t = m \Delta v$$

$$F_f = \mu F_N = \mu mg$$

$$\mu mg \Delta t = m \Delta v$$

$$\mu g \Delta t = \Delta v$$

$$\Delta t = \frac{\Delta v}{\mu g}$$

$$\Delta t = \frac{(12 \text{ m/s})}{(0.6)(10 \text{ m/s}^2)}$$

$$\Delta t = 2.0 \text{ s}$$

299. The amount of work is the area under the force–displacement graph. The work for the first 4 m of displacement is the area of the 12 N by 4 m rectangle, which is 48 J. The work for the next 4 m of displacement is the area of the 12 N by 4 m triangle, which is ½ (4) (12) = 24 J. The total amount of work done on the object is 48 J + 24 J = 72 J.

300. The work–energy theorem is used to find the final kinetic energy of the object:

$$W = \Delta K$$

$$W = K_f - \frac{1}{2} m v_i^2$$

$$K_f = W + \frac{1}{2} m v_i^2$$

$$K_f = 72 \text{ J} + \frac{1}{2}(15 \text{ kg})\left(4.0 \frac{\text{m}}{\text{s}}\right)^2$$

$$K_f = 72 \text{ J} + 120 \text{ J} = 192 \text{ J}$$

301. The final velocity is found as follows:

$$K_f = \frac{1}{2} m v_f^2$$

$$v_f = \sqrt{\frac{2K_f}{m}} = \sqrt{\frac{2(192 \text{ J})}{15 \text{ kg}}} = 5.1 \text{ m/s}$$

302. As the spring compresses and the object stops, all of the 192 J of kinetic energy will transfer to elastic potential energy of the spring:

$$(K+U_s)_{initial} = (K+U_s)_{final}$$
$$(K+0)_{initial} = (0+U_s)_{final}$$
$$192 \text{ J} = \frac{1}{2}kx^2$$
$$x = \sqrt{\frac{2(192 \text{ J})}{650\dfrac{\text{N}}{\text{m}}}} = 0.77 \text{ m}$$

Chapter 7: Rotational Motion

303. (D) The pry bar is in equilibrium, so the sum of all the moments about the tip (the fulcrum) must be zero.

$$\Sigma\tau = 0$$
$$r_\perp F + r_\perp F = 0$$
$$(0.02 \text{ m})(-F) + (1 \text{ m})(20 \text{ N}) = 0$$
$$F = 1{,}000 \text{ N}$$

304. (A) The beam is in equilibrium when it is held by the guide rope, so the sum of all the moments must be zero. The guide rope is 23 m from the fulcrum, and the center of mass is 2 m from the end. The weight of the beam is F = mg = (5.0 kg/m * 50.0 m) * 9.8 N/kg = 2,450 N.

$$\Sigma\tau = 0$$
$$r_\perp F + r_\perp F = 0$$
$$-(2 \text{ m})(2{,}450 \text{ N}) + (23 \text{ m})F = 0$$
$$F = 210 \text{ N}$$

305. (C) The lever is in equilibrium, so the sum of all the moments must be zero.

$$\Sigma\tau = 0$$
$$r_\perp F + r_\perp F = 0$$
$$(0.50 \text{ m})(1{,}000. \text{ N}) - (1.5 \text{ m})F = 0$$
$$F = 330 \text{ N}$$

306. (D) The perpendicular distance from the pivot to the line of action of the force defines the lever arm.

307. (B) 100 N is found by the summation of moments about the rear wheels. The baby and carriage weight act downward 30 cm in front of the back wheels, and the handle is forced downward 30 cm behind the back wheels.

$$r_\perp F + r_\perp F = 0$$
$$(0.30 \text{ m})(5 \text{ kg} + 5 \text{ kg})(10 \text{ N/kg}) - (0.30 \text{ m})F = 0$$
$$F = 100 \text{ N}$$

308. (E) For a system to be in equilibrium, the net force about each axis must be zero as well as the net torque about each axis.

309. (D) Angular momentum must be conserved in the system, so as the skater draws his arms into his body, he is decreasing his moment of inertia. Thus, his angular velocity must increase to conserve his angular momentum.

310. (B) Unlike degrees, which are arbitrarily determined, radians are based on the properties of a circle.

311. (D) According to Newton's first law, objects maintain constant velocity as long as there is no unbalanced force. The ball flies off tangent to the circle because the string is no longer holding the ball to the circular path; therefore, the ball has a velocity tangent to the circle. At the instant the string is cut, the velocity of the ball at that moment dictates how the ball will move.

312. (A) The angular velocity must first be converted to radians per second:

$$\omega = \left(12\frac{\text{rev}}{\text{sec}}\right)\left(2\pi\frac{\text{rad}}{\text{rev}}\right) = 24\pi \ \frac{\text{rad}}{\text{sec}}$$

Next, the angular momentum is calculated as follows:

$$L = I\omega$$
$$L = (mR^2)(24\pi) = 24\pi(mR^2)$$

313. (D) For the hour hand:

$$\omega = \left(\frac{2 \ \text{rev}}{24 \ \text{hours}}\right)\left(\frac{2\pi \ \text{rad}}{\text{rev}}\right)\left(\frac{1 \ \text{hour}}{3,600 \ \text{seconds}}\right) = \pi/21,600 \ \frac{\text{rad}}{\text{sec}}$$

For the minute hand:

$$\omega = \left(\frac{1 \ \text{rev}}{\text{hour}}\right)\left(\frac{2\pi \ \text{rad}}{\text{rev}}\right)\left(\frac{1 \ \text{hour}}{3,600 \ \text{seconds}}\right) = \pi/1,800 \ \frac{\text{rad}}{\text{sec}}$$

314. (E) 7,770 m/s is given by the formula $v = R \times \omega$, in which v is the orbital velocity, R is the radius of the junk's orbit, and ω is the angular rotation of the junk, $2\pi/(90 \times 60)$ radians/s.

$$v = R\omega = (6.38 \times 10^6 + 300,000 \text{ m})\left(\frac{2\pi}{90*60}\frac{\text{rad}}{\text{s}}\right) = 7,770 \text{ m/s}$$

315. (D) The translational kinetic energy of the orbiting body is dependent on the mass and its speed. The kinetic energy = ½ m v^2 = ½ (3 kg)(7,770 m/s)^2 = 9.06 × 10^7 J.

316. (D) The distance traveled in a complete orbit is the circumference of the orbit, and the time is the period. Speed is the ratio of distance to time:

$$v = \frac{d}{t} = \frac{2\pi R}{\text{period}} = \frac{2\pi \; (385,000,000 \text{ m})}{(27.3 \; \cancel{days})*\left(24\frac{\cancel{hours}}{\cancel{day}}\right)\left(3,600\frac{\text{sec}}{\cancel{hour}}\right)} = 1,030 \text{ m/s}$$

317. (C) When an object has dimensions, then forces may act off-axis and result in a torque that angularly accelerates the object. For objects that may not be modeled as a point particle, Newton's first law has six equations that equal zero: the three for summation of forces along the three axes and the three summations of moments about the three axes.

318. (D) A net torque results in an angular acceleration.

319. (C) Every point on the rotating platform makes the same number of revolutions per second, and thus has the same rotational speed.

320. (B) Linear speed is the amount of meters covered each second. The girl is making a circle with twice the circumference (circumference = $2\pi R$) in the same amount of time and thus has twice the linear speed.

321. (B) Angular momentum is directly proportional to angular speed ($L = I\omega$), so if the angular speed triples, the angular momentum will triple.

322. (A) Rotational kinetic energy is directly proportional to the square of the angular speed $\left(K = \frac{1}{2}I\omega^2\right)$, so if the angular speed triples, the rotational kinetic energy is nine times as much.

323. (E) Since there is no net torque applied to the skater, her angular momentum will remain the same. Extending her arms outward will increase her moment of inertia, and her angular velocity will decrease.

324. (D) The angle is calculated as follows:

$$\Delta\theta = \omega_0 t = \left(0.50\frac{\text{rad}}{\text{s}}\right)(12 \text{ sec}) = 6 \text{ rad}$$

$$\Delta\theta = (6 \text{ rad})\left(\frac{360°}{2\pi \text{ rad}}\right) = 340°$$

325. (A) The initial velocity is $\omega_0 = 0$, the angular acceleration is $\alpha = 12$ radians/sec^2, and the angular displacement is $\Delta\theta = 90° = \dfrac{\pi}{2}$ radians.

$$\Delta\theta = \omega_0 t + \frac{1}{2}\alpha t^2 = (0)t + \frac{1}{2}\alpha t^2$$
$$\Delta\theta = \frac{1}{2}\alpha t^2$$

Solving for t:

$$t = \sqrt{\frac{2\Delta\theta}{\alpha}} = \sqrt{\frac{2\left(\dfrac{\pi}{2}\,\text{rad}\right)}{12\dfrac{\text{rad}}{s^2}}} = 0.51\text{ s}$$

326. (B) Angular speed, ω, is calculated as follows:

$$L = I\omega$$

$$\omega = \frac{L}{I} = \frac{18\dfrac{\text{kg}\cdot\text{m}^2}{s}}{12\text{ kg}\cdot\text{m}^2} = 1.5\frac{\text{rad}}{s}$$

327. (E) The initial angular speed is $\omega_0 = 150\dfrac{\text{rad}}{s}$, the final angular speed is zero, and the angular acceleration is $\alpha = -25\dfrac{\text{rad}}{s^2}$.

$$\omega = \omega_0 + \alpha t$$

$$t = \frac{\omega - \omega_0}{\alpha} = \frac{0 - 150\dfrac{\text{rad}}{s}}{-25\dfrac{\text{rad}}{s^2}} = 6.0\text{ s}$$

328. (D) The seesaw is in equilibrium, so the sum of all the moments must be zero.

$$\Sigma\tau = 0$$
$$r_\perp F + r_\perp F = 0$$
$$(2.0\text{ m})\left(42\text{kg}*10\frac{N}{\text{kg}}\right) - (R)\left(35\text{ kg}*10\frac{N}{\text{kg}}\right) = 0$$
$$R = 2.4\text{ m}$$

329. **(A)** The following relationship on the equation guide may be solved for elapsed time:

$$\Delta L = \tau\, \Delta t$$

$$\Delta t = \frac{\Delta L}{\tau}$$

$$\Delta t = \frac{L_2 - L_1}{\tau}$$

$$\Delta t = \frac{I\,\omega_2 - I\,\omega_1}{\tau}$$

330. **(D)** The rotational kinetic energy of the tire transfers to thermal energy. To calculate the rotational kinetic energy, first convert the rotational speed of the tires into radians per second:

$$\omega = \left(25\,\frac{\text{rev}}{\text{s}}\right)\left(\frac{2\pi\ \text{rad}}{1\ \text{rev}}\right) = 157\,\frac{\text{rad}}{\text{s}}$$

According to the work–energy theorem, the energy transferred to heat equals the change in kinetic energy of the tire:

$$E = \frac{1}{2}I\omega_f^2 - \frac{1}{2}I\omega_i^2$$

$$E = \frac{1}{2}(1.5\ \text{kg m}^2)\left(157\,\frac{\text{rad}}{\text{s}}\right)^2 - 0$$

$$E = 19{,}000\ \text{J}$$

331. **(C)** The weight of the mass ($0.025\text{kg} * 9.8\ \text{N/kg} = 0.254\ \text{N}$) multiplied by the radius of the pulley (0.45 m) provides the net torque applied to the pulley. The angular acceleration is calculated as follows:

$$\vec{\alpha} = \frac{\vec{\tau}_{\text{net}}}{I}$$

$$\vec{\alpha} = \frac{(0.254\ \text{N})(0.45\ \text{m})}{0.15\ \text{kg m}^2} = 0.74\,\frac{\text{rad}}{\text{s}^2}$$

332. **(D)** Angular momentum is the sum of the angular momentum of all the components. The masses have a linear velocity of $v = R\omega$, and since they are located at a distance of half the rod length $\left(\dfrac{L}{2}\right)$ from the center of the barbell, this may be written as $v = \dfrac{L}{2}\omega$. Their linear momentum is calculated as $p = mv = m\left(\dfrac{L}{2}\omega\right)$. The angular momentum of these masses is found by multiplying this linear momentum by the distance from the axis to the line of motion of the object: $L = m\left(\dfrac{L}{2}\omega\right)\left(\dfrac{L}{2}\right) = m\omega\left(\dfrac{L}{2}\right)^2$.

The total angular momentum of the rod and the two masses is calculated as follows:

$$L_{total} = L_{rod} + L_{mass\ 1} + L_{mass\ 2}$$

$$L_{total} = I\omega + m\omega \left(\frac{L}{2}\right)^2 + m\omega \left(\frac{L}{2}\right)^2$$

$$L_{total} = I\omega + \frac{m\omega(L)^2}{2}$$

$$L_{total} = \left(I + \frac{m(L)^2}{2}\right)\omega$$

$$L_{total} = \left(1.5\ kg\ m^2 + \frac{3.0\ kg(2.2\ m)^2}{2}\right)\left(0.50\frac{rad}{s}\right)$$

$$L_{total} = \left(1.5\ kg\ m^2 + \frac{3.0\ kg(2.2\ m)^2}{2}\right)\left(0.50\frac{rad}{s}\right)$$

$$L_{total} = 4.4\frac{kg\ m^2}{s}$$

333. (C) Torque is calculated by $\tau = r_\perp F = r\ F_\perp$. Assuming the rod length L, the individual torques are calculated as follows:

   I. $|\tau| = r\ F_\perp = LF$

   II. $|\tau| = r\ F_\perp = LF - (L/2)\ F = \dfrac{LF}{2}$

   III. $|\tau| = r\ F_\perp = (L/2)\ F + L\ (F/2) = LF$

   IV. $|\tau| = r\ F_\perp = L\ [2F\cos(30°)] = LF$

This rank as follows: I = III = IV > II

334. (B) The angular acceleration may be written as $\alpha = \dfrac{\Delta\omega}{\Delta t} = \dfrac{\omega - 0}{\Delta t} = \dfrac{\omega}{\Delta t}$.

The angular displacement is $\Delta\theta = \omega_0 t + \dfrac{1}{2}\alpha t^2 = 0 + \dfrac{1}{2}\alpha(\Delta t)^2$.

Substituting the first equation into the second: $\Delta\theta = \dfrac{1}{2}\left(\dfrac{\omega}{\Delta t}\right)(\Delta t)^2 = \dfrac{\omega\Delta t}{2}$, in radians.

Converting radians to revolutions, the final answer is:

$$\Delta\theta = \left(\frac{\omega\Delta t}{2}\ \cancel{rad}\right)\left(\frac{1\ revolution}{2\pi\ \cancel{rad}}\right) = \frac{\omega\Delta t}{4\pi}$$

335. (D) The period of rotation, T, is the amount of seconds for each revolution. First, the angular velocity is converted into revolutions per second:

$$\omega\left(\frac{rad}{s}\right) = \frac{\omega}{2\pi}\left(\frac{rev}{s}\right)$$

The period is the inverse of frequency:

$$T = \frac{1}{\omega} = \frac{1}{\dfrac{\omega}{2\pi}\left(\dfrac{\text{rev}}{\text{s}}\right)} = \frac{2\pi}{\omega}\left(\frac{\text{s}}{\text{rev}}\right)$$

336. **(D)** The initial angular speed is not relevant in this problem. The moment of inertia, I, is determined as follows:

$$\vec{\alpha} = \frac{\vec{\tau}_{net}}{I}$$

$$I = \frac{\vec{\tau}_{net}}{\vec{\alpha}} = \frac{55 \text{ Nm}}{5.0\,\dfrac{\text{rad}}{\text{s}^2}} = 11 \text{ kg} \cdot \text{m}^2$$

337. **(A)** The ratio is calculated as follows:

$$\frac{K_{translation}}{K_{rotation}} = \frac{\dfrac{1}{2}mv^2}{\dfrac{1}{2}I\omega^2}$$

$$\frac{K_{translation}}{K_{rotation}} = \frac{\dfrac{\cancel{1}}{\cancel{2}}\cancel{m}v^2}{\dfrac{\cancel{1}}{\cancel{2}}\left(\dfrac{2}{5}\cancel{m}R^2\right)\omega^2}$$

$$\frac{K_{translation}}{K_{rotation}} = \frac{5v^2}{2R^2\omega^2}$$

338. **(C)** The final angular velocity is calculated from the rotational kinetic energy:

$$K = \frac{1}{2}I\omega^2$$

$$\omega = \sqrt{\frac{2K}{I}} = \sqrt{\frac{2(800 \text{ J})}{4 \text{ kg m}^2}} = 20\,\frac{\text{rad}}{\text{s}}$$

Next, the elapsed time, Δt, for the acceleration is found as follows:

$$\omega = \omega_0 + \alpha\,\Delta t$$

$$\Delta t = \frac{\omega - \omega_0}{\alpha} = \frac{(20-0)\dfrac{\text{rad}}{\text{s}}}{5\,\dfrac{\text{rad}}{\text{s}^2}} = 4 \text{ s}$$

339. (C) The angular displacement is calculated as follows:

$$\Delta\theta = \omega_0 t + \frac{1}{2}\alpha t^2$$

$$\Delta\theta = \left(11\frac{rad}{s}\right)(6.0\ s) + \frac{1}{2}\left(-1.5\frac{rad}{s^2}\right)(6.0\ s)^2$$

$$\Delta\theta = 39\ radians$$

340. (E) The rotational kinetic energies may be equated and solved for the rotational velocity of Object 2:

$$K_1 = K_2$$

$$\frac{1}{2}I_1\omega_1^2 = \frac{1}{2}I_2\omega_2^2$$

$$\omega_2^2 = \frac{I_1}{I_2}\omega_1^2$$

$$\omega_2^2 = \frac{8\ kg\ m^2}{2\ kg\ m^2}\left(1\frac{rad}{s}\right)^2 = 4\left(\frac{rad}{s}\right)^2$$

$$\omega_2 = \sqrt{4\left(\frac{rad}{s}\right)^2} = 2\frac{rad}{s}$$

341. (C, D) When the force goes through the axis of rotation, no torque is applied, so this eliminates choices A, B, and E. Choices C and D both have forces that do not go through the axis of rotation and have a component perpendicular to the lever arm, and thus torque is applied.

342. (A, E) The moment of inertia is the rotational equivalent of inertial mass, and thus is the resistance something has to rotational motion. It can also be found from the rotational analogue to Newton's second law:

$$\vec{\alpha} = \frac{\vec{\tau}_{net}}{I}$$

Solving for I:

$$I = \frac{\vec{\tau}_{net}}{\vec{\alpha}}$$

Thus, the moment of inertia is the ratio between torque and angular acceleration.

343. (D, E) The question asks which accelerations are NOT possible, so you can begin by eliminating the choices that ARE possible. An object moving in a circle must be accelerating toward the center with a centripetal (inward) acceleration, so choice A must be eliminated. The object may also be spinning with an angular acceleration if there is net torque acting on it, so choice C must be eliminated. If there is a net force tangent to the circle, the object will accelerate with a tangential acceleration, so choice B must be eliminated. This leaves

choices D and E. An object moving in a circle will NOT experience an outward ("centrifugal") radial acceleration, or it would not stay in the circle, so choice D must be selected. Since there are unbalanced forces on every object moving in a circle and its velocity is changing, zero acceleration is also not possible, so choice E must be selected.

344. (B, D) When a solid object rotates with a constant angular acceleration, its angular velocity changes at a steady rate. A constant net torque is responsible for a constant angular acceleration according to $\vec{\alpha} = \dfrac{\vec{\tau}_{net}}{I}$.

345. (A, C) A moment of inertia is the resistance a body has to rotation. The more mass the body has and the farther the mass is separated from the axis of rotation, the greater the moment of inertia. The moment of inertia does NOT depend on the state of motion of the body, so choices A and C are the best selections.

346. The net torque on the rod is the sum of the torque contributions from each force. The 12-N force tends to rotate the rod counterclockwise (positive torque), and the 24-N force clockwise (negative torque).

$$\tau_{net} = \tau_{10} + \tau_{20} = r\ F_{\perp} + r\ F_{\perp} = (1.5\ \text{m})12\cos(60°) - (1.5\ \text{m})(24\ \text{N})$$
$$\tau_{net} = -27\ \text{Nm (clockwise)}$$

347. The moment of inertia for a thin rod pinned at the center is:

$$I = \frac{1}{12}ML^2$$
$$I = \frac{1}{12}(12\ \text{kg})(3.0\ \text{m})^2$$
$$I = 9.0\ \text{kg} \cdot \text{m}^2$$

348. Angular acceleration is calculated using the rotational expression of Newton's second law:

$$\vec{\alpha} = \frac{\vec{\tau}_{net}}{I}$$
$$\vec{\alpha} = \frac{-27\ \text{Nm}}{9.0\ \text{kg m}^2} = -3.0\ \text{rad/s}^2$$

349. The angular displacement must first be in radians: $\Delta\theta = -90° = -\dfrac{\pi}{2}$ radians (clockwise).

To solve this, it is assumed that the torque (and thus the angular acceleration) will remain constant throughout the rotation. Thus, the following equation for constant angular acceleration may be used:

$$\Delta\theta = \omega_0 t + \frac{1}{2}\alpha t^2$$

350. Since it starts from rest, the initial angular velocity, ω_0, is zero, and you can solve for time as follows:

$$\Delta\theta = \frac{1}{2}\alpha t^2$$

$$t = \sqrt{\frac{2\Delta\theta}{\alpha}}$$

$$t = \sqrt{\frac{2\left(-\dfrac{\pi}{2}\right)\dfrac{\text{rad}}{\text{s}}}{-3.0 \dfrac{\text{rad}}{\text{s}^2}}} = 1.0 \text{ s}$$

$$\Delta\theta = \frac{1}{2}\alpha t^2 = \frac{1}{2}\left(-3.0 \frac{\text{rad}}{\text{s}^2}\right)(5.0 \text{ s})^2 = -37.5 \text{ rad}$$

$$\Delta\theta = (-37.5 \text{ rad})\left(\frac{1 \text{ rev}}{2\pi \text{ rad}}\right) = -6 \text{ rev}$$

351. Before the collision, the dart has a linear momentum of $\vec{p} = m\vec{v}$. When it hits the 25-cm-tall target 5 cm above the hinge, it is moving horizontally at 2.5 m/s at a distance of 20 cm above the hinge (25 cm – 5 cm). Its angular momentum is the product of the linear momentum times the perpendicular distance to the axis:

$$\vec{L} = R_\perp \vec{p} = R_\perp (m\vec{v})$$

$$\vec{L}_{\text{initial}} = (0.020 \text{ m})\left(0.012 \text{ kg} * 2.5\frac{\text{m}}{\text{s}}\right) = 0.0060\frac{\text{kg m}^2}{\text{s}}$$

Because there is no external torque on the dart/target system, the angular momentum must be conserved, so the final angular momentum of the dart/target system after the collision must also be $0.0060\dfrac{\text{kg m}^2}{\text{s}}$.

352. After the collision, the dart/target system's angular momentum may be written as $\vec{L} = I\vec{\omega}$, with the moment of inertia of the dart/target system found as the sum of the contributions of each (treat the dart as a point particle and the target as a plank pinned on one end):

$$I = I_{\text{dart}} + I_{\text{target}} = m_{\text{dart}} R_\perp^2 + \frac{1}{3} M_{\text{target}} L^2$$

$$I = (0.012 \text{ kg}) (0.20 \text{ m})^2 + \frac{1}{3}(0.095 \text{ kg})(0.25 \text{ m})^2$$

$$I = (0.00048 + 0.00198) \text{ kg} \cdot \text{m}^2$$

$$I = (0.00246) \text{ kg} \cdot \text{m}^2$$

Knowing the angular momentum from part (a), solve $\vec{L} = I\vec{\omega}$ for angular speed:

$$\vec{\omega} = \frac{\vec{L}}{I} = \frac{0.0060 \dfrac{\text{kg m}^2}{\text{s}}}{0.00246 \text{ kg m}^2} = 2.4 \frac{\text{rad}}{\text{s}}$$

Chapter 8: Electrostatics: Electric Charge and Electric Force

353. (D) The electric charge of a single proton is $+1.6 \times 10^{-19}$ C. The object has a charge of $+8.0 \times 10^{-19}$ C. So, divide the object's charge by the single proton charge to find that it has five more protons than electrons.

354. (D) The charge on a proton is 1.6×10^{-19} C. The distance between the protons is 1×10^{-6} m. The protons have the same charge, so the force will be repulsive. Use Coulomb's law to find the magnitude of the force:

$$F = \frac{kq_1 q_2}{r^2}$$
$$F = \frac{(9 \times 10^9 \text{ N} \cdot \text{m}^2/\text{C}^2)(1.6 \times 10^{-19} \text{ C})(1.6 \times 10^{-19} \text{ C})}{(1.0 \times 10^{-6} \text{ m})^2}$$
$$F = 2.3 \times 10^{-16} \text{ N}$$

355. (E) The negatively charged object induces a charge in the neutral object. The negatively charged object repels negative charges in the neutral conductor to the opposite side. The remaining positive charges attract the negatively charged object.

356. (B) The fact that the paper bits accelerated upward is evidence that the upward electrostatic force dominated over the downward gravitational force.

357. (C) The fundamental charge is 1.6×10^{-19} C, which is the magnitude of the charge of an electron or proton, and all charges are integer multiples of this value. Millikan discovered this quantity in 1909 with his famous oil drop experiment. No charge less than this value has ever been detected.

358. (A) According to Coulomb's law, electric force is inversely proportional to the square of the distance between the objects. If the distance is doubled, then the force decreases to one-fourth of what it was.

359. (D) According to Coulomb's law, electric force is directly proportional to the product of the two charges. If one charge is doubled, the electric force doubles. If the other charge is tripled, that triples the already doubled force. Thus, the force is six times the original force.

360. (B) When identical conductive objects touch, they share the electric charge evenly. Therefore, each object has $\dfrac{+6.4 \times 10^{-8} \text{ C}}{2} = +3.2 \times 10^{-8} \text{ C}$.

361. (D) Coulomb's law may be used to find the value of the electric repulsive force:

$$\left|\vec{F}_E\right| = k\,\frac{|q_1 q_2|}{r^2}$$

$$\left|\vec{F}_E\right| = 9.0 \times 10^9\,\frac{\text{Nm}^2}{\text{C}^2}\,\frac{\left|(6.4 \times 10^{-8}\,\text{C})(6.4 \times 10^{-8}\,\text{C})\right|}{(0.0056\ \text{m})^2}$$

$$\left|\vec{F}_E\right| = 1.2\ N$$

362. (A) The charge of a single electron is -1.6×10^{-19} C, so the total number of electrons may be found as follows: # electrons $= (-9.6\ \text{C})\left(\dfrac{1\ \text{electron}}{-1.6\ I \times 10^{-19}\,\text{C}}\right) = 6 \times 10^{19}$ electrons.

363. (E) The only change is that one of the charges is doubled. Since the electrostatic force is directly proportional to charge, the force must double from 100 N to 200 N.

364. (B) In good conductors, the valence electrons may move freely from atom to atom.

365. (A) In the field of electrostatics, objects become charged when electrons transfer between objects (protons are fixed in the nucleus of the atom and will not transfer from atom to atom). When an object becomes positively charged, it must lose electrons. Thus the silk gains electrons and the glass loses electrons.

366. (B) According to the law of conservation of charge, charge cannot be created or destroyed. Thus, the net charge of an isolated system must remain constant. In order for the system to remain neutral, the magnitude of the charge on the negative rubber rod must equal the magnitude of the positive charge on the wool fabric.

367. (A) Electrical attraction occurs between oppositely charged objects but also occurs between neutral objects and charged objects. One can say for certain that at least one of the pieces of tape is charged.

368. (A) The electron has a charge of -1.6×10^{-19} C, and two protons have a charge of $2(+1.6 \times 10^{-19}\,\text{C}) = +3.2 \times 10^{-19}\,\text{C}$. Coulomb's law needs to be solved for the radial distance, r:

$$\left|\vec{F}_E\right| = k\,\frac{|q_1 q_2|}{r^2}$$

$$r = \sqrt{k\,\frac{|q_1 q_2|}{\left|\vec{F}_E\right|}}$$

$$r = \sqrt{\left(9.0 \times 10^9\,\frac{\text{Nm}^2}{\text{C}^2}\right)\frac{\left|(-1.6 \times 10^{-19}\,\text{C})(+3.2 \times 10^{-19}\,\text{C})\right|}{4.8 \times 10^{-7}\,\text{N}}}$$

$$r = 3.1 \times 10^{-11}\,\text{m} = 31\ \text{pm}$$

369. (B) Since the paper is an insulator, the electrons tend to stay within their individual atoms. The positive tape can attract the (negative) electrons within the atoms to the side closest to the tape, and an attraction occurs. This phenomenon is known as electric polarization. Note: The protons are fixed within the nucleus and do not flow through objects; electrons are the "fluid" responsible for electrostatic phenomena.

370. (B) Protons are fixed within the nucleus and do not flow from atom to atom through objects.

371. (D) The leaves are repelling each other, so they both have the same charge, either positive or negative. The electroscope must have been touched by a charged object at some point in time.

372. (D) Electrons are the only subatomic particle that can flow easily through conductors. The (negative) electrons in the electroscope flow up toward the positive rod because opposites attract. Thus the gold leaves are now positive because they are missing electrons. The like-charged leaves now repel.

373. (B) In a positive electroscope, the leaves stand apart because they have like charges. If they come together, that means that they must be approaching the neutral state, and this is achieved by sending electrons to the leaves. A negative rod held near the metal cap will do just that by inducing (negative) electrons to move into the leaves. Note: A positive electroscope still has valance electrons that can flow freely through the electroscope, so transfer of electrons from the rod into the electroscope is necessary.

374. (A) The charges and masses of the particles are available in the AP "Constants and Conversion Factors" table. Coulomb's law may first be used to find the force of attraction between the particles:

$$\left|\vec{F}_E\right| = k \frac{|q_1 q_2|}{r^2}$$

$$\left|\vec{F}_E\right| = k \frac{|q_{electron} q_{proton}|}{r^2}$$

Next, the acceleration may be found by using Newton's second law. Since the electron has less mass, it will accelerate at a greater rate.

$$a = \frac{\vec{F}_{net}}{m} = \frac{\vec{F}_E}{m_{electron}} = \frac{k \dfrac{|q_{electron} q_{proton}|}{r^2}}{m_{electron}}$$

$$a = \frac{9.0 \times 10^9 \dfrac{\text{Nm}^2}{\text{C}^2} \dfrac{|(-1.60 \times 10^{-19}\,\text{C})(1.60 \times 10^{-19}\,\text{C})|}{(1.5 \times 10^{-10}\,\text{m})^2}}{9.11 \times 10^{-31}\,\text{kg}}$$

$$a = 1.12 \times 10^{22} \frac{\text{m}}{\text{s}^2}$$

375. (D) Electrons and protons have the same magnitude of charges, so the force from the proton at (0, 1) is the same magnitude as the force from the electron at (1, 0). The proton applies an upward attractive force on the electron at the origin. The electron at (0, 1) applies a leftward repulsive force on the electron at the origin. The net force on the electron is up and to the left on the coordinate plane, at an angle of 135°.

376. (E) The electric force is found from Coulomb's law, and the gravitational force is found from the universal law of gravitation:

$$\frac{\left|\vec{F}_E\right|}{\left|\vec{F}_g\right|} = \frac{k\dfrac{\left|q_{electron}\,q_{proton}\right|}{r^2}}{G\dfrac{\left|m_{electron}\,m_{proton}\right|}{r^2}}$$

$$\frac{\left|\vec{F}_E\right|}{\left|\vec{F}_g\right|} = \frac{k}{G}\frac{\left|q_{electron}\,q_{proton}\right|}{\left|m_{electron}\,m_{proton}\right|}$$

$$\frac{\left|\vec{F}_E\right|}{\left|\vec{F}_g\right|} = \frac{9.0\times10^9\,\dfrac{\text{Nm}^2}{\text{C}^2}\left|(-1.60\times10^{-19}\,\text{C})(1.60\times10^{-19}\,\text{C})\right|}{6.67\times10^{-11}\,\dfrac{\text{Nm}^2}{\text{kg}^2}\left|(9.11\times10^{-31}\,\text{kg})(1.67\times10^{-27}\,\text{kg})\right|}$$

$$\frac{\left|\vec{F}_E\right|}{\left|\vec{F}_g\right|} = 2.27\times10^{39}$$

377. (A) The conductor is charged positively by contact. This occurs because the (negative) freely moving valence electrons in the conductor are attracted to the positively charged glass rod. The previously neutral conductor is now missing electrons and is positively charged. Protons are fixed in the nucleus and do not flow from atom to atom in a solid object.

378. (B) Coulomb's law may be used to solve for the identical, unknown charges:

$$\left|\vec{F}_E\right| = k\frac{\left|q_1 q_2\right|}{r^2}$$

$$\left|q^2\right| = \frac{\left|\vec{F}_E\right|r^2}{k}$$

$$\left|q\right| = \sqrt{\frac{\left|\vec{F}_E\right|r^2}{k}}$$

$$\left|q\right| = \sqrt{\frac{6.0\times10^{-5}\,\text{N}(0.02\text{ m})^2}{9.0\times10^9\,\dfrac{\text{Nm}^2}{\text{C}^2}}}$$

$$\left|q\right| = 1.6\times10^{-9}\,\text{C}$$

379. (D) This sphere is positive; therefore it must have more protons than electrons. Divide the net charge by the fundamental charge as follows:

$$\text{Excess \# of protons} = \frac{+4.0 \times 10^{-15}\,\text{C}}{+1.6 \times 10^{-19}\,\dfrac{\text{C}}{\text{proton}}} = 25{,}000 \text{ protons}$$

380. (E) Since the positive Object A is attracted to Object B and opposites attract, B must be negative. Since the negative Object B is repelled from Object C and like charges repel, C must be negative. Since the negative Object C is attracted to Object D, then D must be positive.

381. (D) The net charge on both spheres is 12 μC − 8 μC = +4 μC. Since they are both identical conductors, the electrons will flow from one to the other until they share the same charge. When separated, they will each have +2 μC.

382. (E) The positive glass rod will attract many valance electrons to flow into the left sphere. When the spheres are separated, those electrons are now trapped on the left sphere, making it negatively charged. The sphere on the right is missing electrons, and is thus equally positively charged.

383. (D) Neutral objects attract both positive and negative objects. Thus the foil *may be neutral*. Positive and negative objects also attract. Thus the foil *may also be positive* to attract to the negative balloon.

384. (B) The balloon is an insulator, so the charge will not flow throughout the balloon but will rather stay in the location where the friction with the wool cloth caused the charge separation. Since the balloon is negative, excess electrons are on the balloon in the location where it was rubbed on the wool.

385. (C) This process is called "charging by induction and grounding." The negative rod repels many of the valance electrons in the conducting sphere to the person. When the person disconnects his finger, the sphere is now positive because it's missing electrons.

386. (C) Since the nuclei are positive and electrons are negative, the force will be attractive. The force of the nucleus on the electron is equal to the force of the electron on the nucleus because all interaction forces are equal and opposite according to Newton's third law. This can be also be shown with Coulomb's law, $\left|\vec{F}_E\right| = k\dfrac{|q_1 q_2|}{r^2}$, because the same electrostatic force is calculated regardless of which charge is q_1 and which is q_2.

387. (B) Sphere A must have gained electrons in the charging process (the protons stay fixed in the nucleus and are not transferred in solids in an electrostatic experiment). The number of excess electrons on Sphere A are calculated as follows:

$$\text{Excess \# of electrons} = \frac{-1.28 \times 10^{-13}\,\text{C}}{-1.60 \times 10^{-19}\,\dfrac{\text{C}}{\text{electron}}} = 800{,}000 \text{ electrons}$$

The mass of these extra electrons is calculated as follows:

$$800,000 \text{ electrons}\left(9.11\times10^{-31}\ \frac{\text{kg}}{\text{electron}}\right)=7.29\times10^{-25}\ \text{kg}$$

388. (B) Coulomb's law may be solved for the distance between the charges:

$$\left|\vec{F_E}\right|=k\ \frac{|q_1 q_2|}{r^2}$$

$$r=\sqrt{k\ \frac{|q_1 q_2|}{\left|\vec{F_E}\right|}}$$

$$r=\sqrt{k\ \frac{|(e)(4e)|}{F}}$$

$$r=\sqrt{k\ \frac{4e^2}{F}}$$

$$r=\sqrt{k\ \frac{(2e)^2}{F}}$$

$$r=2e\sqrt{\frac{k}{F}}$$

389. (A) When Sphere A and Sphere B touch, the net charge is $+10\ \mu C - 6\ \mu C = +4\ \mu C$, and so each sphere gets $+2\ \mu C$ when they are separated. Now, when Sphere B and Sphere C touch, the net charge is $+2\ \mu C - 4\ \mu C = -2\ \mu C$, and so each sphere gets $-1\ \mu C$ when the spheres are separated.

390. (A) The nuclei have the same charge, so the hydrogen nucleus will be repelled from the helium nucleus. Coulomb's law $\left(\left|\vec{F_E}\right|=k\ \frac{|q_1 q_2|}{r^2}\right)$ predicts that the force between them will decrease significantly as the distance between them increases. Since Newton's second law $\left(a=\dfrac{\vec{F}_{net}}{m}\right)$ states that acceleration is directly proportional to the net force, and it's known that force decreases with distance, then the hydrogen nucleus will move away from the helium nucleus with a *decreasing acceleration rate*.

391. (B, E) The fundamental charge is 1.6×10^{-19} C, which is the magnitude of the charge of an electron or proton, and all charges are integer multiples of this value (e.g., there cannot be a half of an electron or proton charge). Options B and E yield integer values of the fundamental charge.

392. (C, E) Coulomb's law $\left(\left|\vec{F_E}\right|=k\ \frac{|q_1 q_2|}{r^2}\right)$ demonstrates that the magnitude of the electric force depends on the charges of each object and the distance, r, that they are separated.

393. (C, D) Rubber is an excellent insulator. Distilled water is pure water and makes a good insulator. Salt water, on the other hand, has ions that allow for conductivity and is considered a conductor along with the metals listed, gold and aluminum.

394. (D, E) Oppositely charged objects attract. Also, neutral objects are attracted to both positive and negative objects. Objects that are charged in the same way cannot attract each other.

395. (A, B) Coulomb's law $\left(\left|\vec{F}_E\right| = k\,\dfrac{|q_1 q_2|}{r^2}\right)$ may be used to reason through this answer. If both electrons are replaced with protons, they will still repel, and since they have the same magnitude of charge, the magnitude of the force will be the same. (If only one electron is replaced with a proton, the magnitude of the force will remain the same, but the force will change to an attractive force.) Since the electrostatic force is directly proportional to the product of the charges, then if both charges are doubled, the force will quadruple. However, the fact that the distance is doubled cancels this quadrupling effect, because the electrostatic force is inversely proportional to the square of the distance.

396. The $-1.6\ \mu C$ charge repels the $-3.2\ \mu C$ charge to the left, and the $+4.8\ \mu C$ charge attracts the $-3.2\ \mu C$ charge to the left:

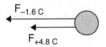

397. The net force is to the left and is the sum of the two forces in the diagram above. Using Coulomb's law:

$$\left|\vec{F}_E\right| = k\,\frac{|q_1 q_2|}{r^2}$$

$$\left|\vec{F}_E\right| = \left(9.0\times10^9\ \frac{\mathrm{Nm}^2}{\mathrm{C}^2}\,\frac{\left|(+4.8\times10^{-6}\ \mathrm{C})(-3.2\times10^{-6}\ \mathrm{C})\right|}{(0.0040\ \mathrm{m})^2}\right)$$

$$+\left(9.0\times10^9\ \frac{\mathrm{Nm}^2}{\mathrm{C}^2}\,\frac{\left|(-1.6\times10^{-6}\ \mathrm{C})(-3.2\times10^{-6}\ \mathrm{C})\right|}{(0.0020\ \mathrm{m})^2}\right)$$

$$\left|\vec{F}_E\right| = (8{,}640\ \mathrm{N}) + (11{,}520\ \mathrm{N}) = 2.016\times10^4\ \mathrm{N} \approx 2.0\times10^4\ \mathrm{N}\ \text{(to the left)}$$

398. The acceleration is calculated from Newton's second law:

$$a = \frac{\vec{F}_{net}}{m}$$

$$a = \frac{2.016\times10^4\ \mathrm{N}}{0.075\ \mathrm{kg}}$$

$$a = 2.7\times10^5\ \frac{\mathrm{m}}{\mathrm{s}^2}\ \text{(to the left)}$$

399. When the −6.4 μC pith ball touches the neutral pith ball and then separates, they each will share the charge and have −3.2 μC.

400. The force diagram looks like this:

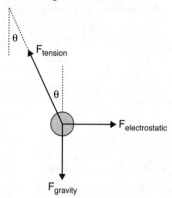

401. The gravitational force is $F_g = \left(9.8\dfrac{\text{N}}{\text{kg}}\right)(0.024\ \text{kg}) = 0.24\ \text{N}$. The electrostatic force is calculated from Coulomb's law:

$$\left|\vec{F}_E\right| = k\frac{|q_1 q_2|}{r^2}$$

$$\left|\vec{F}_E\right| = 9.0\times10^9\ \frac{\text{Nm}^2}{\text{C}^2}\frac{\left|(-3.2\times10^{-6}\ \text{C})(-3.2\times10^{-6}\ \text{C})\right|}{(0.52\ \text{m})^2}$$

$$\left|\vec{F}_E\right| = 0.34\ \text{N}$$

402. The angle theta is half the angle between the threads. To keep the pith ball in equilibrium, the angle is calculated by:

$$\theta = \tan^{-1}\left(\frac{F_{\text{electrostatic}}}{F_{\text{gravity}}}\right)$$

$$\theta = \tan^{-1}\left(\frac{0.34\ \text{N}}{0.24\ \text{N}}\right) = 55°$$

Therefore, the total angle between the threads is 110°.

Chapter 9: DC Circuits (Resistors Only)

403. (D) The electric charge is 2.4 C, and the time interval is 0.10 s. Here is the current:

$$I = \frac{\Delta q}{\Delta t}$$

$$I = \frac{(2.4 \text{ C})}{(0.010 \text{ s})}$$

$$I = 240 \text{ A}$$

404. (A) The voltage is 9 V, and the resistance is 10 Ω. Use Ohm's law to find the current:

$$I = \frac{V}{R}$$

$$I = \frac{(9 \text{ V})}{(10 \text{ Ω})}$$

$$I = 0.9 \text{ A}$$

405. (E) The voltage is 9.0 V, and the current is 3.0 A. Calculate the power dissipated by the resistor:

$$P = IV$$

$$P = (3 \text{ A})(9 \text{ V})$$

$$P = 27 \text{ J}$$

406. (C) To find the equivalent resistance of resistors in series, add all the resistances together:

$$R_{eq} = R_1 + R_2 + R_3$$

$$R_{eq} = 20 \text{ Ω} + 150 \text{ Ω} + 500 \text{ Ω}$$

$$R_{eq} = 670 \text{ Ω}$$

407. (B) First, find the equivalent resistance of the resistors by adding the resistances. Then, use Ohm's law to find the current:

$$R_{eq} = R_1 + R_2 + R_3$$

$$R_{eq} = 3 \text{ Ω} + 1 \text{ Ω} + 2 \text{ Ω}$$

$$R_{eq} = 6 \text{ Ω}$$

$$I = \frac{V}{R_{eq}}$$

$$I = \frac{(12 \text{ V})}{(6 \text{ Ω})}$$

$$I = 2 \text{ A}$$

408. (E) In a series circuit, the current is equal in all parts of the circuit. However, the voltage drops across each resistor follow Ohm's law. Since R_1 has the greatest resistance and it has the same current as the other resistors, it has the greatest voltage drop across it.

409. (D) The total power dissipated by the resistors is the same as the power output of the battery. Power is the product of the total voltage drop (12 V) and the current (2 A):

$$P = IV$$
$$P = (2 \text{ A})(12 \text{ V})$$
$$P = 24 \text{ W}$$

410. (C) The total current in the circuit was found earlier to be 2 A. Use Ohm's law to calculate the voltage drop across the third resistor (2 Ω):

$$\Delta V_3 = IR_3$$
$$\Delta V_3 = (2 \text{ A})(2 \text{ Ω})$$
$$\Delta V_3 = 4 \text{ V}$$

411. (C) In all parts of a series circuit with different resistors, the resistances are different, the voltage drops are different, and the current is the same.

412. (D) When one light in a string of lights goes out and then they all go out, it means the lights are wired in series.

413. (D) In a parallel circuit, the current gets divided among the branches and the voltage is the same across each device. According to Ohm's law, $I = V/R$, so the amount of current flow is inversely proportional to the resistance. Therefore, since $R_3 > R_1 > R_2$, then $I_2 > I_1 > I_3$.

414. (D) The equivalent resistance of a parallel circuit is calculated as follows:

$$\frac{1}{R_{eq}} = \frac{1}{R_1} + \frac{1}{R_2} + \frac{1}{R_3}$$
$$\frac{1}{R_{eq}} = \frac{1}{(8 \text{ Ω})} + \frac{1}{(6 \text{ Ω})} + \frac{1}{(10 \text{ Ω})}$$
$$\frac{1}{R_{eq}} = 0.4 \text{ Ω}^{-1}$$
$$R_{eq} = 2.6 \text{ Ω}$$

415. (B) Once you have calculated the equivalent resistance (2.6 Ω), use Ohm's law to find the total current:

$$I = \frac{\Delta V}{R_{eq}}$$

$$I = \frac{(12\ V)}{(2.6\ \Omega)}$$

$$I = 4.6\ A$$

416. (B) First, find the current flowing through the third resistor by using Ohm's law. Next, calculate the power:

$$I_3 = \frac{\Delta V}{R_3}$$

$$I_3 = \frac{(12\ V)}{(10\ \Omega)}$$

$$I_3 = 1.2\ A$$

$$P = IV$$

$$P = (1.2\ A)(12\ V)$$

$$P = 14\ W$$

417. (C) First, calculate the current from the charge and time. Then, find the voltage from Ohm's law:

$$I = \frac{\Delta q}{\Delta t}$$

$$I = \frac{(40\ C)}{(80\ s)}$$

$$I = 0.5\ A$$

$$V = IR$$

$$V = (0.5\ A)(10\ \Omega)$$

$$V = 5.0\ V$$

418. (E) Use Ohm's law to find the resistance:

$$V = IR$$

$$R = \frac{V}{I}$$

$$R = \frac{(100\ V)}{(2\ A)}$$

$$R = 50\ \Omega$$

419. (C) Combine Ohm's law and the power equation, and then solve for the resistance:

$$P = IV$$
$$V = IR$$
$$P = I(IR)$$
$$P = I^2 R$$
$$R = \frac{P}{I^2}$$
$$R = \frac{(1\times10^5 \text{ W})}{(5 \text{ A})^2}$$
$$R = 4\times10^3 \ \Omega = 4 \text{ k}\Omega$$

420. (A) According to Kirchhoff's laws, the sum of all the voltages around a closed loop is zero. The battery provides 9.0 V, while the voltage decreases across each resistor $[(-2.7 \text{ V}) + (-4.2 \text{ V}) + (-2.1 \text{ V}) = -9.0 \text{ V}]$.

421. (E) First, calculate the equivalent resistance of the resistors in series; then use Ohm's law to find the value of the battery voltage:

$$R_{eq} = R_1 + R_2 + R_3$$
$$R_{eq} = 20 \ \Omega + 10 \ \Omega + 30 \ \Omega$$
$$R_{eq} = 60 \ \Omega$$
$$V = IR_{eq}$$
$$V = (2 \text{ A})(60 \ \Omega)$$
$$V = 120 \text{ V}$$

422. (D) Use Ohm's law to calculate the voltage drop across the 30-Ω resistor when the current is 5 A:

$$\Delta V_3 = IR_3$$
$$\Delta V_3 = (5 \text{ A})(30 \ \Omega)$$
$$\Delta V_3 = 150 \text{ V}$$

423. (A) According to Kirchhoff's laws, the sum of all the voltages around a closed loop is zero.

424. (B) First, calculate the equivalent resistance of the parallel branch of the circuit ($R_{eq\parallel}$). Use that to calculate the equivalent resistance of the series circuits:

$$\frac{1}{R_{eq\parallel}} = \frac{1}{R_2} + \frac{1}{R_3}$$
$$\frac{1}{R_{eq\parallel}} = \frac{1}{(10 \ \Omega)} + \frac{1}{(20 \ \Omega)}$$

$$\frac{1}{R_{eq\parallel}} = 0.15 \; \Omega^{-1}$$

$$R_{eq\parallel} = 6.7 \; \Omega$$

$$R_{eq} = R_1 + R_{eq\parallel} + R_4$$

$$R_{eq} = 10 \; \Omega + 6.7 \; \Omega + 45 \; \Omega$$

$$R_{eq} = 61.7 \; \Omega$$

425. (B) Once you have calculated the equivalent resistance of the resistors R_2, R_3, and the parallel branch ($R_{eq\parallel}$), use Ohm's law to calculate the current moving through the circuit. That current must be equal between the first resistor, the parallel branch of resistors, and the final resistor. So, the current leaving the parallel branch must be the same as that which entered it (Kirchhoff's law):

$$I = \frac{\Delta V}{R_{eq}}$$

$$I = \frac{(120 \; V)}{(61.7 \; \Omega)}$$

$$I = 1.9 \; A$$

426. (A) The resistance of a thermal resistor is calculated from Ohm's law as the ratio of voltage to current ($R = V/I$). When the resistor is used in normal operating conditions, its value is fixed. Thus, when the voltage is doubled, its current doubles proportionately.

427. (D) The resistance of a wire is given by $R = \dfrac{\rho \ell}{A}$. This shows that resistance is inversely proportional to cross-sectional area. Therefore, if you double the area, the resistance will reduce to one-half of its value.

428. (A) The resistivity (ρ) of a wire increases with temperature because greater molecular vibrations in the atoms of the wire make it more difficult for the electrons to flow. Resistance is directly proportional to resistivity $\left(R = \dfrac{\rho \ell}{A} \right)$.

429. (B) The relationship between these variables is given as $R = \dfrac{\rho \ell}{A}$. The cross-sectional area must first be converted to meters: $A = (4.0 \; \text{mm}^2) \left(\dfrac{(10^{-3})^2 \; m^2}{\text{mm}^2} \right) = 4.0 \times 10^{-6} \; m^2$

$$R = \frac{(1.7 \times 10^{-8} \; \Omega m) \; (1.5 \; m)}{(4.0 \times 10^{-6} \; m^2)}$$

$$R = 6.4 \times 10^{-3} \; \Omega$$

430. (C) Power is the rate at which energy transfers from a device; thus the energy transfer may be found by multiplying the power by the time:

$$P = I\Delta V = \left(\frac{\Delta V}{R}\right)\Delta V = \left(\frac{\Delta V^2}{R}\right)$$

$$P = \left(\frac{(120 \text{ V})^2}{12\,\Omega}\right) = 1,200 \text{ W} = 1,200 \text{ } \frac{\text{J}}{\text{s}}$$

$$E_{\text{transferred}} = P\Delta t = \left(\frac{\Delta V^2}{R}\right)\Delta t$$

$$E_{\text{transferred}} = \left(1,200 \text{ } \frac{\text{J}}{\text{s}}\right)(7,200 \text{ s}) = 8.6 \times 10^6 \text{ J}$$

431. (C) The potential difference ΔV across a device is the amount of energy transferred for each coulomb of electric charge that flows through the device. By definition of units, $V = \frac{\text{J}}{\text{C}}$. Thus, a 12-volt car battery transfers 12 joules of energy for each and every coulomb of electric charge that passes through it.

432. (D) According to Kirchhoff's junction rule (i.e., conservation of charge flow), the currents of the two resistors in parallel must add together and feed into the series part of the circuit. Thus, 1.5 A + 1.5 A = 3.0 A. Since current is constant in series, both the 20-Ω resistor and the power supply will get 3.0 A.

433. (B) In a series circuit, the equivalent resistance is $R + R = 2R$. Therefore, using Ohm's law, the circuit's current is $I = \frac{\Delta V}{R_{\text{series}}} = \frac{\Delta V}{2R}$. Plugging this into the power equation:

$$P = I(\Delta V)$$

$$P = \frac{\Delta V}{2R}(\Delta V) = \frac{\Delta V^2}{2R}$$

$$P = \frac{\Delta V^2}{2R}$$

434. (A) Power is the rate at which energy transfers in a device, so this is what needs to be found. In a series circuit, the equivalent resistance is $R + R = 2R$. Therefore, using Ohm's law, the circuit's current is $I = \frac{\Delta V}{R_{\text{series}}} = \frac{\Delta V}{2R}$. Since current is constant in series, each individual resistor gets this current. The power equation needs to be arranged in terms of current and individual resistance using Ohm's law as follows:

$$P = I(\Delta V) = I(IR) = I^2 R$$

Plugging the earlier expression for current in this new expression:

$$P = \left(\frac{\Delta V}{2R}\right)^2 R$$

$$P = \frac{\Delta V^2}{4R}$$

435. (C) Power is the rate at which energy transfers in a device, so this is what needs to be found. Since voltage is constant across each device in parallel, each individual resistor gets the full voltage. The power equation needs to be arranged in terms of this voltage and individual resistance using Ohm's law as follows:

$$P = I(\Delta V)$$

$$P = \frac{\Delta V}{R}(\Delta V)$$

$$P = \frac{\Delta V^2}{R}$$

436. (C) According to $R = \frac{\rho \ell}{A}$, resistance is inversely proportional to cross-sectional area A and directly proportional to length ℓ. Therefore, doubling both variables will result in no net change to the resistance.

437. (D) The junction rule states that the current flowing into any junction in a circuit equals the current flowing out of that same junction. Since current is the rate of flow of electric charge, Kirchhoff's junction rule is an expression of the law of conservation of charge.

438. (C) Kirchhoff's loop rule states that the sum of the potential differences around any complete loop of a circuit must be zero. Electric potential difference (sometimes called voltage) is the energy transferred per unit of charge in a device. As you proceed around a circuit, some devices add energy to the circuit (e.g., a battery) and have a positive potential difference. Other devices transfer energy out of a circuit (e.g., a resistor) and have a negative potential difference. Energy cannot be created or destroyed, so in the end the positive and negative differences in potential must sum to zero. This is an expression of the law of conservation of energy.

439. (B) As the temperature increases, the resistivity of the wire increases. Since resistance is directly proportional to resistivity, the resistance increases. For a fixed potential difference, the current is inversely proportional to resistance, so the current decreases with increasing resistance.

440. (A, D) Every element in a series circuit has the same current, and the equivalent resistance is the sum of all the resistances.

441. (A, E) The resistance of a wire is given by $R = \frac{\rho \ell}{A}$. The ratio of voltage to current is a constant for a wire, so their individual values do NOT affect the resistance.

442. (C, E) The conventional flow of current in a circuit is the positive charge that flows out from the positive terminal, but current actually consists of the flow of the electron charge out from the negative terminal. According to the law of conservation of charge, electrons cannot be created or destroyed, so the electron flow (the current) will be the same throughout the circuit, and the electrons will remain in it.

443. (B, C) Power is defined as the rate of energy transfer in a circuit and is calculated as follows: $P = I\Delta V$.

444. (A, E) Energy cannot be created or destroyed. In a simple circuit, the chemical energy stored in the battery is transferred to thermal energy at the resistor. When the battery "dies," the chemical reactions are complete and the resistor and the environment have now been heated.

445. Calculate the equivalent resistance of the parallel branch of the circuit ($R_{eq\parallel}$); then use that to calculate the equivalent resistance of the series circuits:

$$\frac{1}{R_{eq\parallel}} = \frac{1}{R_2} + \frac{1}{R_3} + \frac{1}{R_4}$$

$$\frac{1}{R_{eq\parallel}} = \frac{1}{(5.0\ \Omega)} + \frac{1}{(2.5\ \Omega)} + \frac{1}{(20\ \Omega)}$$

$$\frac{1}{R_{eq\parallel}} = 0.65\ \Omega^{-1}$$

$$R_{eq} = 1.54\ \Omega$$

$$R_{eq} = R_1 + R_{eq\parallel}$$

$$R_{eq} = 10\ \Omega + 1.54\ \Omega$$

$$R_{eq} = 11.5\ \Omega$$

446. Use Ohm's law, the voltage, and the equivalent resistance to calculate the current flowing through the circuit:

$$I = \frac{\Delta V}{R_{eq}}$$

$$I = \frac{(120\ V)}{(11.5\ \Omega)}$$

$$I = 10.4\ A$$

447. $\Delta V = IR$

$$\Delta V_1 = IR_1 = (10.4\ A)(10\ \Omega) = 104\ V$$

$$\Delta V_2 = \Delta V_3 = \Delta V_4 = IR_{eq\parallel} = (10.4\ A)(1.54\ \Omega) = 16\ V$$

448. $I = \dfrac{\Delta V}{R}$

$I_1 = \dfrac{\Delta V_1}{R_1} = \dfrac{(104 \text{ V})}{(10 \,\Omega)} = 10.4\text{A}$

$I_2 = \dfrac{\Delta V_2}{R_2} = \dfrac{(16 \text{ V})}{5 \,\Omega} = 3.2\text{A}$

$I_3 = \dfrac{\Delta V_3}{R_3} = \dfrac{(16 \text{ V})}{(2.5 \,\Omega)} = 6.4\text{A}$

$I_4 = \dfrac{\Delta V_4}{R_4} = \dfrac{(16 \text{ V})}{(20 \,\Omega)} = 0.8\text{A}$

449. (a) The equivalent resistance increases linearly as you increase the number of resistors in series. In contrast, the equivalent resistance decreases as you increase the number of resistors in parallel because more pathways are open.

(b) The current in the power supply decreases as you increase the number of resistors in series because current is inversely related to resistance for a fixed voltage (rearrange Ohm's law to get $I = V/R$) and the equivalent resistance is increasing. In contrast, the current increases linearly as you increase the number of resistors in parallel because the equivalent resistance decreases.

450. (a) In the series circuit, the equivalent resistance increases with an increasing number of resistors, and the power decreases inversely for a fixed potential difference as follows:

$$P = I\Delta V = \left(\dfrac{\Delta V}{R_{eq}}\right)\Delta V = \left(\dfrac{\Delta V^2}{R_{eq}}\right)$$

In contrast, in the parallel circuit, the equivalent resistance decreases with an increasing number of resistors, and so the total power increases linearly with the number of resistors.

(b) Power is the rate of flow of energy and corresponds to the brightness of the bulbs. Since the current is constant in a series circuit, the power in each individual bulb may be calculated as follows: $P = I\Delta V = I(IR) = I^2 R$. Since the current of the circuit decreases as the number of lightbulbs in the string increases, the brightness of the bulbs also decreases. For a parallel string of lights, the power of each bulb is calculated as follows:

$$P = I\Delta V = \left(\dfrac{\Delta V}{R}\right)\Delta V = \left(\dfrac{\Delta V^2}{R}\right)$$

Since each bulb gets the same voltage in parallel, the lights will get the same power and stay equally bright (although this happens within limits).

Chapter 10: Mechanical Waves and Sound

451. (C) Of the waves listed, only sound is an example of a longitudinal wave in which the particles vibrate in the direction of the wave.

452. (E) The amplitude of a wave is defined as the distance between the peak of the crest and the equilibrium position of the medium, or the bottom of the trough and equilibrium.

453. (B) The period of a wave whose frequency is 100 Hz can be calculated as follows:

$$T = \frac{1}{f}$$

$$T = \frac{1}{(100 \text{ Hz})}$$

$$T = 0.01 \text{ s}$$

454. (D) Here's how to calculate the velocity of a wave with a frequency of 100 Hz and a wavelength of 1.0 m:

$$v = f\lambda$$

$$v = (100 \text{ Hz})(1.0 \text{ m})$$

$$v = 100 \text{ m/s}$$

455. (D) A sound wave travels at 343 m/s. The wavelength of the sound wave is 17.2 cm $(1.72 \times 10^{-2} \text{ m})$. Calculate the frequency as follows:

$$v = f\lambda$$

$$f = \frac{v}{\lambda}$$

$$f = \frac{(343 \text{ m/s})}{(1.72 \times 10^{-2} \text{ m})}$$

$$f = 1.99 \times 10^{4} \text{ Hz, or 20 kHz}$$

456. (C) The sound wave broadcast through the headphones is 180° out of phase with the one from the jackhammer. The two waves interfere with each other and cancel out. The result is that the operator does not hear the jackhammer noise. This is an example of destructive interference.

457. (D) Since half of a wave fits into the 0.50-m tube, the wavelength is 1.00 m. The speed of sound is 343 m/s. Calculate the fundamental frequency of the tube ($n = 1$):

$$\lambda = \frac{v}{f}$$

$$f = \frac{v}{\lambda}$$

$$f = \frac{343 \frac{m}{s}}{1.00 \text{ m}}$$
$$f = 343 \text{ Hz}$$

458. (D) The two waves will add together, and the resulting wave will have the amplitude 2A/3.

459. (C) The figure depicts the phenomenon of destructive interference.

460. (D) After the waves meet, they will travel on. One wave (+A) will travel to the right, while one wave (−A/3) will travel to the left.

461. (B) The frequency of the tuning fork is 440 Hz. At the temperature specified, the speed of sound is 343 m/s. We are looking for the length, L, of the air column when the first ($n = 1$) resonance sound is heard. A standing wave with one antinode and one node is a quarter of a wavelength; therefore $L = \frac{\lambda}{4}$.

$$\lambda = \frac{v}{f}$$

$$\lambda = \frac{343 \frac{m}{s}}{440 \frac{\text{waves}}{s}} = 0.78 \text{ m}$$

$$L = \frac{\lambda}{4} = \frac{0.78 \text{ m}}{4} = 0.19 \text{ m}$$

462. (C) The tsunami wave's velocity is 720 km/h (200 m/s). The period of the wave is 10 min (600 s). Calculate the wavelength:

$$v = \frac{\lambda}{T}$$
$$\lambda = vT$$
$$\lambda = (200 \text{ m/s})(600 \text{ s})$$
$$\lambda = 1.2 \times 10^5 \text{ m, or } 120 \text{ km}$$

463. (A) The speed of a radio wave is the speed of light (3×10^8 m/s), and the frequency is 100 MHz (1×10^8 Hz). Calculate the wavelength of the radio wave:

$$v = f\lambda$$
$$\lambda = \frac{v}{f}$$
$$\lambda = \frac{(3 \times 10^8 \text{ m/s})}{(1 \times 10^8 \text{ Hz})}$$
$$\lambda = 3 \text{ m}$$

464. (D) The change in frequency of a wave emitted from a moving object as that object passes you is called the Doppler effect.

465. (C) The beat frequency is the difference between the two frequencies of the tuning forks (444 Hz − 440 Hz = 4 Hz).

466. (C) The two waves will add together, and the resulting wave will have the amplitude 3A/2.

467. (E) A wavelength is the length of one complete wave pattern. It can be measured as the distance from crest to crest or trough to trough.

468. (C) The volume of sound corresponds to amplitude, so a loud sound correlates to a large amplitude. The pitch of the sound corresponds to frequency, so a low pitch is a low frequency.

469. (A) When six waves pass a buoy in 3.0 seconds, two waves must pass by each and every second, so the frequency is 2.0 Hz. The 1.5-m distance between the waves is the wavelength. The speed of the waves is calculated from the wave equation:

$$\lambda = \frac{v}{f}$$
$$v = f\lambda$$
$$v = \left(2\,\frac{\text{waves}}{\text{s}}\right)\left(1.5\,\frac{\text{m}}{\text{wave}}\right) = 3.0\,\frac{\text{m}}{\text{s}}$$

470. (C) As a wave is generated, an increase in frequency results in a smaller wavelength $\left(\lambda = \frac{v}{f}\right)$. For a fixed wave speed, frequency and wavelength are inversely proportional.

471. (A) Pitch is the average of the two frequencies: $f_{\text{pitch}} = \frac{f_1 + f_2}{2} = \frac{256\text{ Hz} + 252\text{ Hz}}{2} =$ 254 Hz. The beat frequency is the absolute value of the difference between the frequencies: $|f_1 - f_2| = 256\text{ Hz} - 252\text{ Hz} = 4\text{ Hz}$.

472. (A) The period is the time it takes for one complete wave to pass by. Six waves passed by in three seconds, so two waves pass by every second. That means every wave takes a half a second to pass by.

473. (C) $f = \dfrac{v}{\lambda} = \dfrac{16\,\frac{\text{m}}{\text{s}}}{4\,\frac{\text{m}}{\text{wave}}} = 4\,\frac{\text{waves}}{\text{s}} = 4\text{ Hz}$

474. (B) Amplitude is the (vertical) distance between the equilibrium position (the zero line) and the crest of the wave, which is 20 cm in this diagram. Wavelength is the (horizontal) distance of one complete wave, which is approximately 5 cm in this diagram.

475. (C) This is a question about the Doppler effect. As a source of sound approaches an observer, a higher frequency than normal is heard, and as it leaves the observer, a lower frequency is heard. The speed stays the same because the medium does not change.

476. (A) Sound beats are a result of the interference between two sounds of almost the same frequency.

477. (E) A sound beat is a changing amplitude (loudness) that occurs at a particular frequency. That frequency is the difference between the two frequencies making the sound.

478. (D) According to the AP Physics 1 Course and Exam Description, "A wave is a disturbance that carries energy and momentum from one place to another without the transfer of matter."

479. (B) A wave is classified by the way the medium vibrates as the wave energy travels through it. In a transverse wave, that vibration is perpendicular to the motion of the wave (as opposed to the parallel vibration in the case of longitudinal waves).

480. (E) Frequency (measured in Hertz) is defined as the number of vibrations that occur per second.

481. (D) Wavelength and frequency are inversely proportional, so an increase in frequency will decrease the wavelength. Speed depends solely on the medium and will stay the same in this case.

482. (D) Waves travel at a constant speed. Using the constant rate equation:

$$d = vt = \left(344\frac{m}{s} \right)(2 \text{ s}) = 688 \text{ m}$$

483. (B) $\lambda = \dfrac{v}{f} = \dfrac{345\frac{m}{s}}{256\frac{waves}{s}} = 0.740\dfrac{m}{wave}$

484. (B) Frequency and period are inverse of each other. If the frequency is the same, then the period will also be the same.

485. (B) Sound is a longitudinal wave, so the medium (air particles) must vibrate along lines parallel with the motion of the wave energy.

486. (A) Once a mechanical wave is generated, its frequency is fixed, even when it changes speed from one medium into the next. Thus, according to $v = f\lambda$, wavelength will change proportionately with speed.

487. (B) The two-way time is given, so to find the one-way distance, the time will be divided in half:

$$d = vt = \left(1{,}400\,\frac{m}{s}\right)\left(\frac{0.15\ s}{2}\right) = 105\ m$$

488. (A, D) The speed of sound increases slightly with temperature, going up about 6 m/s for every 10° Celsius above zero. Sound travels about 18 times faster in steel than air.

489. (A, B) Standing waves form when the medium is disturbed at its natural frequency. This resonance occurs because the wave reflects off a boundary and interferes with oncoming waves to form nodes (destructive interference) and antinodes (constructive interference).

490. (D, E) The speed of a mechanical wave depends only on the medium and its characteristics.

491. (B, D) When a wave hits a boundary, three things occur: reflection, transmission (refraction), and absorption. So the phenomena that do NOT occur are a change in frequency and an increase in energy.

492. (C, D) Resonance occurs when something is forced to vibrate at its natural frequency and a dramatic growth in amplitude occurs. The tuning fork and the wineglass are perfect examples of this.

493. Wavelength is the length of one complete vibration (crest and trough). Since there are two-and-a-half waves in the picture, the wavelength is $\lambda = (2.5\ m)/(5/2) = 1.0\ m$. Another way to see this is by dividing the wave into five 0.5-m segments and recognizing that the wavelength is two of those segments. The amplitude is the distance from the equilibrium (undisturbed center line) and the crest, which is half of the 0.6-m distance, or 0.3 m.

494. Period is the inverse of frequency:

$$T = \frac{1}{f} = \frac{1}{5.0\,\dfrac{vibrations}{s}} = 0.20\,\frac{s}{vibration}$$

495. Speed is calculated with the wave equation: $v = f\lambda = \left(5.0\,\dfrac{vibes}{s}\right)\left(1.0\,\dfrac{m}{vibe}\right) = 5.0\,\dfrac{m}{s}$.

496. The wave must travel 2.5 m to the wall and 2.5 m back, for a total of 5.0 m. Since the speed is 5.0 m for each and every second, the time will be one second.

497. Frequency does not affect the speed of a mechanical wave. Frequency and wavelength, however, are inversely proportional. Thus, if frequency is doubled, wavelength will be cut in half to 0.5 m.

498. The distance between compressions is the wavelength of the sound wave:

$$\lambda = \frac{v}{f} = \frac{343\dfrac{m}{s}}{25{,}000\dfrac{waves}{s}} = 1.4 \times 10^{-2} \frac{m}{wave} = 1.4 \frac{cm}{wave}$$

499. To travel to the cave wall and back again, the sound travels a distance of 3.5 m + 3.5 m = 7.0 m. Using $d = vt$ and solving for time:

$$t = \frac{d}{v} = \frac{7.0\ m}{343\dfrac{m}{s}} = 0.020\ s$$

500. The stationary bat will observe the Doppler effect as the moving bat goes by. The frequency (pitch) will be higher than 25,000 Hz as the sounding bat approaches, and lower than 25,000 Hz after it passes.